Eastern European Roma
in the EU

Eastern European Roma in the EU

Mobility, Discrimination, Solutions

Anca Pusca, editor

International Debate Education Association

New York, London & Amsterdam

Published by
International Debate Education Association
400 West 59th Street
New York, NY 10019

Library of Congress Cataloging-in-Publication Data

Eastern European Roma in the EU : mobility, discrimination, solutions / Anca Pusca, editor.

p. cm.

ISBN 978-1-61770-024-8

1. Romanies--Europe, Eastern. 2. Romanies--Government policy--European Union countries . 3. Romanies--Legal status, laws, etc.--European Union countries. 4. Romanies--European Union countries--Social conditions. 5. European Union countries--Ethnic relations. 6. Social integration--European Union countries. I. Pusca, Anca.

DX210.E37 2011

305.891'497047--dc23

2011038483

 **IDEBATE Press**

Printed in the USA

Contents

Introduction:
Moving Toward a Common EU Framework for Roma Integration

THE CONTEXT

Since 1989, the European Union (EU) has played a critical role in advocating for Roma rights, funding Roma initiatives, and incentivizing national governments to develop clear policies for the protection of Roma within their borders . While there is room for improvement, the EU has slowly, but clearly, been moving toward the establishment of a common EU framework for Roma integration that will offer better protection against anti-gypsyism as well as a clearer and more cohesive mechanism for Roma inclusion in European societies.

The aim of this book is not so much to assess the potential success of such a framework—it is too early for that—but rather to examine the different stages that have led the EU toward a common policy on the Roma, the motivations behind these actions, and the kind of challenges that this policy initiative has encountered along the way. The book is divided into four sections: Roma in Eastern Europe, Roma and the EU Accession Process, Roma Political Mobilization, and Proposed Solutions. The four sections follow a loose temporal line that examines the treatment of Eastern European Roma before 1989 and the various legacies of such treatment; the EU involvement in the Roma question after 1989 through the EU accession process; and the post-accession challenges that the EU is currently facing, particularly in terms of Roma migration.

Before 1989, communist East European states had various Roma policies, ranging, for the most part, from forced assimilation to looser policies of integration—particularly within the former Yugoslavia, where the question of minorities was much more sensitive. It is safe to say that the EU had, at that point, no Roma policy outside of member states such as the United Kingdom, which had devised specific settling rights for the so-called travelers, many of whom were Roma, and an overall informal agreement across the EU to grant refugee status to Roma coming from communist Europe.

Faced with the prospect of new accessions and a quickly disintegrating former Yugoslavia after 1989, the EU, initially through the Council of Europe and the Organization for Security and Cooperation in Europe (OSCE), and later through the European Commission's enforcement of the so-called Copenhagen Criteria,[1] began to develop a set of different policies aimed at fighting Roma discrimination "at home"—meaning within the new accession states—and incorporating into national law the protection of Roma rights, including the right to housing, health care, education, and employment. The coupling of these new national Roma policies and legislation with the requirement that nations adopt these as a condition for admission to the EU resulted in a relatively successful and, in some cases, quick adoption of new legislation. Implementation was a different matter, however.

The carrot-and-stick approach of the accession negotiation process proved effective for acknowledging and addressing the so-called Roma problem in Eastern Europe; however, it also helped peg the problem to this particular region, suggesting that discrimination was largely a question of the communist legacy rather than a wider issue that could easily transplant itself to other EU member states through migration. As such, a double standard was set, whereby Eastern European accession countries carried all of the burden for addressing and fixing "the problem," while Western European EU members were spared the need to address "the problem" at all.

Not until the late 1990s, with the extension of the visa-free regime to include new accession countries, did the EU finally acknowledge the Roma issue as an EU-wide one. Numbers of initial border crossings after the extension of the visa-free regime show that, in most cases, a large percentage of those who crossed into Western Europe were East European Roma. Facing increasing economic and social pressures from these new migrants, Western EU member states continued to consider Roma to be an East European problem that had to be solved by and within the states of Eastern Europe—either through a forceful return of these new migrants or encouragement of voluntary return through different economic incentives. These included stipends to open up new business at "home," as well as targeted EU funding aimed at helping the Roma better integrate into East European societies and find jobs there.

The idea that East European migrants, Roma in particular, were not at "home" in Western Europe, even with the legal right to free movement, appears to have been present from the beginning of the accession process—where the ideal of offering Eastern Europe a friendly hand and an opportunity for reunification lay in stark contrast with the practicalities of actually opening up borders and accepting the fact that East Europeans, including Roma, would be looking for better opportunities within the richer countries of Western Europe.

Not until this new wave of Eastern European and Roma migration did the EU acknowledge the need to rethink and reconfigure its Roma policy as an EU-wide policy, as opposed to one that was mainly related to the accession process.

With much of Eastern Europe now a part of the EU and this stage of the accession process concluded, the enforcement mechanism provided through the Copenhagen Criteria was no longer available, thus, new mechanisms for enforcement needed to be found. Funding for Roma communities through the European Social Fund, the European Regional Development Fund, and the European Agricultural Fund for Rural Development became the main means for continuing to secure the protection of Roma communities and the enforcement of already adopted legislation. The success of this new mechanism remains questionable, however, particularly when taking into account that "the EU has spent close to 350 million euros on Roma projects, without a comprehensive strategy"[2] and is now faced with increasingly radical responses to Roma immigration, such as forced evacuations and expulsions, destruction of Roma camps, and rising signs of violence against the Roma communities across the EU.

The visibility of the "Roma problem" increased with the Italian expulsion of Roma in 2007[3] and, more recently, the French expulsion of Roma in 2010.[4] These expulsions served to put the issue of anti-gypsyism high on the European agenda, raising concerns about the ability of EU countries to protect the basic rights of European citizens—including the right to free movement—as well as the need to address anti-gypsyism not only in the new accession countries but throughout the EU. The EU response to the Italian and French crises has been largely disappointing—neither the Italian nor the French governments have been found to break EU law through their actions, highlighting once again the bias toward the diplomatic appeasement of founding EU states. The crises did, however, lead to a closer investigation of how the EU 2004 Directive on Free Movement[5] has been integrated into national legislation within different EU states and the extent to which a nation's laws meet the requirement of avoiding discrimination, particularly on the grounds of nationality and belonging to an ethnic minority.

The two recent crises in Italy and France clearly point to a serious problem of discrimination against Roma across the EU, which is related not only to a wider anti-immigration sentiment, but also, and more worrisome, to a clear anti-gypsy sentiment that appears to be on the rise. Political scientist Ivan Krastev[6] attributes this to a wider shift across the EU from a *democratic imagination*—which has shaped an optimistic, self-confident Europe that saw an opportunity to change itself and the world—to a *demographic imagination*—which "terrifies us with the prospect that the world will change us,"[7] in the context of the current global economic crisis. The *demographic imagination* has led majorities to feel like minorities betrayed by their elites and victims of a process of globalization that was supposed to offer prosperity, not take it away.[8] This has, in turn, fed and been fed by the populist turn throughout Europe, which has placed the rights of minorities—such as the Roma—in direct opposition to the rights of the majority.

While Krastev is perhaps more pessimistic than most, he does point to the extent to which the so-called Roma problem is much wider and involves a political turn to the right that cannot be addressed purely through legislation. The passing of new laws to protect Roma rights or even a platform for Roma inclusion needs to be complemented by a clearer political platform to directly address the fears of the majority and defend the rights of minorities. This political platform cannot be negotiated only within Brussels, however—it needs to address specific national pressures that different EU member states are experiencing.

Faced with such radical pressures, the EU put forward a new EU Framework for National Roma Integration in April 2011 as a complement to its wider EU 2020 Framework that seeks to target poverty through the promotion of smart, sustainable, and inclusive growth. The framework is inspired by the Decade of Roma Inclusion 2005–2015,[9] which brings together governments, nongovernmental organizations, and Roma activists to work on increasing the welfare of Roma communities throughout Europe. The Decade has gathered an unprecedented commitment from European governments and institutions to improve Roma welfare with support from a series of international institutions and foundations, including the Open Society Foundations, the World Bank, the United Nations Development Programme, and the European Roma Rights Center. The Framework seeks to build on this commitment in order to secure a stronger legal, institutional, and collaborative structure that could address Roma issues across the EU.

The new Framework for National Roma Integration recognizes the challenges that the EU faces with regard to its Roma minority policy to be EU-wide, seeks to remove the double standard created through the accession mechanism, and outlines clear steps that all EU member states should follow to improve Roma access to education, employment, health care, and housing within their borders. While it is expected that the Framework will evolve into a stronger institutional structure, as it stands today, it fails to create a clear political mechanism that Krastev and others suggest is needed to address the issues that it acknowledges, beyond the creation of national contact points responsible for coordinating the development and implementation of the strategy. The Framework also fails to vigorously push for a more active inclusion of Roma in the decision-making process, as recommended by Roma activists such as Valeriu Nicolae.[10] Nevertheless, the Framework is an important first step that could evolve into a much needed EU common policy on the Roma.

DEBATES AND CONTROVERSIES

Many debates surround the EU "Roma problem." These include: 1) debates about Roma identity, which are often tied to debates on Roma origins and way of life; 2) debates about Roma political status and whether they should seek representation as an ethnic minority or a special interest group; 3) debates about Roma rights and whether they should be addressed separately or together with the rights of other minority groups; and 4) debates about Roma migration and whether it can be treated as a special kind of migration. This listing is certainly not exhaustive but serves simply to point to the variety of issues and opinions found in the literature.

This volume focuses on four main debates that serve both to provide a certain historical sense of the creation and evolution of EU policy toward the Roma since 1989 and also to focus attention on the four issues that are often considered critical to any discussion of discrimination against Roma:

1. the impact of the communist legacy on post-1989 attempts for Roma inclusion;

2. the double standard imposed through the EU accession process that placed highly unequal burdens on EU member states vs. EU accession states;

3. opportunities for Roma political mobilization and their limits; and

4. solutions to Roma inclusion and their limits.

Section I focuses on the two different temporalities in which the European Roma debate often occurs. One begins after 1989 with a broad assumption of cohesiveness and similarity of problems across all Eastern European Roma groups. The other begins much earlier, taking into account significant differences in the communist policies toward Roma and their impact on different Roma groups' ability to organize politically as well as to be recognized by the wider majority. While these views need not always contradict one another and could, in some cases, be seen as complementary, they do offer significantly different perspectives on how these different temporal assumptions can alter the debate.

In Chapter 1, James Goldston focuses his analysis mainly on post-1989 Europe in which the EU, through the EU accession process, emerges as the much needed advocate for Roma rights—just in time to meet persistent and intensifying stereotypes that would have otherwise further threatened the already precarious position of the Roma throughout Eastern Europe. He underlines the sheer luck of timing that saw the fight for Roma rights after 1989 coincide with the EU's attempt to build a stronger political union through eastward enlargement and integration. He also wonders about the extent to which the Roma rights movement in Europe would have had a chance without the EU's significant role in funding Roma rights initiatives, pushing for Roma rights legislation in applicant states, and offering Roma a chance to bring their plight to judicial review through the European Court of Human Rights. While applauding the EU's commitment to the protection of Roma rights, Goldston also acknowledges that racism and xenophobia continue to be a growing problem in Europe that the EU will not be able to address alone. To address xenophobia, Goldston argues that the EU will need the direct support of each of its member states as well as the support of civil society—particularly that of the wider majority.

Goldston's optimism and trust in the EU is slightly counterbalanced by Zoltan Barany's chapter, which sees the ability of the EU to address the Roma problem as significantly limited by a communist legacy that will be difficult to erase. In Chapter 2, Barany offers a much longer timeframe as well as a more careful distinctions between different groups of Roma across Eastern Europe. Barany argues that the capacity for Roma activism and political participation post-1989 was not just a result of EU funding and government pressures but, rather, was deeply influenced by state policies before 1989. While communism significantly improved the objective condition of many Roma through an active politics of assimilation—making education and wage labor mandatory—it led to the dispersal of compact communities and destruction of tight family networks.

With the exception of Yugoslavia, the Czech Republic during the Prague Spring, and Hungary (which mainly worried about the fate of ethnic Hungarian minorities abroad), little recognition was given to Roma as a separate minority group; hence, the group enjoyed little autonomy during communism. Barany argues that the authority of Roma leaders diminished not only in countries where they had enjoyed little autonomy but also in countries where they were forced to collaborate with the state authorities and the police, thus undermining their credibility within the community. According to Barany, Roma ability to organize politically after 1989 was deeply influenced by their political presence before 1989 either as Communist Party members or community leaders, their participation in Roma community groups and organizations, and the presence of Roma intelligentsia that had been educated through the mandatory education policies.

Section II debates the double standard imposed through the EU accession process, which pressured new member states to develop specific policies on the Roma aimed at protecting and empowering the community and effectively entitled old member states to see the "Roma problem" as largely an East European one that needed to be solved outside of their borders. Maria Spirova and Darlene Budd as well as Michael Johns acknowledge the important role that EU conditionality—the need to adopt the main requirements of European Union law, including the nondiscrimination and minority protection requirements, before EU accession—has played in creating Roma policies throughout Eastern Europe. Socialization alone almost certainly would not have been able to achieve such legislation. Yet, they each offer a series of criticisms concerning the bias inherent in the implementation of conditionality through the accession process alone. Noting a significant difference between EU discourse and EU actions—particularly the actions of old member states—this section underlines the continued East–West divide during and after the accession process. It is this divide that, some argue, has led to the recent expulsions in France, Italy, and underlay earlier expulsions from Finland, Germany, the Netherlands, and the United Kingdom.

In Chapter 3, Maria Spirova and Darlene Budd discuss the different EU tools—including the Copenhagen Criteria, and funding distribution through the Decade of Roma Inclusion, OSCE, and Council of Europe—that forced the adoption of new Roma policies in Hungary, the Czech Republic, Bulgaria, and Romania. Arguing for the importance of recognizing group minority rights across the EU, Spirova and Budd point to the slow ratification of the Council of Europe Framework Convention on National Minorities, particularly by older EU member states, in a context where candidate countries for EU membership were being pressured to ratify. They also suggest that the success of EU conditionality in Eastern Europe, which resulted in the creation of not only new protection policies but also clear mechanisms and organizations to implement them—such as Hungary's program for Roma integration, the Czech Republic's Board for Roma Community Affairs, Bulgaria's Framework for Equal Integration, and Romania's Roma Framework Convention—needs to extend to all member states. Pointing to the growing gap in Roma poverty and lessening access to education, as well as Roma surveys that continue to show deep disillusionment with the current state of affairs, Spirova and Budd clearly underline the need to try new strategies to ensure a move from simply talking about protecting Roma rights to actually enforcing them.

In Chapter 4, Michael Johns builds on Spirova and Budd's arguments by underlining once again the double standard implicit in the area of Roma protection and antidiscrimination in the EU, a double standard that he refers to, as the title of his piece suggests, as a "do as I say, not as I do" policy. Johns is also quick to point out the extent to which an overall ethnic and minority policy that has largely focused on conflict prevention since the 1990s will not satisfy the needs of specific minorities. According to Johns, the inherent correlation between minority rights and ethnic conflict that lies at the base of much of the EU's minority politics serves to reinforce the double standard by treating Western Europe as somehow immune from conflict and, as such, exempt from the need to create specific protection policies. Not only EU discourse but also EU institutions such as the OSCE continue to support this divide by focusing their country recommendations almost exclusively on the East. Johns points to the extent to which the pressure to implement strict minority protection policies has put many former communist countries, such as Latvia and Estonia, in a position of having to choose between two of their main goals: joining the EU and protecting the culture and society of their newly formed states.

Section III debates the opportunities and limits for Roma political mobilization across the EU, assessing the success of mobilization through the normal political process, affirmative action, or grassroots actions. The articles in this section do not look for definitive conclusions about each of these processes but, rather, underline the extent to which success of a particular process is largely dependent on the unique conditions within each country. Accordingly, the three articles point to overall challenges to Roma political mobilization across the EU, assess the success of unique mobilization models encountered in Slovenia's local government, and investigate how the Internet can act as both a promoter and an inhibitor of Roma political mobilization.

Chapter 5 provides a quick summary of the nature of political participation of Roma, traveller and Sinti communities across the EU. Compiled by the European Roma Information Office, an EU office that collects and distributes information on the Roma minorities across Europe, this fact sheet underlines the extent to which Roma exclusion is particularly pronounced in Western Europe— supporting the double-standard arguments presented in the previous section. The fact sheet examines some of the most prominent factors that contribute to the failure to include Roma communities in the political process, including prejudice and stereotypes, lack of political experience and networks, institutional discrimination within political systems, and citizenship and residency. The fact sheet also offers an overview of the more prominent tools for promoting participation, including the promotion of Roma participation in mainstream political parties, Roma-based political parties, and Roma politicians.

In Chapter 6, Irena Baclija and Miro Haček discuss the specific case of the election of Roma councilors in 19 Slovenian municipalities and their ability to influence local politics to provide needed services for Roma. While they do not question that Roma political participation is critical for securing Roma rights, Baclija and Haček draw a series of important lessons from the experience of the first 13 years of post-1989 democracy in Central and Eastern Europe. According to them, these initial years helped dispel two important illusions: 1) "that Roma concerns can be effectively addressed and their rights promoted within the ordinary political process"[11] and 2) "that a token number of Roma in the public administration can make a difference."[12] Instead, they suggest that governments need to learn how to engage with Roma partners in a way that does not alienate Roma political representatives or leaders from their own communities, involve Roma in Roma-related policy formation early in the process, look for broad representation and transparency, and involve Roma communities in the implementation and evaluation of Roma-related programs.

In Chapter 7, Neda Atanasoski directs her attention to the way in which the Internet has been used both to raise awareness of Roma issues across the world and to give Roma a political voice. While Atanasoski criticizes the extent to which Roma Internet presence is dominated by the voices of non-Roma advocates—which often silence the voices of the Roma themselves—she does point to a series of interesting projects, such as the Kosovar Roma Oral Histories Project, that manage to offer an alternative to the dominant narratives. Atanasoski, like some of the other writers in this volume, is concerned by the EU's double-standard approach to Central and Eastern Europe vs. Western Europe. She argues that this is reflected in the use of a double narrative that, when present online, risks turning the Roma into a "virtual" subject of rights with technologies such as the Internet acting as "emancipatory tools." This virtual presence risks not only discrediting the desperate material needs of the Roma, creating the illusion of a political online voice that is, in fact, less persuasive and empowering than one might expect, but also, once again, prioritizing Western perspectives that fail to acknowledge how the West, itself, is implicated in the process of discrimination.

Section IV debates the effectiveness of currently proposed solutions to the problems of integrating Roma children into schools and housing across a series of countries, including Hungary, Slovakia, and the Czech Republic. While most Roma activists agree that Roma problems require more than awareness raising, passing legislation, and ensuring political participation, a common agreement on how to achieve equal access to education, housing, health care, and employment has not been reached. The fact that problems may be similar in different countries does not guarantee that similar strategies will have equal levels of success. Case study after case study has shown that the best solutions arise from addressing specific local needs through both political and practical compromises that can only be achieved at that particular time. Hence, attempts to replicate solutions through similar compromises may not always work but are, instead, dependent on the commitment of key actors to find both short-term fixes and long-term solutions that are not dependent on the continuing involvement of these key participants.

In Chapter 8, Vera Messing compares a series of attempts to integrate Roma children into the schools in Hungary, Italy, and Switzerland— focusing in particular on the success of the Hungarian Learnery after-school initiative in Turna and Satu. Messing argues that while a clear correlation exists between educational attainment, employment, and Roma integration, higher educational attainment alone does not guarantee greater inclusion in the labor market. While past communist regimes were able to guarantee employment based on educational qualifications, liberal market regimes are unable to do so; hence, the increasing gap in Roma employment must be addressed on several fronts, not solely through education. Addressing discrimination and segregation in the labor market is thus as important as achieving a lower dropout rate among the Roma. The success of the Learnery after-school initiative in reducing the Roma dropout rate does not necessarily translate into these students' ability to gain college admission and obtain jobs equivalent to their level of education.

In Chapter 9, a case study by the European Union Agency for Fundamental Rights, developed by Marek Hojsík and Tatjana Peric, assesses the success of two different housing projects for the Roma communities in Val'kovna and Nalepkovo in Slovakia. They argue that the move from housing as a right during communism to housing as an individual responsibility after 1989 had a significant and lasting negative impact on the Roma communities of that nation. The privatization of housing left the provision of housing for economically disadvantaged households in the hands of the government and local municipalities, neither of which had the means or skills to ensure these often growing households access to adequate housing. Overcrowding has left Roma communities to fend for themselves, resulting in the construction of illegal and dangerous camps, the significant lowering of housing standards, and the ghettoization of many of these communities. Because solutions to the Roma housing problem have only been seriously addressed in the last few years, problems have been compounded by significantly increasing levels of poverty, crime, and xenophobic reactions to the Roma community. Housing development plans are often bound for failure from their inception because: 1) the inability of local council members to address the xenophobia of the majority; 2) the actions of local non-Roma who often sabotage the building of the projects; and 3) architectural plans that fail to take into account the specific and unique needs of each community. Just like Messing, Hojsík and Peric conclude that the success of housing projects is largely dependent on addressing wider discrimination and segregation.

As each of the four sections shows, the implementation of the Common EU Framework for National Roma Integration has not been easy. EU's long-standing commitment to the Roma has produced both positive and questionable results, with the last 20 years having taught us much. The latest iteration of the EU Framework shows a commitment to resolve the double-standard problem created by the accession process, an awareness of the uniqueness of the Roma issue, and an acknowledgment of the need for more concrete and stable EU-wide policy structures to address it. Whether the Framework will be able to meet the expectations of many of its stakeholders, however, remains to be seen.

Notes

1. For more information, see http://europa.eu/rapid/pressReleasesAction.do?reference=DOC/93/3 &format=HTML&aged=1&language=EN&guiLanguage=en.

2. George Soros, "Time to Break the Vicious Circle of Roma Exclusion," in *Roma: A European Minority*, ed. Monika Flasikova-Benova et al., 39–44 (Brussels: European Parliament Press, 2011).

3. After a Romanian Roma was accused of robbing and murdering an Italian 47-year-old woman on October 30, 2007, the government of Romano Prodi issued a decree for the deportation of European citizens deemed to be a threat to public security. The decree was clearly targeting the Roma population, leading to fingerprinting of Roma for purposes of criminalization, destruction of Roma camps, and deportation of Roma, while at the same time feeding violence against the Roma that led to several incidents of arson in Roma camps in Naples and beyond. For more information, see Claudia Aradau in *Radical Philosophy* (January/February 2009), http://www.radicalphilosophy.com/commentary/the-roma-in-italy.

4. The recent Roma expulsions in France are, unlike those in Italy, not so much a response to a particular event but rather a result of an accretion of tighter immigration policy and a so-called tightening of French identity; this "tightening" targeted not only the Roma population but also the wider immigrant population in France. The Roma expulsions became an issue mainly after the Romanian accession to the EU in 2007, when the French government decided to keep access to its labor market limited and established a legal mechanism to incentivize Romanian and Bulgarian Roma to leave (through the so-called notice of Obligation de Quitter le Territoire Francais [OQTF]) if they become an unreasonable burden for the French social assistance system. In 2010, an intense crackdown on Roma camps led to the delivery of hundreds of such notices, with Roma forced to sign so-called voluntary agreements to leave the country and then put on planes to take them back "home." To ensure that the agreements

would be respected and also to provide a stronger incentive to leave, the French authorities destroyed a series of Roma camps across the country. For more information, see Dominic Thomas in *Radical Philosophy* (January/February 2009), http://www.radicalphilosophy.com/commentary/sarkozy%E2%80%99s-law.

5. For more information on the 2004 directive, see http://eur-lex.europa.eu/LexUriServ/LexUriServ.do?uri=OJ:L:2004:229:0035:0048:EN:pdf

6. Ivan Krastev, "Roma and the Politics of Demographic Imagination," in *Roma: A European Minority*, ed. Monika Flasikova-Benova et al., 45–52 (Brussels: European Parliament Press, 2011).

7. Ibid., 45.

8. Ibid., 46.

9. For more information, please see: http://www.romadecade.org.

10. Valeriu Nicolae, "Why 'Fixing' the Roma Is the Wrong Approach," in *Roma: A European Minority*, ed. Monika Flasikova-Benova et al., 89–99 (Brussels: European Parliament Press, 2011).

11. Irena Baclija, and Miro Hacek, "Limited Opportunities for Political Participation: A Case-study of Roma Local Councillors in Slovenia," *Romani Studies* 17, no. 2 (2007): 156.

12. Ibid., 157.

Section 1:
Roma in Eastern Europe

The year 1989 acts as a convenient dividing line for analyzing the treatment of Roma in contemporary Europe. Prior to 1989, the communist regimes of Southern and Eastern Europe were among the first to recognize and actively target discrimination against the Roma. While the solutions were not always in line with broader international principles of respect for the social, political, and economic rights of ethnic minorities, communist regimes took the issue of Roma integration seriously and devised elaborate social plans that required strong economic and bureaucratic commitment. The integration of the Roma played an important role in the development of education curricula, housing and urban planning, job allocation and skills development, and demographic control. Although many of these policies actively discriminated against the Roma as a minority group, many were nonetheless successful in providing Roma populations with unprecedented access to state services.

The collapse of these communist regimes also marked the collapse of this carefully designed integration system and the resurgence of strong prejudice against the Roma. The economic and political pains of transition as well as the availability of new opportunities with the opening up of borders pushed many Roma out of Eastern Europe into Western Europe. This migration created a new set of political and economic pressures that could no longer be solved within specific borders, but rather required pan-European solutions. The EU has shown an eagerness as well as reluctance to take over this search for new solutions. The chapters in this section showcase these two radically different models for Roma integration—the pre-1989 vs. the post-1989 models—and discuss the advantages and disadvantages of both.

Chapter 1: Roma Rights, Roma Wrongs

by James A. Goldston*

EUROPE'S GYPSY PROBLEM

Several years ago, a Western law-enforcement adviser working in Romania—a country where police abuse has been widely reported, noticed a common explanation for the country's astronomically high conviction rate: nearly every prosecution commenced with the defendant's confession. All the more surprising, then, that one of the nation's most infamous crimes—a 1993 case in which a raging mob in the town of Hadareni murdered three men and burned down more than a dozen homes—was stymied in the courts. No indictment. No trial. The reason, as the local mayor made clear at the time: the victims were "Gypsies," and prosecution of their killers would not have been popular.

Today, after more than eight years of international pressure and several protracted court proceedings, the families of the Hadareni victims are still waiting for justice. And Romania hardly enjoys a monopoly on impunity for violence against Roma (the name many Gypsies use for themselves). Throughout much of Europe, Roma are among the most hated, misunderstood, and mistreated of people. Their renown as musicians, dancers, and palm-readers is surpassed only by the near-universal belief among the *Gadze*—or non-Roma—that Gypsies are also liars, thieves, and cheats. Robert Jordan, the sympathetic hero of Hemingway's *For Whom the Bell Tolls*, could have been speaking for many contemporary Europeans when he said, "The gypsy . . . is truly worthless. He has no political development, nor any discipline, and you could not rely on him for anything."

In Europe today, negative myths about Gypsies penetrate childhood stories, family legends, and the fabric of everyday life. People reveal their anti-Roma prejudice unhesitatingly, in the most casual conversations. "I don't like them," says a Budapest florist as she wraps up some daisies. "Can't trust them," warns a taxi driver. The stereotypes about Gypsies are so insidious that even some leading human rights activists share the tendency to minimize the extent of Roma mistreatment, to react defensively when their national governments are criticized for their Roma policies, or to blame the Roma for their own troubles.

Fortunately, conditions may finally be beginning to change for Europe's most despised minority. With the fall of communism, many Roma in central and eastern Europe—where the vast majority of Roma live—have rediscovered their ethnicity and formed their own community and advocacy groups. Meanwhile, Europe's accelerating process of political integration offers the prospect of improved legal protection for the Roma and other minorities, through human rights laws and strict conditions imposed on countries eager to join the European Union. And accession may also lead the EU's older members to look inward and address their own shortcomings in this area.

Such a positive future for the Roma is by no means secure, however. In recent years, the Roma have been subjected to physical attacks, discrimination, and exclusion from many aspects of mainstream life. Economic hardships have created a fertile environment for the exploitation of racial prejudices, and more than a few European politicians have eagerly taken advantage of these opportunities.

STRANGERS AMONG US

Lacking a territory or government of their own and numbering only eight million to ten million, the Roma today are in many ways Europe's quintessential minority. Although they have lived in the region for 500 years, the Roma's history in Europe has been characterized by alienation, persecution, and flight.

Even the details of their identity are contested. The term "Gypsy"—by which most Roma are known to the outside world—was given to them by others, probably in the mistaken belief that the Roma came from Egypt. The word has often been used to denote itinerants rather than members of a specific ethnic group. Although some Roma continue to live in caravans and move from place to place, most have long since settled. In recent years, as political awakening has encouraged collective expression, the umbrella term "Roma" has increasingly come to embrace not only the Romani ethnic group found mostly in the Balkans and central and eastern Europe, but also peoples with different languages, cultures, and physical appearances: the "Gitanos" of Spain, the "Travelers" of England and Ireland, and the "Sinti" of Germany and Italy. The word *rom*—which means "man" in the Romani language—has provided a fitting foundation for the universality to which many Roma increasingly aspire.

The ethnic Romani are generally believed to have arrived in Europe from India in the fourteenth century. Oppression soon followed and then lasted for centuries. They were enslaved in Romania well into the 1800s and subjected to pogroms and banishment in many parts of Europe. During the Romani genocide in World War II, more than 500,000 Romani are thought to have perished throughout Nazi-dominated Europe.

Less deadly but still destructive were the efforts to assimilate the Roma and end their wandering that were launched under the Hapsburgs and accelerated apace when communist governments took power in eastern and central Europe after 1945. These governments suppressed the notion of ethnic difference in the name of class unity, forcing their Roma citizens to settle and discouraging them from expressing—or even acknowledging—their identity. Motivated by subtle—and not so subtle-racism, communist-era policies such as segregated education and the sterilization of Roma women were premised on the assumption that a backward and degenerate people had to be either forcefully dragged into the modern age—or prevented from making the trip.

E Pluribus Unum

Over the past decade, however, the possibility of a genuine and lasting improvement in the condition of the Roma has emerged, thanks to an extraordinary piece of luck: timing. Just as the movement for Roma rights began to gain ground, the European Union intensified its struggle to transform itself from a free trade zone into a more meaningful political union. Thus, as the EU has begun to incorporate ten postcommunist countries where many Roma live, these two trends—the assertion of Roma rights and European integration—have increasingly converged. Today, the plight of the Roma has rightly come to be seen as a major test of Europe's constitutional pretensions. How can Europe's much-vaunted human rights and equality provisions be taken seriously, the thinking goes, unless they improve the lives of the union's most vulnerable citizens? Simultaneously, the prospect of being allowed to join the EU has become the single most important catalyst for changes in individual government policies toward the Roma.

The round of EU enlargement now being debated will be unlike any the organization has ever experienced. Incorporating central and eastern European states has the potential not only to ease the democratic transitions in these countries, but also to infuse the European project itself with a greater sense of purpose. As Günter Verheugen, EU commissioner for enlargement, observed, "the next enlargement will . . . give us the opportunity to unite the European continent—on the basis of shared ideals and agreed common values." Advocates of European integration aim to do far more than just expand the union's geographic reach, and they have set their sights high: they hope to build a new model of cooperative democratic governance, one capable of abolishing internal armed conflict, securing economic prosperity, developing lasting legitimacy for public institutions, and safeguarding individual freedoms.

Of course, much of what is actually being discussed in the accession negotiations with Hungary, Poland, the Czech Republic, and several other countries concerns technical matters, such as the regulation of fisheries, telecommunications, and agriculture. But the protection of minority rights—and hence of the Roma—has become a core issue as well.

Why are minority rights so important to the European project? There are several reasons. First, there is Europe's past to consider. The continent's ethnic minorities have already suffered horrific atrocities. This history influenced the creation of treaties such as the U.N. Charter, the Universal Declaration of Human Rights, and the European Convention of Human Rights, which helped establish the post-World War II order and still cast a long shadow today. It is no accident that both the Universal Declaration and the European Convention specifically prohibit discrimination on grounds of "race," "color," and "national or social origin."

Then there is Europe's present. One need only remember the role that ethnic hatred played in inspiring the violent disintegration of Yugoslavia to appreciate the dangers posed to regional stability if minority rights are ignored.

And this leads to the third reason minority rights have become so important to Europe: the future. Anti-immigrant and anti-minority political messages have grown more popular on the continent in the last few years: witness the electoral success of Jorg Haider's Freedom Party in Austria and the recent marked increases of political support for anti-immigrant parties in Belgium, Denmark, Norway, and Switzerland. This xenophobic trend has rightly disturbed many European leaders. But the EU's hasty imposition of sanctions against Austria in early 2000 and their quiet retraction several months later only underlined the absence of a permanent mechanism for monitoring negative developments and enforcing a whole new model of adherence to European norms of equality.

Finally, sheer common sense demands that the treatment of minorities become a major issue in European integration. After all, Europe itself is, at its core, a community of minorities in the most fundamental sense. No state contains even close to half the population of the EU. Although English is increasingly becoming a universal second language, no first tongue commands a majority. The union's diffuse population is also reflected by its political structure; the EU's ruling Council of Ministers makes many decisions through a complex process known as "qualified majority voting," designed to ensure that a blocking minority of member states can veto any action by the majority that threatens their own interests.

As enlargement proceeds, the EU's heterogeneity will only increase, with the union becoming more and more an agglomeration of diverse political and linguistic groups. The union's leadership is already starting to recognize this trend. When the European Commission's president, Romano Prodi, recently proclaimed on a visit to Budapest that the "equal treatment of minorities is a cornerstone of the new united Europe," he was proclaiming a fundamental principle—and stating the obvious.

COURTING EQUALITY

So much for Europe's aspirations. How much progress has the region actually made on sensitive issues such as minority protection?

Ten years ago, for most Europeans the word "Roma" meant nothing more than a city in Italy, whereas "Gypsy" was used as a pejorative to describe the bands of thieves who preyed on tourists from Barcelona to Budapest. Ignorance and stereotypes so deeply embedded in the popular consciousness will not be erased overnight. But the awakening of several million Europeans to their Roma roots has begun to effect profound changes, and the EU has played an important role in this process.

Since 1990, Brussels has contributed more than $10 billion to help candidate countries prepare for membership, and some of this cash has been specifically designated to aid minorities. Supported by grants from the EU, individual governments, and private donors, scores of Roma youth are today studying law, public administration, and other professions in the hope that they can start to overcome a historical deficit of formally educated leadership. Furthermore, a number of European governments that previously ignored racism have now begun to acknowledge its presence in their midst, creating some programs to combat discrimination and promising others. One country, Romania, even adopted provisional legislation in 2000 that, if confirmed by both houses of parliament, would prohibit racial and other forms of discrimination in most areas of public life and provide for legal remedies. Comprehensive antidiscrimination laws still do not exist in other postcommunist states, although, partly in response to pressure from Brussels, initial drafts are now circulating in several of them.

Also encouraging is the growth of Romani media participation in several eastern European countries. In the Czech Republic and Hungary, for example, Roma journalists have increasingly started to appear on mainstream television programs. Meanwhile, next door in Slovakia, five new Romani newspapers have appeared since 1999. Others have started up in Poland and Slovenia. And in early 2001, the Hungarian media board granted an FM broadcast license to the first full-time radio station run by and for Roma.

The development that has perhaps the greatest significance, however, is the growing number of Roma who, over the last five years, have started to use legal means to fight their oppression. Bolstered by a nascent public-interest law movement, dozens of Roma have gone to court seeking—and, at times, winning—legal redress for discrimination and violence against them. And so in 1997, a Hungarian court found for the first time that a pub owner's refusal to serve Roma clients—an everyday event—violated the law. The court even awarded damages to the Roma victims and ordered that the defendant pay to publish a written apology in the country's most popular daily newspaper. Since then, other courts in Hungary and the Czech Republic have followed suit, fining bar and disco owners for not admitting Roma.

Where domestic courts have not produced results, Roma have also turned to the European Court of Human Rights in Strasbourg. This tribunal hears cases brought under the European Convention of Human Rights, a treaty signed not just by all EU countries but by all 43 member states of the Council of Europe. And some of these lawsuits have started to pay off. Thus four years ago—in its first decision in a case brought by a Romani applicant from a post-communist country (Bulgaria)—the court ruled that public authorities are required to conduct an "effective official" investigation whenever a complainant presents "arguable" evidence of police ill-treatment. This decision represented a major victory for Roma living in eastern Europe, where such abuse remains far too common and is rarely prosecuted. And in March 1999, a Roma advocacy group filed an application with the court contesting racial exclusion orders that explicitly barred all Roma from entering two towns in Slovakia. A month later, before the court had even ruled on the case, the Slovak government lifted the bans.

Roma have also started to use courts to challenge racial segregation in education—winning in Hungary, but losing at the domestic level in the Czech Republic. An appeal of the latter case—brought by 18 Czech Romani primary school students—is now pending in Strasbourg.

As lawsuits proliferate, the "Roma problem"—once considered the result of an intractable mixture of local mores and ancient prejudices—is increasingly seen as a question of rights and remedies that state institutions have the capacity, and the obligation, to secure. And the implications of this transformation are being felt outside the courtroom, as increasing numbers of Roma, spurred by a heightened sense of entitlement to full political citizenship, challenge official practices and push for change. Thus a Roma organization in Vidin, Bulgaria, for example, has sought to leapfrog years of litigation by providing supplemental training and transport to 400 Roma children who previously attended segregated schools, to help them move into the mainstream school system.

As such self-help measures suggest, international legal remedies for abuse, although salutary, are not a panacea. The European Court of Human Rights may be the most effective regional judicial mechanism yet established; it issues binding rulings that, slowly but surely, are giving rise to a genuinely common European law of human rights. This tribunal cannot, however, replace domestic courts—and was never intended to. Indeed, prior to filing an application in Strasbourg, a claimant must have exhausted every domestic avenue of relief. Moreover, the court's procedures are slow, often taking more than five years from filing to judgment. Finally, the Strasbourg system is already overstretched. Court staff therefore look carefully for any reason not to consider individual cases on their merits—and often find several.

In short, Europe's own regional mechanisms may be able to prod, push, and plead with national governments to improve their conduct, but they cannot substitute for the responsibility of states to enforce their own laws. Moreover, even where European integration has led to new domestic legislation, actual improvements in minority protection have been limited by the fact that relatively few domestic judges and lawyers are familiar with antidiscrimination laws or with international human rights standards. Civil rights litigation remains a rarity in most countries, and the European Court has yet to find a government guilty of discrimination on grounds of race or ethnicity.

Despite these shortcomings, there have been significant advances so far, and the prospect of EU expansion has played an important part in bringing them about. Over the past several years, Roma rights—a concept previously unheard of—has soared to the top of the EU agenda. Hardly a month passes without the Roma being made the subject of a pan-European gathering. The European Commission's annual reports on candidate countries also underscore the importance of minority rights, as do periodic statements on the subject by senior EU officials and visits to the countries that are the worst offenders. In the autumn of 2000, at a preparatory meeting for last year's World Conference against Racism in Durban, South Africa, 41 European governments committed themselves to "guarantee equality to all," and to "bring to justice those responsible for racist acts and the violence to which they give rise."

In June 2000, furthermore, the EU enacted a binding regional prohibition against racial discrimination. This "Race Directive" defines discrimination broadly and mandates liberal standards of proof and effective judicial redress for violation. And the law requires that its provisions be transposed into domestic law in all EU member states by 2003. It also establishes a floor of legal protection that countries hoping to join the union will have to internalize as a condition of their accession.

WORDS INTO DEEDS

The prospect of membership in the world's richest intergovernmental club has helped change popular attitudes and official policy in candidate countries. And yet, despite some advances, most of these governments still must significantly improve their protection of minority rights.

Many governments continue to deny the presence of racism, and ongoing hate speech by officials poisons public discourse. Such language is not always confined to the fringes, either: Vadim Tudor, a member of the Romanian parliament who won more than a quarter of the vote in the 2000 presidential election, reportedly stated, "We are not interested in what Gypsies want. All [Gypsies] should be put in jail. There is no other solution." And in April of last year, a deputy prime minister of Slovakia showed how little some things have changed when, in an interview with the international press meant to trumpet the country's reforms, he made no mention of racism or discrimination but simply repeated communist-era shibboleths about Roma "need[ing] to know what is good for them" and having "to change their way of life."

Perversely, the EU accession process has also led to the scapegoating of Roma by officials embarrassed by asylum applications in the West or criticism from Brussels. This was evident when, two years ago, Romania's then foreign minister expressed frustration that a "few thousand Gypsies . . . are preventing the country from getting off the EU visa blacklist." In another incident, in August 2000, after a group of Roma from the village of Zamoly fled Hungary to seek asylum in France, one Hungarian official accused them of "going abroad to discredit Hungary" and "making groundless allegations against the state and government." The mayor of a nearby town was more direct: "The Roma of Zamoly have no place among human beings. Just as in the animal world, parasites must be expelled." Far from condemning these statements, Prime Minister Viktor Orbán exhorted Hungary's Roma to "try to study and work more." (Since then, French authorities have granted asylum to two dozen of the Zamoly Roma.) And last April, following a well-publicized request for asylum in Belgium by a number of Roma from his country, the Slovak foreign minister warned, "We would consider it very unfair if the Iron Curtain fell on Slovakia because of 90 Romani asylum applicants."

In view of these bitter official attitudes, it is no surprise that central and eastern Europe's Roma continue to suffer hostility and harassment. In recent years, skinhead attacks against Roma have been recorded in large numbers in Bulgaria, the Czech Republic, and Slovakia. Police abuse of Roma is widely reported in Bulgaria, Hungary, and Romania. And just this past July, two Romani men were killed: one in Slovak police custody, having been reportedly bound to a radiator and beaten to death; the other, having been fatally stabbed in a Czech bar following a barrage of racial insults.

All too frequently, Roma complaints receive short shrift and the perpetrators of racially motivated crimes escape justice or receive lenient punishments. International monitoring bodies and local activists complain that the police in several candidate countries have refused to record victim statements and sometimes even pressure Roma victims to withdraw their complaints. The Czech government has conceded that "in several cases of serious violent attacks against [Roma] and foreigners . . . the bodies responsible for penal proceedings tended to trivialize the matter." Yet when a prominent Romani activist filed a complaint after being physically attacked in his Czech home in July 2000, the town's deputy mayor said, "A mountain is being made out of a molehill."

When neo-Nazi groups broke windows and sprayed racist graffiti on the houses of Roma families in the Polish town of Brzeg in December 2000, the local police commander reportedly suggested that it was the Roma themselves who had painted the graffiti in order to claim asylum in western Europe. And in another incident last March, a Romani woman from Kosice, Slovakia, alleged that a group of 15 skinheads had beaten her and her ten-year-old daughter, doused her in gasoline, and tried to set her aflame while shouting, "Die, Gypsy bitch." Although the woman received hospital treatment for multiple wounds, the chief of the district police publicly questioned whether the beating had actually taken place. "In my opinion, she made it up," he told a newspaper. "I don't know why she would do it, but the Roma are probably preparing the ground work to leave [the country]."

Of course, when there exists sufficient political will, anti-Roma violence does get prosecuted. Last spring, a chorus of international condemnation led to the conviction and seven-year jail sentence of a Slovak soldier for brutally murdering a 49-year-old Romani mother of eight. Such convictions remain the exception, however, and seem to require both intense international scrutiny and high level political involvement.

If violence offers the most graphic demonstration of anti Roma prejudice, racial segregation in education may have the worst long-term effects. In the

Czech Republic, Hungary, and Slovakia, Roma have for decades been shunted into "special schools" for those deemed "retarded" or "mentally deficient." Thousands of Roma students each year are thus given only second class education and are denied basic opportunities for economic advancement. In Ostrava, the Czech Republic's third-largest city, Roma children outnumber non-Roma in special schools by 27 to 1. Although Ostrava's Roma represent fewer than 5 percent of all primary school students, they constitute 50 percent of the special school population. And nationwide, approximately 75 percent of Romani children attend special schools.

In other spheres, Roma suffer similar treatment. They are routinely denied access to housing, jobs, restaurants, bars, and even health care simply because of their ethnicity. And such discrimination is an equal opportunity phenomenon; no Roma are too important to merit exemption. Thus, on the eve of the annual human rights meeting of the Organization for Security and Cooperation in Europe (OSCE) in Warsaw in September 2000, three Roma—including the OSCE's highest-ranking official on Roma issues—were forcibly removed from a downtown cafe after refusing to leave when denied service.

Studies in Bulgaria, the Czech Republic, and Hungary suggest that Roma charged with crimes have received disproportionately harsh treatment: they are detained prior to trial more frequently and for longer periods and sentenced more severely upon conviction. Verifying these allegations is difficult, however, thanks to a paucity of ethnic data and the fact that most governments resist monitoring racial bias. Ironically, this resistance is shared by many Roma, who remember all too well that government registration of ethnic origin has often led to abuse.

ON THE INSIDE

The EU accession process has focused most attention on the rights of Roma and other minorities in the candidate countries. Western European leaders, determined to forestall a large influx of Roma fleeing the east, have lectured their foreign colleagues on how to do better. But this attention on eastern and central Europe has at times obscured the fact that EU member states have also struggled, with limited success, to address racism and xenophobia in their own ranks. The numbers of Roma in the EU may be smaller, and violence against them less common, but western Roma, and Roma refugees from outside the EU, also suffer serious discrimination.

The anti-Roma sentiment in the EU may reflect a broader hostility toward migrants and foreigners and the emergence of racist attitudes in countries—such as Finland, Ireland, and Sweden—where they had previously been less evident. Although general xenophobia may exist, however, the Roma still suffer special vilification. According to one report, Roma in Italian schools suffer worse discrimination than do foreign students. Teachers reportedly find it "impossible to blend the nomad culture with ours"—despite the fact that, as in most places, few of Italy's 100,000 Roma are actually nomadic.

In Greece, members of the more than 150,000-strong Roma community suffer frequent ill-treatment from the police, including excessive use of force and verbal abuse. Yet police are rarely disciplined or prosecuted for such offenses. In Germany, Bavarian police records single out Roma and Sinti for preventive crime measures; in Spain, non-Roma parents protest the integration of Roma children into schools; and in Ireland, Travelers are excluded from pubs.

Nor have all EU governments proved equally determined to address racial discrimination, despite the union's equality provisions. The United Kingdom and the Netherlands boast strong antidiscrimination laws, public bodies that investigate complaints, and lawyers and minority activists capable of effective advocacy and litigation. Six EU states, however, have still not ratified the principal European convention securing the rights of national minorities, and legislation in a number of other EU countries is seriously deficient. Last February in Greece, a man was convicted of the crime of "disseminating false information" for distributing a leaflet that acknowledged the presence of minority languages in the country. The court reasoned that the leaflet could "incite anxiety among citizens and create the impression that in Greece minorities exist."

Part of the problem is that in the EU, as in the candidate countries, governments have frequently sought to recast racial discrimination as a social and economic problem. However well intended, such thinking often focuses on the Roma—on their insufficient skills, their purportedly inadequate emphasis on education, or their alleged "unadaptability" to hard work—rather than on the discriminatory treatment they receive. Such arguments displace official responsibility and hinder reform by suggesting that the majority need do little to change. Although improved opportunities for adequate jobs, health care, and housing are essential, real progress requires that governments directly confront discriminatory practices and entrenched racist attitudes among their populations.

PUTTING IDEALS INTO ACTION

Expanding the EU is commonly seen as the best way to spread democratic values and respect for human rights from the west of Europe to its east. And there is much truth to this notion, as can be seen from the way the rule of law was consolidated throughout the accession region over the past decade. EU expansion will have even greater significance, however, if it is not a one-way street but can be made into a vehicle for broadening protection of human rights—including minority rights—throughout Europe. The very process of asking membership candidates to satisfy certain standards requires articulating those standards and the shared ideals and agreed common values for which Europe stands. And simple fairness demands that EU member states subject themselves to the same principles.

As the United States and other countries with legacies of racial discrimination continue to learn, centuries of prejudice are not easily overcome. The EU and national governments have already made substantial progress in this regard, but they should now use the accession process to more fully realize their progressive ideals. These governments should start this process by establishing yardsticks that are clear, unconditional, and apply to all EU members—new and old. To this end, the union's current 15 members should set an example by bolstering their own legal measures to conform to the Race Directive, improving the enforcement of their laws against racial violence, and ensuring that all Roma and others with genuine asylum claims receive due consideration.

The European Commission should also make these political and legal issues more prominent in its annual reports on the candidate countries. It should make clear that, although the accession negotiations will involve some flexibility as prospective members struggle to harmonize their laws and economies with the EU's, no extensions will be granted on standards relating to equality and minority rights. And it should underline that, although accession is a political process, the independence of evaluations of candidate countries' performance will not be compromised. Furthermore, since monitoring has inherent value, instead of ceasing once accession takes place, it should continue and be extended to encompass EU member states as well. Expanding monitoring would accomplish two goals. By making clear that the political criteria apply equally throughout the union, it would dispel any suspicion that candidate states are judged by higher standards. And by providing for regular review, it would encourage systematic development of EU human rights policy and avoid the appearance—fatal to the sanctions on Austria in 2000—that Brussels' actions are haphazard or partisan.

Finally, the commission should do a better job of involving civil society—including Roma and other minority groups—more directly in the accession process. The widely criticized "democratic deficit" within the EU has been replicated in EU-candidate relations: the terms of enlargement have mostly been negotiated between governments and behind closed doors. Over the past decade, EU and other funding has supported a constellation of NGOs with a wealth of accumulated expertise on minority rights issues. The commission and individual governments should capitalize on this experience by treating such NGOs as full partners in the design, implementation, and evaluation of minority policies. One immediate improvement would be to simplify application procedures and make EU funding for antidiscrimination measures more accessible.

The EU can only do so much, however; primary responsibility for protecting minority rights rests with national governments. Senior officials should therefore repeatedly and publicly acknowledge that racism is pervasive and declare it unacceptable. Governments must enact comprehensive antidiscrimination legislation and establish effective enforcement bodies to monitor compliance and remedy violations. In addition, they should increase support for Roma education and legal aid programs. Most important, however, candidate governments should use the accession process not just as a checklist for club membership but as a means to jump-start their transition to diverse and tolerant societies. Too often, newly minted national programs have seemed to be aimed at pleasing Brussels rather than truly protecting minorities. For example, when the Bulgarian government announced in 1999 a series of pledges to combat discrimination and protect the rights of the Roma, its declaration was greeted with much international fanfare. Yet a number of Bulgarian members of parliament learned of the program's existence only when European Commission President Prodi praised it in a subsequent speech. And three years later, most of the proposals lie dormant.

In all likelihood, many of the present EU candidates will soon be members. This is undoubtedly for the good. But if, during this period of heightened scrutiny, candidate governments go through the motions but fail to fully invest in the implementation of minority rights, an extraordinary opportunity will have been missed. Accession offers an unprecedented chance to institutionalize reform both within the EU and in the candidate states. These changes can permanently ground the new Europe on a foundation of respect for human rights. This chance must be seized—for who knows when Europe will get another one like it?

*James A. Goldston is the founding executive director of the Open Society Justice Initiative. Prior to his tenure with OSI, Goldston served as legal director of the European Roma Rights Center.

James A. Goldston, "Roma Rights, Roma Wrongs," *Foreign Affairs* 81, no. 2 (2002): 146–162.

Chapter 2: Politics and the Roma in State-Socialist Eastern Europe

by Zoltan Barany*

ABSTRACT

This article is a comparative analysis of state-socialist policies towards the East European Gypsies (Roma). I make two related arguments. First, the Gypsy policies of East European states evolved differently and resulted in considerable variation. Second, notwithstanding the state-socialist social control policies, a measure of independent Romani activism did emerge laying the groundwork for post-socialist Gypsy mobilization.

INTRODUCTION

In the communist period the East European states replaced the often brutal exclusionary policies of preceding eras with a fundamentally inclusive approach toward the Roma (Gypsies). The new regimes did their best to assimilate the Roma and bring them under state control. Although they remained at the bottom of virtually all socio-economic indicators, employment policies, free education and healthcare, state assistance in housing and child-rearing, and a number of positive discrimination programs had considerably improved the objective conditions of many Gypsies. The cost of Romani integration was high, however, not only in terms of state expenditure and growing inter-ethnic tensions, but also in the loss of Gypsy traditions.

This article focuses on political matters: state policies targeting the Gypsies and developments in Romani political mobilization. It is often assumed that the Gypsy policies of socialist states were hardly distinguishable from each other. Another commonly held view contends that no autonomous Romani activism could develop under socialist rule. I make two related arguments at odds with these positions. First, the Gypsy policies of East European states evolved differently and resulted in considerable variation. Second, notwithstanding the state-socialist social control policies, a measure of independent Romani activism did emerge laying the groundwork for post-socialist Gypsy mobilization.

PART I: POLICIES TOWARDS THE ROMA
General Aims and Principles

The basic goal of communist systems was to exert their control over as large a spectrum of socio-economic and political activities as possible. East European elites envisioned a process of homogenization to which unruly nationalities posed a potential obstacle. The Roma, with their "deviant" lifestyles, did not fit into the communist design of a new society. Therefore, the fundamental goal was to assimilate them and to transform them into productive, cooperative, and supportive socialist citizens. The party-state pursued several integral policies to ensure speedy Romani assimilation: dispersal of compact Gypsy communities and subsequent resettlement, mandatory education, and compulsory wage labor. These policies received ideological support from Lenin who viewed assimilation as an inevitable historical process and condoned actions that would accelerate it with the exception of coercive operations (a point often conveniently forgotten by his disciples).

One of the main political questions pertaining to the Roma was the issue of what type of administrative status should be granted to them. By Stalin's criteria of national minorities the Gypsies came up short on several counts. They did not possess a common language let alone a territorial base, the majority of both communists and Roma were unaware of Romani history, and they did not have a uniform culture. Since they did not "measure up," there was no need to endow them with "national minority" status such as given to Hungarians in Czechoslovakia or Germans in Romania. Consequently, there was no ideological justification for granting them the type of institutions (such as schools with instruction in their mother tongue, socio-cultural organizations, etc.) that national minorities—who in many cases comprised much smaller populations—ordinarily received. Still, there were some important differences in the type of administrative status granted to East European Romani communities.

The 1971 Bulgarian Constitution, unlike its predecessor promulgated in 1947, made no specific references to ethnic minorities but referred to "citizens of non-Bulgarian origins". The authorities in Sofia went as far as denying the very existence of a Gypsy minority (as an ethnic category they were absent from censuses after the 1950s) to ease the execution of the regime's assimilationist policies. Nevertheless, the Roma were officially referred to as a "minority" until 1974 when they disappeared from all statistical data and were seldom mentioned officially afterwards. In 1948 the "nationality" status Roma enjoyed in inter-war Czechoslovakia was revoked and thence the Gypsies officially comprised an ambiguously defined ethnic group, a category that was confirmed by the 1960 Constitution. Experts loyal to the regime took pains to explain on "scientific grounds" why the Gypsies were not and would never become a nationality and that the only correct policy was to assimilate them (Sus, 1961, pp. 97–100). In censuses the Roma were compelled to declare themselves as members of a constitutionally recognized nationality (in the 1980 census 75% declared themselves as Slovaks, 15% as Hungarians, and 10% Czechs) (Ulc, 1988, p. 323). After the Prague Spring, Romani activist Miroslav Holomek advanced the concept of Gypsy nationality but did not get anywhere in the repressive political climate of the time. In official documents and statistics the Roma usually appeared under the rubric of "other and non-stated nationalities." Polish documents customarily referred to the Roma as a "population of Gypsy origin" thus avoiding the formulation of a precise status (Mirga, 1993, p. 71). Until 1989 Polish authorities viewed Roma in an ethnographic context. Romania's Gypsy minority was tabulated under the residual category of "other nationalities." Although the 1965 Constitution went farther (at least in theory) than the 1947 basic law in guaranteeing special educational and cultural minority rights, the Roma were not included in these changes.

In Hungary the Roma's administrative status had evolved gradually in concert with the liberalization of the state. In the 1950s minority experts insisted time and again that the Gypsies did not comprise a nationality and therefore could not be granted national minority status. A 1961 resolution of the Central Committee (CC) of the Hungarian Socialist Workers' Party (HSWP) contended that, although the Roma did not comprise a nationality (based on the Stalinist criteria) they had to be endowed with the same "developmental and constitutional privileges" as national minorities owing to their substantial numbers. Champions of the assimilationist policy defended it in the same terms as in Czechoslovakia: "The Gypsies are not a nationality, the solution to their problem is complete assimilation," opined one in 1962 (Turoczi, 1962). In 1984, after an extensive debate, authorities in Budapest "decided" that the Gypsies did comprise a unique ethnic group after all and, in 1988, the Politburo (PB) of the HSWP granted nationality status to the Roma (Santa, 1991). In many respects the most generous East European state towards the Roma was Tito's Yugoslavia. According to the 1974 Yugoslav Constitution all nationalities, including the Gypsies, were equal but republican constitutions did not include references to them. From 1981 the federal state extended nationality status to the Roma and allowed them to display their own symbols although only Bosnia–Herzegovina and Montenegro uniformly conferred the attendant privileges (Poulton, 1995, pp. 139–140). Other republics continued to view the Gypsies as an ethnic group, the lowest in the three-tier system of "nations" (Croats, Serbs,

Macedonians, etc.), "nationalities" (Albanians, Hungarians, etc.) and "other nationalities and ethnic groups" (Vlachs, Jews, etc.) (Poulton, 1993a, p. 5).

The variation in the Roma's administrative status hints at the important differences between the East European states' approaches toward them. Although some of the disparities may seem subtle, they signified notable differences in political strategy which, in turn, reflected the increasingly dissimilar political paths of the region's states. Generally speaking, the Roma received little political attention until the 1950s as communist elites had to concentrate on consolidating their power and leading the postwar reconstruction efforts. By the mid-1950s "what to do with the troublesome Gypsies?" became an important question across Eastern Europe. The main goal (assimilation) was the same; the approaches were different. These disparities justify extended discussion.

Pattern I: Consistent Coercion (Czechoslovakia, Bulgaria)

The year 1958 was a momentous turning point in the destiny of Gypsies in several East European countries. The CC of the Czechoslovak Communist Party (CSCP) decided in favor of a rapid and comprehensive campaign to settle and assimilate the Roma throughout the country. The resultant legal instrument (Law 74/1958) deprived "nomads" of the right to travel and forced them to find regular employment. This law was tantamount to an administrative attempt to define Roma as a social group (great care was taken to specify a way of life and avoid mentioning the word "Gypsy") (Guy, 1975, p. 222). The Prague government established the National Council for Questions of the Gypsy Population in 1965 to coordinate Gypsy policy. In the same year, authorities in Slovakia recommended to local administrators that no community should include more than 5% Gypsies. The only and all-too-brief period of enlightened minority policy coincided with the Prague Spring and its aftermath (1968–1969). In the early 1970s government resolutions in the Czech Lands (1972)/231) and Slovakia (1972)/94) subjected the Roma to displacement from their settlements to communal apartments in urban areas (Sedivy and Marosi, 1996, p. 21). Schools punished the use of the Romani language even during breaks between classes. Assimilationist pressures did not subside in the 1970s and 1980s and full employment, retraining, and the elimination of Romani crime remained key priorities (as witnessed by the government resolution 1974/29).

One of the most controversial policies towards the Roma in all of Eastern Europe was the sterilization of Gypsy women in Czechoslovakia. The program commenced in 1966 offering women—the applicant had to be at least 35 years old and must have had a minimum of three children—the possibility of sterilization. In 1986 the regulations were modified to allow women as young as 18 years of age to have themselves sterilized even if they had no children. To make it attractive, the authorities paid those who underwent the procedure up to 25,000 crowns (about ten months' good salary). The sterilization policy intended primarily to slow the rapid growth of the Romani population though the two major pertinent decrees of the Ministry of Health and Social Affairs of the Czech Socialist Republic in 1972 and 1988 did not explicitly mention them. In fact, the number of sterilized women as well as the proportion of Roma among them had increased from 500 a year in the early 1980s to 2,000 in 1988; and from 36% in 1987 to nearly 50% in 1989 (though the Gypsies constituted only about 2.5% of the population), respectively (Fisher, 1993, p. 55). According to one source, doctors often sterilized Romani women without their consent, following abortions or Caesarean sections (Hockenos, 1993, p. 220).

After a short period of relative tolerance, Bulgaria began its assimilationist campaign in 1953–1954. Local authorities, particularly in the northern plain where many of the nomadic tribes lived, started to enforce a strict sedentarization policy. This program received additional impetus in 1956 when the USSR ordered that all nomadic groups be settled as soon as possible.[1] A 1958 Bulgarian government decree (No. 258) prohibited Gypsy travel and in the following year the Bulgarian Communist Party's (BCP) CC directed local authorities to ensure full Romani employment. In 1962 Bulgarian minority experts decided to create a segregated Gypsy school system since their education in integrated settings did not produce the anticipated results quickly enough. The fundamental aim was to unify Bulgarian society which meant the rejection of basic minority rights of Turks, Gypsies, and Pomaks (Bulgarian-speaking Muslims). The regime's methods in service of this objective included changing Muslim names to Slavic ones, forced emigration (to Turkey), and religious persecution. A series of government decrees and party resolutions prescribed measures for "reforming" Romani lifestyle and "developing" their culture. After 1984 the Gypsies were prohibited from speaking Romani, dancing and playing unique Romani musical instruments in public and, in 1987, the authorities halted the publication of (Bulgarian language) Gypsy newspapers and closed down the Romani theater. Bulgaria's assimilationist policies were consistent. They succeeded in raising the living standards and educational attainments of the Romani minority and continued to deny them the right to preserve their language, religion, and culture.

Authorities in both Bulgaria and Czechoslovakia actively discouraged objective scholarly research on aspects of Romani life, culture, and language in order to erode Gypsy identity. The writings of Milena Hubschmannova, one of the few eminent independent Romanologists of the region, were heavily censored.

In Bulgaria only two dissertations on the Roma (both supporting the party line) were completed throughout the entire communist period. One of them argued that all (foreign) organizations engaged in studying the Gypsies were formed with the purpose of creating a "fifth column of imperialism" in Bulgaria (Helsinki Watch, 1991a, p. 13).

Pattern II: Erratic Intrusion (Poland, Romania)

In the early 1950s Poland became the first East European state to try to integrate nomadic Gypsies by offering them housing and employment. A 1952 government decree established an Office for Gypsy Affairs under the aegis of the Ministry of Internal Affairs' Department of Social Administration which remained the institutional locus of Romani policy until 1989. The offer was accompanied by minimal coercion and the majority of peripatetic Roma refused to settle. A 1960 meeting of the Polish United Workers' Party's (PUWP) Central Committee recognized the meager results borne by this more or less constructive approach to the problem and decided to apply more direct pressure on the Roma, drawing on the experiences of Czechoslovakia (Mirga, 1993, pp. 72–73). In 1964 a more forceful assimilation campaign commenced which included the registration of Roma by local authorities, restrictions on travel and gatherings, and control of Gypsy cultural organizations (Bartosz, 1994, pp. 16–17). The new tactic brought results in a short time. Within a few years 80% of formerly nomadic children were registered in schools and dispersal policies proved reasonably effective (Fraser, 1992, p. 275). Still, a larger proportion of Roma (both male and female) were able to remain self-employed and Gypsy educational standards stayed lower—due to high absenteeism—than in any other East European state. After the mid-1960s no special legislation was aimed at the Gypsies in Poland but the militia randomly enforced various laws (e.g., on forest maintenance and highway movement) to keep them in check. Owing to the lack of comprehensive legislation and the uniform enforcement of existing regulations Polish Roma were more successful in resisting assimilationist pressures than their counterparts elsewhere in the region.

Romania was the first state that intended to sedentarize nomadic Gypsies by confiscating their horses and wagons as early as 1946 and dispersing compact communities in 1951.[2] By the early 1950s the majority of nomadic Roma were settled. As elsewhere in the region, full Romani employment was an important government objective (in fact, reluctant Gypsies were often sentenced to forced labor under the provisions of Decree 153/1970) but this policy was not pursued as vigorously as in Czechoslovakia, for instance. A 1977 Romanian Communist Party (RCP) CC report admitted the half-hearted implementation of the government decree 1976/25 that called for increases in regular Romani employment and education standards. The party's renewed assimilationist campaign included the prohibition of traditional meetings, confiscation of the gold coins that were often the only possession of value Roma owned, and herding more Gypsies to the factories (Remmel, 1993, pp. 74–75). The results, according to a 1983 RCP CC document remained mixed and depended largely on the zeal of local jurisdictions.

Actually, after the mid-1970s (and especially following the only partially effective renewal of the RCP's dispersal and education campaign), state attention to the "Gypsy problem" had considerably diminished. In any case, the demand that local authorities demonstrate more vigilance directly contradicted the RCP's 1972 declaration that it had solved the country's ethnic problems. Officials even told a foreign filmmaker planning a documentary on the Gypsies that "there are no more Romanie [sic] in our country" (Erich, 1995, p. 16). A 1980 RCP CC position broke with the previous strong pro-natalist policy and decided not to encourage couples with more than five children to have more unless one of the parents was employed in a "useful social activity" and all school-age children regularly attended school.[3] The clear target of this change in policy was the Gypsy community as many Roma shunned work in favor of living on per-child subsidies and did not pressure their children to go to school.

Pattern III: Decreasing Pressures (Hungary)

In stark contrast to its sister party to the north, a 1958 HSWP PB resolution endorsed a policy of active support for Gypsy culture and education and stressed the importance of each minority's national organizations in these efforts. The party resolution of 1961—that officially recognized, for the first time, the abject poverty and profound socio-economic marginality of the Roma—was a turning point that began the process of forceful assimilation. In 1964 and 1968 HSWP CC documents deplored the unimpressive results of the party's educational, employment, and resettlement policies and acknowledged that bridging the gap between the Roma and the rest of society might well take decades of painstaking work and a large amount of resources. Unlike other East European states, however, Hungarian authorities sponsored Gypsy research which yielded several fine sociological studies that were to become the foundations of the regime's changed policies.[4] For instance, the 1974 decision of the HSWP CC's Agitation and Propaganda (Agitprop) Committee ran directly counter to the 1961 resolution by encouraging the formation of Romani clubs, ensembles, and other socio-cultural organizations, supporting Gypsy intellectuals, calling for the establishment of a Gypsy newspaper and even for bilingual education (in areas where Romani children were in a majority). To ensure high quality scholarly work on the Roma, in 1982 the HSWP and the Ministry of Education established the Scientific Council for the Coordination of Gypsy Research within the Institute of Social Sciences of the Hungarian Academy of Science.

By the early 1970s the HSWP had realized that its policies should take into account the Gypsies' unique ethnic identity and specific socio-economic problems. In 1977 a Ministry of Education position paper was the first open break with the assimilationist policy and was followed by several important HSWP resolutions. Most significant of these was the 1979 HSWP PB resolution that criticized the 1961 document and called for expanding the political presence of "deserving" Roma. The 1984 report and resolution of the HSWP CC Agitprop Committee signalled the end of the assimilationist approach by declaring that the Roma could freely choose between alternative methods of social integration: through preserving its culture, traditions, and ethnic identity or by voluntary assimilation (Seewann, 1987, p. 27). In many respects (primary education, employment, culture) the resultant policies improved on the Roma's situation although in several regards (such as higher education) they were rather more superficial. Notwithstanding the HSWP's propaganda efforts, Gypsies did not receive their proportionate share of state resources and, in 1984, two-thirds of them still lived below the official poverty line (Macfarlane, 1990, p. 217). There is no doubt, however, that Hungary's Gypsy policies were more successful in integrating the Roma than other East European states with the notable exception of Yugoslavia.

Pattern IV: Constructive Interference (Yugoslavia)

The cornerstone of Yugoslav nationality and minority policy was to establish and, if necessary, strictly enforce ethnic harmony in the multinational state. After World War II Yugoslav communists viewed the Roma favorably and Tito even considered, albeit briefly, the establishment of a "Gypsy autonomous area" in Macedonia to compensate for the Roma's "fanatical commitment to the partisan cause" (Crowe, 1995, p. 222). In contrast to other East European states, the government and the League of Communists of Yugoslavia (LCY) clearly preferred integration to assimilation. In general, the Roma enjoyed a more secure social status and benefitted from a more tolerant state, particularly in the latter years of Tito's rule, than elsewhere in Eastern Europe. Especially after 1974 (the year of the new constitution that enlarged the autonomy of republics), the Yugoslav government had increased the political visibility of smaller ethnic minorities and the Roma benefited from the policy. In contrast to the other countries of the region, Yugoslav Gypsies were allowed to have a large number of cultural and social organizations relatively free of state control. Another important difference was that the Roma were well served by the party-state's land distribution schemes as many became owners of small farms (particularly in Serbia) (Poulton, 1993b, p. 43). At the same time, their situation remained a "serious basic social issue." According to a 1978 government report the integration of Roma into Yugoslav society lagged far behind the regime's expectations, particularly in terms of their educational attainments and living standards (Crowe, 1995, p. 227).

Even after Tito's death, efforts were made to accelerate Romani integration particularly in the field of education. In areas with large Gypsy communities a growing number of schools offered Romani as the language of instruction in the first grade to ease the pupils' transition into the educational system. Openly discriminatory policies toward the Roma were pursued by republic-level authorities which, along with traditions and history, go far in explaining the substantial differences of the Gypsies' conditions in various republics. For instance, local authorities in Slovenia—the most advanced republic and home to only a small Romani population—followed a policy of territorial segregation and forced socio-economic integration whereas officials in Macedonia and Serbia tended to adopt more relaxed attitudes toward the Roma. Within the East European context Macedonia became the most hospitable place for the Roma (Barany, 1995). After the 1963 earthquake city and republic authorities in Skopje poured large sums of money into building up Shuto Orizari (a suburb of the capital) that had quickly grown into the largest Romani community in the world with a population of approximately 40,000 people in the 1980s. Gypsies there could elect their town council and delegate a member into the Macedonian legislature.

The Reasons for Policy Disparities

Czechoslovakia and Bulgaria were singular among the East European states for their consistent and rigorous pursuit of Romani assimilation from the early 1950s, when communist elites began to seriously consider the "Gypsy question," until 1989. In the case of Czechoslovakia the Prague Spring and its immediate aftermath brought a brief respite from intolerant state policies but with the beginning of "normalization" all reforms were reversed by the new political leadership. As Milena Hubschmannova recalls, "in Czechoslovakia activists and Roma experts considered Hungary and Yugoslavia the examples of how communist parties could actually have acceptable, progressive policies toward the Roma."[5]

Throughout the four decades of their rule Czechoslovak and Bulgarian communists perceived the Roma as a major problem that hindered their efforts toward building a new society. They considered assimilation the only answer to the dilemma the Gypsies represented to them. It is important to note that Czechoslovak authorities treated the other large ethnic minority, Hungarians, relatively well (particularly after the late 1940s) whereas policies toward Bulgaria's large Turkish minority were just as discriminatory as they were toward the Roma. There were many complex reasons for this situation but two important ones go far in yielding a satisfactory explanation. First, ethnic Hungarians were far better integrated into Czechoslovak society than the Roma in both states or the Turks in Bulgaria. Second, fraternal relations with neighboring Hungary were important to politicians in Prague whereas Bulgaria did not concern itself much with antagonizing Turkey until 1989. The Roma, of course, had no protectors in or outside of these states.

Romania and Poland seem like an unlikely pair to fall under the erratic intrusion pattern. After all, Romania was one of the most repressive dictatorships in the region whereas Poland was one of its most liberal states. A further major difference is that Poland had the smallest Romani population whereas Romania the largest. Nonetheless, both states' policies toward the Gypsies were inconsistent but for different reasons. In the Polish case the Roma constituted roughly 0.1% of the population and even if they did not conform to Warsaw's expectations, they did not signify a major threat to building socialism. In any case, the early efforts of assimilation brought mediocre results and the state ended up not pressing the issue although this was unlikely to have been the outcome of a conscious decision. For the increasingly nationalist Romanian regime, on the other hand, the Roma comprised a relatively small problem compared to the more cohesive and larger Hungarian minority. Though Bulgaria, Czechoslovakia, and Romania were conservative communist regimes till the end of the state-socialist period, the Gypsy question in Romania simply did not receive the same attention as in the other two states.

Starting with the early 1960s Hungary had become the most liberal communist state in the Soviet Bloc. Minority policies were partially motivated by Budapest's concern with the fate of ethnic Hungarians in neighboring countries and its efforts to create state-minority relations that it hoped these states would emulate. The most important implication of this comparatively tolerant approach to the Gypsies was the party-state's willingness to re-evaluate its own policies and its efforts to understand the magnitude and attributes of the Romani predicament. Although the regime's growing preference for integration versus forced assimilation, promotion of objective research on the Gypsies, and other initiatives did not alter the basic character of its policies, the evolutionary change in Hungary's approach had been indisputably advantageous to the Roma. After the late 1940s socialist Yugoslavia's policies were not affected by Soviet expectations. In this multinational state nationality policies received far more attention than elsewhere in Eastern Europe and the coercive assimilation of ethnic minorities was not a state policy. More than anywhere else in the region, Yugoslavia's Gypsy policies were marked by tolerance and the intention to foster Romani integration.

PART II. PROGRESS IN ROMANI MOBILIZATION
From Traditional to Modern Leaders

The introduction of centrally planned economies and state efforts to disperse hard-to-control compact Romani groups dealt a devastating blow to the life of traditional Gypsy communities. Many traditional Gypsy leaders fell victim to this process and, given that they were generally woefully uneducated in the formal sense, they could rarely deal effectively with the *gadje* (non-Gypsy) and their complex bureaucracies. As a result, the influence wielded by traditional Romani leaders declined everywhere in Eastern Europe albeit not to the same degree. In areas where nomadism and established lifestyles survived longer conventional Gypsy leaders were better equipped to maintain their authority in their bailiwick. The state devised different ways to deal with them. In many areas of Hungary and Romania, for instance, local officials and the police coerced them to report on their own people, call the authorities in emergencies, and assist state policies through exercising their personal influence.[6] Local authorities across the region customarily blamed uncooperative Gypsy chiefs for unsuccessful policies, and accused them of preserving their power, keeping the "naive" Roma under their influence, and actively resisting resettlement and dispersal. In Poland, on the other hand, the more *laissez faire* attitude of the authorities, the cohesion of some Gypsy communities, and the strong influence traditional leaders had historically enjoyed, often allowed them to maintain their elevated position in Romani society.

The emergence of a small but critically important Romani intelligentsia was a development corresponding to the waning influence of traditional Gypsy leaders. The sheer numerical results yielded by the socialist states' emphasis on education were unimpressive with respect to the number of Romani university graduates. Nonetheless, many of those who did acquire post-secondary education became active in politics as well as in organizing Gypsy cultural and, wherever possible, mobilization projects. An interesting facet of this issue is that those Roma who studied humanities and social sciences were more likely to become participants in political activities than those who studied natural sciences.[7] Many of the latter—probably due to more attractive employment opportunities and personal considerations—attempted to assimilate and shake off, as it were, their Gypsiness.

It is difficult to estimate the size of the East European Romani intelligentsia but it seems fair to say that by 1989 it comprised approximately two to three thousand people. Among their ranks were dozens of eminent sociologists, writers, painters, poets, teachers and, of course, musicians.

In order to hasten Romani integration all East European communist parties actively recruited Gypsy members. The party tried to present them in the media as role models to be emulated by their brethren. A BCP CC document reveals that 3500 Roma had joined the party's ranks by 1959 and thousands more were members of its youth organization (Helsinki Watch, 1991a, p. 63) There were probably as many as 10–12,000 Romani communist party members in Eastern Europe in the mid-1970s who constituted an important support base for the socialist states. None rose to higher prominence than Emil Rigo, a member of the CSCP Politburo in 1968 and keen supporter of its assimilationist policies. Another eminent Gypsy leader, Slobodan Berberski, was a member of the Yugoslav communist party's Central Committee as well as a prominent figure in the international Romani movement. In the late 1940s Shakir Pashov, along with several other Roma, gained seats in the national legislature in Sofia while Gospodin Kolev became a BCP CC member three decades later. Faik Abdi, an economist by training, served as a member of the Macedonian Republican Assembly in 1969–1974. Bekir Arif was for 12 years the elected president of Shuto Orizari's municipal council. Many hundreds of Roma across the region were also employed in various capacities (usually at lower levels) as state and party officials. For instance, in 1965 Roma held 46 seats in district councils of Baranya County, Hungary while in 1983, 433 Gypsies served as council deputies in Czechoslovakia (Puxon, 1973, p. 16; and Kostelancik, 1989, p. 319).

Although the authorities strictly controlled office-holders (whether Roma or not), the political participation of hundreds of Gypsies benefited the entire Romani population. Those who held political or bureaucratic positions gained valuable experience and acquired organizational and administrative skills that could be useful resources once the post-communist transition removed obstacles to ethnic mobilization. At the same time the diminishing role of traditional leaders and the growing authority of modern intellectuals created deep cleavages within the Romani communities, fissures that were to have a damaging impact on Gypsy mobilization.

State-controlled Gypsy Organizations

Although a number of Romani organizations existed in the communist period, they were either entirely controlled by the authorities or enjoyed minimal independence. Most were the toadies of communists and served to bolster the regimes' hollow claim of wide-based social legitimacy. As in most other respects, in this area, too, there were major differences between East European states. Generally speaking, the states where communist rule was more liberal (Hungary, Poland, and Yugoslavia) tended to enable Romani organizations to gradually enjoy increasing autonomy. In contrast, more conservative communist regimes (Bulgaria, Czechoslovakia, Romania) either did not permit the formation of Gypsy organizations or subjected them to stifling control.

In 1957 Czechoslovak party officials refused the requests of Romani spokesmen to establish their own association (one similar to that of other ethnic minorities). In early 1968 the rapidly improving political milieu leading to the Prague Spring allowed for the formation of the Union of Gypsies–Roma, under the aegis of the National Front (a party-controlled umbrella organization, similar to the Fatherland Front in Bulgaria or the Patriotic People's Front [PPF] in Hungary). The Union had separate organizations in the Czech Lands and in Slovakia. By its first national meeting more than 5,000 Roma joined its membership. It organized festivals promoting Romani culture, published a magazine, and pursued anti-defamation activities (Kalvoda, 1991, pp. 102–103). The Union was relatively independent of state control and, as such, it was obviously not suitable for the "normalization" policy. In 1973 the authorities unceremoniously disbanded it because it "failed to fulfill its integrative function" and due to serious financial mismanagement (the Union leadership was unable to account for 7.5 million crowns of state funds).[8] From 1973 all Romani political organizations were prohibited by the state. Taking advantage of the political instability in the immediate post-war period, Roma founded the Cultural Enlightenment Organization of the Gypsy Minority in Bulgaria in 1946 which soon mushroomed into a federation with over 200 local chapters (Crowe, 1995, p. 21). Bulgaria's assimilationist policies included the termination of the Gypsy Cultural and Educational Society which replaced the two interwar era organizations (Egypt Society and Future) in 1953 and the incarceration of Shakir Pashov, the country's most prominent Romani leader, in 1954.[9]

The evolutionary nature of socialist Hungary's Gypsy policies is quite well traceable through the country's Romani organizations. In 1961 the Cultural Association of Hungarian Gypsies, organized only four years earlier, was dissolved in concert with the regime's assimilationist policies. In 1974, reflecting the changing direction of policy a new body, the Gypsy Federation, was called to life by the authorities under the supervision of the PPF whose leadership usually consisted of relatively liberal communists. The PPF also actively supported the creation of the National Gypsy Council in 1979 and, in 1986, the Cultural Association of Hungarian Gypsies. All of these organizations were supervised by the regime, primarily through the PPF. By the mid-1980s, however, Roma leaders within and without these organizations had become increasingly vocal in demanding the termination of state control which nonetheless continued until 1988. Starting with the early 1970s the regime also supported dozens of Gypsy clubs and folklore ensembles which organized art exhibitions, readings by Romani authors, and sport activities. By 1989 approximately 150–200 such groups existed (Agoston, 1994, p. 6).

In Poland Roma could form cultural associations whose activities were overseen by the Ministry of Internal Affairs (Bartosz, 1994, pp. 17–18). The most prominent of these was established in Tarnow in 1963 and has survived the communist period. Other organizations catering to the cultural needs of local Romani communities were formed in Gdansk, Olsztyn, Andrychow and elsewhere. The state remained the sole source of financial support for these organizations, providing facilities—usually in houses of culture—and salaries to employees. In many cases the majority of the membership was comprised by interested non-Roma. The state financed but did not control the Federation of Yugoslav Gypsies which had become a relatively independent representative of Romani interests. In 1986 the International Romani Union and the Yugoslav government organized and paid for a large international conference on Romani language and history in Sarajevo. The Roma in Yugoslavia also enjoyed the opportunity to maintain regional associations and cultural organizations. Perhaps the most successful of these was the Romani theater, Phralipe, established in Skopje in 1971, that gained international awards and popular acclaim for its staging of contemporary plays. Romania was at the other end of the spectrum. Although Gypsy activists resuscitated the interwar era's General Union of Romanian Roma in 1946, the RCP abolished it eight years later and afterwards permitted no formal Gypsy organizations.

In some East European states (e.g., Hungary, Yugoslavia) a few newspapers and magazines were published for the Roma, and an even smaller number of radio and television programs (in Yugoslavia) catered to a Gypsy audience. The Gypsy media was financed entirely by the state. In the more conservative countries their undisguised aim was to hasten Romani assimilation while in more liberal states the Gypsies could actually make independent and relatively uncensored contributions to publications and programming. In every case, however, the Roma's involvement in the media endowed them with new experiences and skills that became especially valuable after 1989.

Independent Efforts

One of the quintessential attributes of communist states is their hostility to an independent civil society. The East European regimes' strong push for assimilation posed serious obstacles to maintaining let alone nurturing Romani identity, traditions, and language. Still, the Roma had proved time and again that they possessed a strong desire to preserve their culture and create independent organizations though most of their initiatives had failed due to state opposition.

In orthodox communist systems even such seemingly innocuous activities as putting together sport teams could rarely survive for long without state intrusion. A fitting example is the soccer team organized in the mid-1960s by a group of Roma in the Bulgarian town of Lom. The authorities objected to the club's Gypsy name and all-Roma roster. Team members broke up the squad rather than to give in to the authorities' demand of including at least five ethnic Bulgarians. In Brno, Czechoslovakia, a group of Romani activists started a Gypsy museum in 1969 but the state dissolved the group and put the collection in storage in 1973. Still, a 1972 law allowed the Roma to organize state-supervised folklore groups which also served as the institutional locus of informal political discussions. In Sokolov (northwestern Bohemia) Emil Scuka founded the Theater "Romen" in 1983, based on the already existing folklore group and inspired by the Romani theater of the same name in Moscow.[10] In the same year Romanian Gypsies created an unofficial association in Sibiu that was never acknowledged by the authorities and ultimately disappeared. In essence, the only autonomous Romani formations that existed in the communist period were the loosely knit informal organizations of the drastically diminished number of travelling or semi-nomadic Roma (particularly in Poland and Romania) who were able to maintain their traditional ways despite official interference.

It should not be forgotten that Gypsies took an active part in the popular uprisings of the socialist period. In 1956, hundreds of Roma—among them the colorful character Gabor Dilinko a.k.a. "Bizsu" and his men—fought courageously against the Soviet forces in Budapest and elsewhere.[11] During the August 1968 Warsaw Pact invasion of Czechoslovakia "Gypsy youths went into battle against the tanks" and bravely expressed their solidarity with their fellow citizens (Ulc, 1988, p. 310). Twenty years later a large number of Roma again proved their valor fighting against communist forces in Romania. Few East Europeans are aware of the Gypsy contribution to their struggles against tyranny.

Dissident organizations did not ignore the Roma. From its birth, Czechoslovakia's Charter 77 called attention to their plight and discriminatory state policies. In December 1978 an important samizdat study by Charter signatory and one-time spokesman, Jozef Vohryzek, analyzed the Gypsies' situation and the state's lacking comprehension of their predicament (Vohryzek, 1990, pp. 217–225). In two additional documents (23/1979 and 3/1990) the group scathingly criticized the Czechoslovak government's sterilization program. A prominent dissident and Charter's leader, Vaclav Havel, became a vocal champion of Romani rights in his capacity of Czechoslovak and later Czech president in the 1990s. One of the first Hungarian dissident groups, SZETA, whose main purpose was to publicize the growth of the country's underclass, forcefully castigated the communist state for not intervening more energetically to alleviate the Roma's poverty.

In the late 1980s, taking advantage of the erosion of the communist party's power, Hungarian Gypsies started a number of independent organizations. The first of these was the Democratic Association of Hungarian Gypsies that sprang to life in 1988 with the backing of but independent from the PPF. The Association supported the PPF's liberal policies and received the HSWP's blessing. A more important development was the funding of the Phralipe Independent Gypsy Organization by Roma and non-Roma intellectuals and activists in April 1989. In many ways Phralipe originated in the well-organized and successful resistance of its founders—most importantly the Romani school teacher and activist Aladar Horvath—to the construction of a Gypsy ghetto on the periphery of Miskolc, in order to provide the provincial city's elite with choice apartments in 1988 (Ladanyi, 1991, pp. 45–54). From its inception Phralipe ("brotherhood" in Romani) criticized the regime's Romani policies and the state-created and sponsored Gypsy federations. For a short time at least, Phralipe managed to link Romani and gadje intellectuals with "ordinary" Roma. In Belgrade, Gypsies disappointed by the lack of adequate political representation established the Yugoslav Romany Association (YRA) in July 1989. Sait Balic, the new organization's leader and president of the World Romany Congress, expressed his hope that the founding of YRA would signify an initial step toward wider Romani emancipation (Tanjug, 1989).

The founding of the International Gypsy Committee in 1965 was a momentous development that brought the activities of the international Romani movement into a legitimate institutional framework. Those Roma, particularly from Yugoslavia, who were able to take part in the movement's activities gained a new perspective on the Gypsies' present and future. Faik Abdi, who participated in the first World Romani Congress (London 1971), came away with the conclusion that the Roma were not an inherently apolitical people and cooperation and organizational activities in the international realm might make a substantial contribution to improving their lot.[12] In subsequent congresses (Geneva 1978, Gottingen 1978, Warsaw 1990) Yugoslav Roma managed to gain several top positions in the International Romani Union (IRU), founded at the Gottingen meeting. They were successful in part because Yugoslavia had a large and relatively dynamic Romani community whose activities were not hindered by the state to the same extent as elsewhere in Eastern Europe. Gypsy leaders utilized these international meetings to demand that East European states extend national minority status to Roma and terminate discriminatory policies. Another issue many delegates were concerned with was the state of the Romani language and the alarming decline of the number of people with the ability to use it. Toward that end the organizers planned on formulating a literary Gypsy language and supported the publication of a standardized Romani grammar book, an ambition that was realized in Macedonia in 1980.

Only Yugoslavia and Hungary sent official representatives to the gatherings of the international Romani movement though at times Roma from Bulgaria, Czechoslovakia, and Romania were able to attend as tourists. In 1979 the Roma acquired observer status in the United Nations Council for Social and Economic Questions. Within a decade the IRU attained representation in the Council of Europe and in several United Nations bodies. The vast majority of East European Roma, however, remained unaware of the existence of an international Gypsy movement let alone its achievements.

SUMMARY

The different policies East European states pursued toward the Roma to some extent reflected their overall political attributes: the relative tolerance and liberalism of Hungary and especially Yugoslavia, as well as the orthodoxy of Bulgaria and post-1968 Czechoslovakia. In the case of Poland and Romania the "Gypsy question" received sporadic and temporary attention: in Poland owing to the small proportion of the Romani population while in Romania because of the presence of another larger, more cohesive, and more troublesome ethnic minority. The abysmal socio-economic situation of the Roma across the region served as a major force in shaping state policy. Still, none of these policies generated the magnitude of changes in the Gypsies' socio-economic conditions anticipated by the states as can be gleaned from the many party resolutions and state documents lamenting mediocre results.

Aside from a few isolated examples, the Roma were not permitted to pursue mobilization activities. Thus, their political marginality in this period was rooted in exogenous political causes (e.g. obstacles posed by the state to mobilization). Nevertheless, state-controlled Gypsy organizations and the policy to integrate the Roma into state and party hierarchies served as something of an unintended training ground for the Gypsy activists of the future. As Ivan Vesely, a Slovak Rom who became a prominent Gypsy activist in the Czech Republic, asked me: "Do you think I would be sitting here arguing about Marx and Weber if it were not for the communists? I would be in the ghetto in eastern Slovakia!"[13] Paradoxically, through their social (especially educational) policies the socialist regimes contributed to the development of what they feared most: Romani identity formation and activism.

Acknowledgements

I am grateful to Daniel Chirot and Gary P. Freeman for their comments on the manuscript and to the Ford Foundation and IREX for their financial support of my field research.

NOTES

1. Interview with Ilona Tomova, Adviser to the President on ethnic and religious issues (Sofia, 8 March 1995).

2. This discussion draws on Helsinki Watch ((1991b), pp.17–19).

3. Interview with Catalin Zamfir, a former Romanian Minister of Social Welfare (Bucharest, 1 June 1996).

4. Perhaps the most important product of this crop was Kemeny (1976), an abbreviated version of which is Kemeny (1974).

5. Interview with Professor Milena Hubschmannova (Prague, 27 August 1999).

6. See Bihari (1991) and interview with Vasile Burtea, a Romani official at Romania's Ministry of Labor (Bucharest, 15 March 1995).

7. Interview with Andras Biro (Budapest, 26 July 1996).

8. Interview with the Romani historian, Bartolomiej Daniel, who was one of the Union's leaders (Brno, 2 September 1999).

9. Interview with Krassimir Kanev of the Bulgarian Helsinki Committee (Sofia, 6 March 1995).

10. Interview with Milena Hubschmannova (Prague, 27 August 1999).

11. Patrin/Uzenet (a television program for and about the Gypsies), Hungarian Television 1, (13:00 GMT, 27 October 1997).

12. Interview with Faik Abdi (Skopje, 11 March 1994).

13. Interview with Ivan Vesely (Prague, 16 June 1994).

REFERENCES

Agoston, E., 1994. A cigany munkanelkuli reteg valsag-kezelesenek helyzete. Munkaugyi Miniszterium, Budapest.

Barany, Z., 1995. The Roma in Macedonia: ethnic politics and the marginal condition in a Balkan state. Ethnic and Racial Studies 18 (3), 515–531.

Bartosz, A., 1994. The social and political status of the Roma in Poland. Roma 40, 16–23.

Bihari, T., 1991. Cigany banat, magyar banat. A Vilag (April 24).

Crowe, D.M., 1995. A History of the Gypsies of Eastern Europe and Russia. I.B. Tauris, London.

Erich, R., 1995. In: Figusch, V. (Ed.), Roma People in Slovakia and in Europe. Information and Documentation Centre on the Council of Europe, Bratislava, pp. 15–19.

Fisher, S., 1993. Romanies in Slovakia. RFE/RL Research Report 2 (42), 54–59.

Fraser, A., 1992. The Gypsies. Blackwell, Oxford.

Guy, W., 1975. Ways of looking at Roms: the case of Czechoslovakia. In: Rehfisch, F. (Ed.), Gypsies, Tinkers, and Other Travellers. Academic Press, London, pp. 201–229.

Helsinki Watch, 1991a. Destroying Ethnic Identity: The Persecution of Gypsies in Bulgaria. Helsinki Watch, New York.

Helsinki Watch, 1991b. Destroying Ethnic Identity: The Gypsies of Romania. Helsinki Watch, New York.

Hockenos, P., 1993. Free To Hate: The Rise of the Right in Post-Communist Eastern Europe. Routledge, New York.

Kalvoda, J., 1991. The Gypsies of Czechoslovakia. In: Crowe, D., Kolsti, J. (Eds.), The Gypsies of Eastern Europe. M.E. Sharpe, Armonk, pp. 93–115.

Kemeny, I., 1974. A magyarorszagi ciganylakossag. Valosag 17 (1), 63–72.

Kemeny, I., 1976. Beszamolo a magyarorszagi ciganyok helyzetevel foglalkozo 1971-ben vegzett kutatasrol. MTA Szociologiai Intezet, Budapest.

Kostelancik, D.J., 1989. The Gypsies of Czechoslovakia: political and ideological considerations in the development of policy. Studies in Comparative Communism 22 (4), 307–321.

Ladanyi, J., 1991. A miskolci gettougy. Valosag 34 (4), 45–54.

Macfarlane, L.J., 1990. Human Rights: Realities and Possibilities. St. Martin's, New York.

Mirga, A., 1993. The Effects of State Assimilation Policy on Polish Gypsies. Journal of the Gypsy Lore Society Series 53 (2), 69–76.

Poulton, H., 1993a. The Balkans: Minorities and States in Conflict. Minority Rights Group, London.

Poulton, H., 1993b. The Roma in Macedonia: A Balkan Success story? RFE/RL Research Report 2 (19), 42–45.

Poulton, H., 1995. Who Are the Macedonians? Hurst, London.

Puxon, G., 1973. Rom: Europe's Gypsies. Report #14 of Minority Rights Group, London.

Remmel, F., 1993. Die Roma Rumaniens: Volk ohne Hinterland. Picus, Vienna.

Santa, G., 1991. Sokan vagyunk es semmink sincs: Beszelgetes Osztojkan Belaval II. Beszelo, 18–19, August 10.

Sedivy, V., Marosi, V., 1996. Position of National Minorities and Ethnic Groups in the Slovak Republic. Minority Rights Group, Bratislava.

Seewann, G., 1987. Zigeuner in Ungarn. Sudost-Europa 36 (1), 19–32.

Sus, J., 1961. Cikanska otazka v CSSR. SNPL, Prague.

Tanjug (Yugoslav telegraph agency), 1989. Yugoslav Romany Association Established. Belgrade (July 29).

Turoczi, K., 1962. A ciganysag tarsadalmi beilleszkedeserol. Valosag 5 (6), 72–81.

Ulc, O., 1988. Gypsies in Czechoslovakia: A case of unfinished integration. Eastern European Politics and Societies 2 (3), 306–332.

Vohryzek, J., 1990. O postaveni cikanu-romu v Ceskoslovensku. In: Charta 77, 1977–1989: Od moralni k demokraticke revoluci, Archa, Bratislava, pp. 217–225.

*__Zoltan Barany__ is a professor in the Department of Slavic and Eurasian Studies at the University of Texas at Austin.

Zoltan Barany, "Politics and the Roma in State-Socialist Eastern Europe," *Communist and Post-Communist Studies* 33 (2000): 421–437.

Section II:

Roma and the EU Accession Process

The post-1989 model of Roma integration has largely been shaped by the EU accession process, with integration imposed as a requirement for joining the EU. The model has been widely criticized by those who saw this forced integration as superficial and difficult to achieve despite a series of strong financial incentives and support. Others, however, have praised it as an essential intervention at a time when economic pressures and political uncertainty could have easily made Roma the target of even wider unchecked violence. While these two positions are not mutually exclusive, many analysts have pointed to the damaging effects of the double standard that was effectively implemented through the EU accession process. For a long time, this standard allowed Western Europe to escape any responsibility for the plight of the Roma, while considering Eastern Europe to be both the problem and the solution. The neat separation of responsibilities, with Western Europe playing the role of an apparent neutral arbitrator and Eastern Europe the problem child that needed to be reined in, resulted in deep resentment and distrust as well as a general questioning of Western Europe's commitment to Roma integration. With the legacy of the double standard likely to continue to cast a shadow over future debates and frameworks for Roma integration, the EU—Western Europe in particular—needs to show a new kind and level of commitment to Roma integration. Whether it is ready to do so or not is questionable, however. This section looks at the extent to which this renewed commitment is likely to be embraced (or not) given EU's past history.

Chapter 3: The EU Accession Process and the Roma Minorities in New and Soon-to-be Member States

by Maria Spirova and Darlene Budd*

The Roma have been referred to as a 'European Minority,' reflecting both their nature as a truly transnational minority and their importance for the process of European integration in Eastern Europe. Research generally argues that the European accession process, which has greatly influenced the development of politics in the region, has had a very direct effect on the states' policies towards this disadvantaged minority. This paper proposes to investigate the link between European Union (EU) accession and minority policy by comparing the situation of the Roma in Hungary, the Czech Republic, Bulgaria, and Romania. The paper uses survey data to compare the differences that exist between the situation of the Roma and members of the majority groups along several socio-economic indicators in these four countries. Our findings add to a body of literature that finds limited support for the role of EU accession in influencing Roma policy in Eastern Europe. The EU accession process seems to have narrowed the gap between Roma and the majority in several areas, while not achieving the expected result in a few others.

INTRODUCTION

The Roma have often been referred to as a 'European Minority,' reflecting both their nature of a truly transnational minority and their importance for the process of European integration in Eastern Europe (Liegeois *et al.*, 1995; Tubbax, 2005; EUMC, 2005). Unlike other minorities in Eastern European countries, the Roma have no kin state and are not politically mobilized. This not only makes them a 'transnational' minority, but also leaves them largely dependant on the policies of the state for both socio-economic development and political representation. Research generally argues that the European integration process, which has greatly influenced the overall development of politics in the region, has had a very direct effect on state policies towards this disadvantaged minority.

Most work, however, focuses on the mechanisms through which the European Union (EU) has influenced changes in policy carried out by candidate countries;[1] little has been done to link EU influence over policy with the actual conditions of minorities. This article proposes to expand the focus of previous research by investigating whether the condition of the Roma minorities in several countries is related to the position of each state in respect to the EU accession process. These countries include Hungary and the Czech Republic, representing the newly accepted member states at the time of the analysis, and Bulgaria and Romania, which at the time could be considered soon-to-be-member states. The data used in the article come from two surveys of Roma minorities: the United Nations Development Program (UNDP) survey *Avoiding the Dependency Trap*, carried out in five Eastern European countries in 2001–2002;[2] and the *UNDP Vulnerable Groups Dataset*, conducted by the UN Development Program in 10 Eastern European states and Kosovo during 2004.[3] The article draws some tentative conclusions about the impact of the EU accession process on the Roma minorities in the four countries.

THE EU AND MINORITY PROTECTION IN CANDIDATE STATES

That the EU accession process has been a major factor in the development of democracy in the post-communist world is by now a well-established fact. In many ways, the case of the EU is an anomaly; the literature on democratization and international political economy seldom finds evidence to make the claim that external actors may 'tip the political scales in favor of reform' by using conditionality to change elite behavior (Haggard and Webb, 1994, 5; as cited in Vachudova, 2001, 4).

As joining the EU and NATO has been the dominant foreign policy goal of the majority of the Eastern European countries, the European process has impacted the pace and nature of political reforms and the policy-making process (Smith, 2001, 32).[4] The benefits of membership into the 'most highly developed international institution in the world' (Vachudova, 2001, 34) are used as leverage to influence the domestic politics of credible future member states. In fact, the vast disparity between the bargaining power of the Western and Eastern European states has allowed for the extraordinary influence of the EU integration process on domestic political development in the candidate states (Williams in Linden, 2002).

The way the membership process is set up contributes to EU success in influencing policy. The EU is open to all European states, and the Commission uses a merit-based system to motivate states toward membership. A candidate state moves up the list and closer to membership based on the progress made toward fulfilling EU membership requirements (the Copenhagen Criteria) (Vachudova 32). This process has called on candidate states to change current policies and implement new ones in order to achieve the requirements specified in the Copenhagen Criteria. As a result, policy change in the areas covered by the criteria has often been attributed to 'European conditionality' (Pridham, 1999).

In addition, the EU uses other mechanisms, such as funding distribution and specific programs, to influence policy in candidate states; the *Decade of Roma Inclusion* introduced in 2005 is one example. The Commission also encourages the acceptance of certain international norms and cooperation with other international organizations such as the OSCE and the Council of Europe in the area of minority rights provision.[5] While most work focuses on the 'conditionality' mechanism, which is often equated with EU influence, in this paper we take a broader approach and consider the EU influence to include the mechanisms implied in the conditions for entry as well as other policies and initiative by the EU.

The rights of people belonging to ethnic minorities are addressed on two different levels by the EU. Firstly, several EU documents provide for the non-discrimination of individuals based on race and ethnicity. For example, the Charter of Fundamental Rights of the EU (article 20) states that 'everyone is equal before the law.' Article 21 deals more specifically with the question of discrimination based on a variety of factors. Clauses 1 and 2 state that:

1. Any discrimination based on any ground such as sex, race, color, ethnic or social origin, genetic features, language, religion or belief, political or any other opinion, membership of a national minority, property, birth, disability, age or sexual orientation shall be prohibited.

2. Within the scope of application of the Treaty establishing the European Community and of the Treaty on the European Union, and without prejudice to the special provisions of those Treaties, any discrimination on grounds of nationality shall be prohibited (European Parliament, 2000).

Secondly, the democratic norms promoted through the expansion process go beyond the provisions for non-discrimination to call for the protection of minorities on the group level. At its 1993 meeting, the European Council established a set of criteria that the countries of Central and Eastern Europe had to satisfy in order to be admitted into the EU. The Council specified that:

> Membership requires that the candidate country has achieved stability
> of institutions guaranteeing democracy, the rule of law, human rights and
> respect for and protection of minorities, the existence of a functioning

market economy as well as the capacity to cope with competitive pressure and market forces within the Union (European Council, 1993, 12).

The inclusion of minority rights in these criteria signaled the emerging concern of Western Europe 'over stability in the face of the serious outbreak of (ethnic-based) violence in South Eastern Europe,' which was also reflected in the actions of other multilateral organizations such as the UN, CSCE/OSCE, and the Council of Europe (Bokulic et al., 2006, 66).

Since the 1993 meeting, the EU has maintained its concern for the overall well-being of minorities and has made 'the status of minorities' an important part of the Annual/Progress Reports commissioned by the European Commission.[6] These reports evaluate the progress of each country in terms of its fulfillment of the Copenhagen criteria and are used by the European Council in making policy recommendations and allocating financial assistance to EU candidate states (Bokulic et al., 2006, 67).

Not only has the EU pushed for the adoption of legislation and policies providing for minority rights by linking such legislation and policies to entry into the EU, but it has also used specific programs to promote the implementation and enforcement of non-discrimination policies. The low socio-economic status of the Roma in the candidate states has been a major focus of concern for the EU, and funding has been specifically directed to projects in the areas of education, housing, and healthcare. For example, between 2001 and 2003, the main pre-accession assistance program PHARE provided over 77 million euro to Roma-related projects in the then candidate countries for infrastructure, public awareness, and sector-specific projects (European Commission, 2004, 15).

One of the major challenges to the EU's minority policies in candidate countries has been the claim that minority protection is something the EU has preached rather than practiced. As already mentioned, group minority rights are not part of the EU *acquis*. Some older member states have a long way to go to satisfy the criteria imposed on the candidate states in the late 1990s (Johns, 2003) and some have yet to ratify the Council of Europe's Framework Convention on National Minorities, a document that the EU strongly urged candidate states to ratify in the mid-1990s.

Despite this often-cited inconsistency among EU member countries, research shows that the EU accession process has 'induced change and served as a catalyst at a domestic level' (Bokulic et al., 2006, 37) in candidate states and has had a positive impact on the status of minorities. For example, Kelley (2004) argues that the EU accession process has been necessary to change behavior toward ethnic minorities in candidate states. She makes an even stronger argument by claiming that it is *conditionality* and not merely the socialization-based efforts[7] of the EU that has made the EU policy a successful one. Based on her research, she concludes that 'when European institutions used only socialization-based efforts—which they did quite frequently—governments rarely changed their behavior' (Kelley, 2004, 426). Ram (2003) also examines the impact of European integration on minority rights in the Czech Republic and Romania. Using several legislative developments in the Czech Republic and Romania as examples, she finds that EU conditionality has had a substantial impact on the development of minority policies in the two states (Ram, 2003). Using evidence from Bulgaria, Romania, and Slovakia, Brusis argues that the European accession process has promoted consociational power-sharing arrangements regarding minority protection in accession countries (Brusis, 2003) while Papagianni finds substantial evidence to link the progress made in minority policy in Latvia and Estonia to membership in the EU (Papagianni, 2003).

The evidence, however, is not entirely consistent. Vermeersch, for example, acknowledges a correlation between EU pressures and minority policy shifts in Hungary, the Czech Republic, and Poland, but is skeptical about the overall impact of the European integration process on the status of the Roma. Instead, he concludes that policy changes are often motivated by short-term political and regional considerations (Vermeersch, 2003). Hughes and Sasse (2003) focus on the role of the EC and its reports but come to similarly skeptical conclusions regarding the role of the EU in changing minority policy in candidate states for the better. Guglielmo (2004) is equally ambivalent; she sees great potential in the ability of the EC to effect change in domestic policy towards the Roma, but remains doubtful about its lasting effect 'unless corresponding changes in contextual attitudes, behaviors, social norms, and political culture take place' (55). The conclusions of this recent but impressive body of literature are thus quite diverse, and the consequence of the EU accession process for minority policy in candidate state remains a contested issue.

EU ACCESSION AND THE ROMA IN BULGARIA, THE CZECH REPUBLIC, HUNGARY, AND ROMANIA: CASE SELECTION AND METHODOLOGY

Research to date has focused primarily on the nature and type of governmental policies dealing with minorities or shifts in policy, and has tried to link these shifts to the EU accession process. This research is important as it provides evidence of the efforts made by individual countries to improve the living conditions of minorities—a prerequisite for EU membership. Our research takes a different approach; we investigate the impact of the EU on minority policy in candidate states by studying whether the EU focus on Roma policy has had an impact on the conditions in which these minorities live. While policy may or may not change, the more important outcome would be specific improvements for the Roma in the candidate state.

For the purposes of this study, four countries were selected for analysis: Bulgaria, the Czech Republic, Hungary, and Romania. As mentioned above, these countries were selected for this study based on two criteria. First, each country has a Roma minority, and second, in 2004, each pair of countries was at a different stage of the EU accession process.

Hungary and the Czech Republic

Hungary applied for EU membership in 1994, the Czech Republic applied in 1996, accession negotiations with both were opened in 1998 and completed in 2002, and Hungary and the Czech Republic joined the EU in May 2004. At this point, they are expected to have satisfied all the conditions and criteria for entry and to have provided adequate protection for their minorities. The two countries are relatively homogenous; the majority constitutes about 94% of the population in both Hungary and the Czech Republic while their minority populations are made up of several small groups. The Roma represent between 1.9–5% of the population in Hungary and 0.1–2% of the population in the Czech Republic (CIA, 2005; UNDP, 2005). Official census data report the lower figures; however, due to the stigma attached to being Roma, experts estimate a substantial degree of underreporting among the group. The higher figures thus reflect the estimates of various experts and NGOs.

Bulgaria and Romania

Both Bulgaria and Romania applied for EU membership in 1995, but accession negotiations were not opened until 1999 and their accession negotiations were not signed until 2004. Both joined the EU in January 2007. The ethnic make-up of these two countries is quite different from that of Hungary and the Czech Republic. The two countries have clear dominant majorities (85% in Bulgaria and 89% in Romania), but also a single and concentrated minority (Turks in Bulgaria and Hungarians in Romania), a substantial but scattered second minority (Roma), and a multitude of smaller ethnic groups. The Roma minority is larger in these two countries than in Hungary and the Czech Republic. The percentages of Roma reported by the Census Bureaus for Bulgaria and Romania are 4.68 and 2.5%, respectively. Unofficial estimates are as high as

8% for both countries (UNDP, 2005). With these higher estimates increasing, one may argue that the situation of the Roma in these two states impacts not only them, but to a great extent the demographic and socio-economic profiles of each country.

A brief review of EU policies and instruments, and state policies towards the Roma in the four countries reveal that there is a reason to believe that the EU has been a factor in accelerating state efforts to improve the minority situation. The four states have been on the receiving end of the EU policy recommendations and financial assistance for Roma-specific programs since the early 1990s. The conditions of the Roma were highlighted as an obstacle to EU membership in all four countries in the early EC annual reports and all four were pushed to increase their efforts in that area. In the 1998 annual report, the EC observes:

> The situation of the Roma continues to be problematic as the candidate countries concerned have made little progress in addressing the issue. Although their legal status and rights remain stable, the Roma suffer discrimination and social exclusion, in particular in Hungary, Slovakia, Bulgaria and the Czech Republic. Home to several million Roma, Romania needs to step up its efforts to improve the situation of this minority (EC, 1998).

Financial assistance was also provided to encourage the formulation of policy and implementation of programs to improve the conditions of the Roma. Between 1994 and 2001, Bulgaria received close to 12 million euro, Romania—close to 9 million, Hungary—about 16 million, and the Czech Republic—about 9 million to develop Roma-specific programs (EC, 2002a).[8]

The combined effects of policy recommendations and funding from the EU appear to have had an impact on the state policies towards the Roma. Moreover, the timing of the implementation of major state programs seems to be linked to the major steps towards EU accession. In Hungary efforts started earliest and were most consistent:

> during 1994 to 1998, the government elaborated a program for Roma integration. This program was implemented by the successor government [. . .] In 1999, the government adopted a mid-term program concerning improvements in the social position and quality of life of the Roma (UNDP, 2002, Annex).

In the Czech Republic several bodies were set up in 1995–1996, including the Czech Republic's Advisory Board for Roma Community Affairs and the Inter-ministerial Commission for Roma Community Affairs, which is specifically aimed at formulating policies on behalf of the Roma. In Bulgaria, the *Framework Program for Equal Integration of Roma in Bulgarian Society* was not adopted until April 1999, and the *Romanian Roma Framework Convention* was adopted in 2001 (UNDP, 2002, Annex).

By the early 2000s, the four countries were clearly on two different tracks regarding their Roma policies. In Hungary and the Czech Republic efforts to improve the situation of the Roma were consistent through the late 1990s, and by 2002 'progress ha[d] been made with the implementation of national action plans to improve the difficult situation the members of these communities are facing' (EC, 2002b).

In contrast, in Bulgaria and Romania conditions did not begin improving until 2002 and 2004, respectively. In Romania by 2002, 'the Government has made steady progress in implementing the Roma Strategy' (Commission of the European Communities, 2002), but by 2003 the EC concluded that results have been uneven (Commission of the European Communities, 2003a). In 2004, '[i]mplementation of the Roma Strategy adopted in 2001 continued in the sectors of education, health, employment and relations with the police (Commission of the European Communities, 2004a).' In Bulgaria, by 2002 'there has been very little change in the situation of the Roma minority [. . .] and there are no significant developments in their socio-economic situation and living conditions' and in 2003 'the situation of the Roma minority has barely improved' (Commission of the European Communities, 2003b). By 2004, however, some progress had been made through the 'elaboration of a long-term Action Plan in line with the "Roma Inclusion Decade" and "Action Plan 2003–2004 for the implementation of the Framework Programme" [. . .] [h]owever, no adequate legislative reforms were envisaged in key areas, such as education, health care and housing' (Commission of the European Communities, 2004b).

Overall, based on a review of the evolution of EU instruments and the development of state policies, it appears that the EU has had an accelerating effect on the state policies toward the Roma in all four countries. Criticism and recommendations to improve minority protection records seems to have influenced countries to introduce and implement Roma-specific policies with momentum clearly picking up speed as accession negotiations intensified. In our research, however, we look for evidence elsewhere.

In this study we search for improvements in the overall conditions of the Roma and focus on basic necessities such as employment, education, and housing, in addition to assessing poverty rates of Roma communities. We use two complementary sets of indicators. The first comes from a cross-sectional comparison of the status of the Roma in four countries—Hungary, the Czech Republic, Bulgaria and Romania—in 2004, a point at which the former two had just acceded into the EU and the latter two were (at least) 3 years away. In other words, at this point, the Czech Republic and Hungary had satisfied the Copenhagen criteria and Bulgaria and Romania had not. These indicators allow us to see whether the country's position in terms of EU accession is associated with a much better or worse state of Roma affairs. The data come exclusively from the 2004 UNDP Vulnerable Groups Dataset.

The second set of indicators attempts to capture changes in the status of the Roma in the four countries during the 1997–2004 period using comparable data reported in several surveys. This time period was arguably of critical importance for the EU accession of the four countries—the accession treaties of both Hungary and the Czech Republic were signed in 2003, while Bulgaria and Romania were in the middle of their accession negotiations. We can expect this to be a time period during which previously implemented policies come to fruition and new policies are introduced as all four countries attempt to satisfy Copenhagen performance criteria. We anticipate that the impact of minority policies will be reflected in the status of the Roma minorities over the 1997–2004 period.

Before we go further, however, we need to add an important caveat. It may be argued that even if we do find that the status of the Roma has improved, we may not be able to attribute these improvements solely to the EU accessions process. The spread of democracy throughout Eastern Europe undoubtedly has contributed to the protection and improved status of all minority groups. However, we believe there is sufficient evidence to link changes in the status of the Roma to EU influence and pressure. Activists and analysts alike agree that the plight of the Roma has been, and continues to be a very low priority item on East European domestic political agendas.[9] Proportionally speaking, the Roma are a small group with limited resources and political influence. They are the region's most unpopular social group and are generally viewed as a drain on the limited economic resources of the state (Barany, 2002, 284). Highlighting this fact is a 1993 opinion poll administered in Czechoslovakia revealing that 67% of respondents believed that 'minority rights should be restricted in the interest of the majority' (CIDM, 1995). This makes the domestic political systems particularly unwilling to deal with the issues of the Roma minorities. Political support, public support, and ironically, minority support are often lacking for the formulation and implementation of any policies aimed at improving the status of the Roma (Guglielmo, 2004). The NGO sector is the only segment of the domestic political scene in Eastern Europe that has consistently pushed for the improvement of the Roma's plight (and their actions have also been influenced by the EU and other international donors). Thus, if the impact of the EU is viewed as insufficient, the domestic political process would presumably have achieved even less.[10]

Another potential argument might link any observed differences in the conditions of the Roma in the four countries to the different economic situations of the countries as a whole. Arguably, Bulgaria and Romania have both significantly lower GDP values and higher levels of income inequality than Hungary and the Czech Republic.[11] We attempt to isolate the effects higher GDP levels and greater income inequality in two ways: the measures we use from the 2004 data set, reflect differences between the minority and majority groups living in similar socio-economic conditions. These comparisons were included specifically to isolate minority-specific vulnerability factors from those 'due to regional disparities or depressed local economies' and thus 'allow for cross-country comparisons' (UNDP, 2005). Thus, we believe that the differences captured in the gap measures will reflect minority-specific efforts on behalf of the government, rather than the general economic situation in the country. In addition, we also track changes over time, which should allow us to estimate changes in the majority situation as compared to changes among the minority and thus also see whether things improve for the Roma in isolation from the general country situation.

EU ACCESSION AND THE ROMA IN FOUR COUNTRIES: EMPIRICAL INDICATORS

The belief that accession to the EU motivates countries to improve minority rights records (among other democratic indicators) is tested by comparing the levels of differential situation of the Roma in Hungary and the Czech Republic with those in Bulgaria and Romania, as well as over time within each country. To assess these levels, we use UNDP survey data to create several indicators of disparities between the Roma and comparable groups in the majority population ('gap' indicators).

The gaps for 2004 reflect the differences in the values of several socio-economic indicators for the Roma and the 'majority.' These values are aggregated from the survey answers for the Roma and majority as a group. The 'majority' population is, in fact, comprised of individuals living in close proximity to the Roma, a deliberate effort by the UNDP to account for socio-economic variation and regional disparities (UNDP, 2005). The gap measure is calculated for socio-economic indicators from three categories: economic situation; education; and housing and living conditions. We assess the level of differential treatment of the Roma minority in each country by comparing the gaps along these indicators.

For all indicators the gaps are calculated in such a way as to reflect the extent to which the Roma are worse off than the majority. For example, the gap in poverty reflects the difference between the poverty level of the Roma and the majority ($Gap(P)=P_R-P_M$), while the gap in the proportion of people with 4 years of education reflects the difference between the majority and the Roma ($Gap(E)=E_M-E_R$). Their values are positive indicating that the Roma are worse off than the majority on all accounts. Overall, the higher the gaps, the worse off the Roma are compared to the majority and the higher the discrimination against them. The tables contain both the absolute percentages for the Roma and the majority populations, and the relative gap values for each socio-economic indicator. The use of this relative measure allows us to compare the status of the Roma across countries.

Our expectation is that the differences between the Roma minority and the majority population in 2004 will be smaller in the newly acceded states of Hungary and the Czech Republic than in Bulgarian and Romania, indicating less discrimination towards the Roma. In terms of the gaps, we expect Bulgaria and Romania to have larger gap values than Hungary and the Czech Republic.

Poverty and Unemployment

Table 1 contains the percentages of Roma and majorities living in poverty in the four countries. Poverty is determined using the World Bank standard of individuals with daily incomes or expenditures below $4.30 purchasing power parity (PPP)[12] per day (UNDP, 2005). We report the absolute values and the gap values using both the income-based and expenditure-based poverty rates.[13] Overall, the gap figures support our argument that the EU accession process has led to the improved status of the Roma minority. The gaps in Romania are 47 and 41% for the two poverty indicators, signifying that the rate for Roma in Romania living in poverty (based on income estimates) is higher by 47 percentage points than the rate for the majority living in poverty. The gaps for Bulgaria are 40 and 39%, illustrating a similarly high disparity in the status of the Roma and majority. The gaps in the Czech Republic and Hungary are substantially lower, indicating that the proportions of Roma and the majority living in poverty in both countries are more similar for the two groups. While the gaps in the Czech Republic are substantial at 16 and 27%, they do not reach the levels of discrimination experienced by the Roma in Bulgaria and Roma in Romania. Hungary's gaps of 3 and 1% imply an almost equal status of the Roma and the majority in the lower echelon of society—which is significant.

Acknowledging that measurements of poverty vary in their methodology and are subjective in nature, the following assessment of poverty rates over time in the four case-study countries provides some additional support for the accession hypothesis. It is important to note that the 1990s poverty calculations included for each country differ from each other and from the method used in the United Nations 2005 report. However, analyzing poverty rates among nations over time allows us, at a minimum, to determine a positive or negative trend towards closing the gap between Roma and non-Roma poverty figures.

Table 1:
Poverty Rates: Percentage of People Living on Less Than $4.3 a Day, 2004

	Income-based poverty rates		Expenditure-based poverty rates	
	Percentage of Roma/majority (%)	Gap (%)	Percentage of Roma/majority (%)	Gap (%)
Hungary	8/5	3	9/8	1
Czech Republic	25/9	16	45/18	27
Bulgaria	51/11	40	49/10	39
Romania	69/22	47	67/26	41

According to a household survey administered by the World Bank, 84% of the Roma in Bulgaria were living below the poverty line in 1997 compared to 36% of the total population, resulting in a 48% gap (Ringold, 2000, 11).[14] In Romania, 79% of the Roma were living in poverty in 1997 compared to the national poverty rate of 31%, resulting in an equally sizable 46% gap (Ringold, 2000, 11).[15] In both countries, the relative gap measures of poverty decreased between 1997 and 2004 expenditure-based poverty rates. Data from a 1998 survey administered in Hungary revealed a similar demographic pattern. The panel format of this survey assessed the duration and frequency of poverty experienced from 1992 to 1997. While Roma comprised only 5% of the population, 33% of the long-term poor were Roma (Ringold, 2000, 11).[16] The percentage of the total Hungarian population living below the poverty line during the same time period was approximately 10% resulting in a 23% gap (UNDP, 2001, 152).[17] The poverty levels of the Roma have dropped from 1997 to 2004, and the gaps between the general population and the Roma are smaller in 2004 than in 1997. The gaps are consistently larger in Bulgaria and Romania than in Hungary. While reports reveal that 7.6% of the total population in the Czech Republic was living in poverty in 1996 (UNDP Millennium

Development Goals, 2004),[18] the percentage of Roma living below the poverty line is not reported.

The unemployment rates for the Roma and majority groups are reported in Table 2. Based on the data specifications, the indicators are reported by age groups. 'Labor Force' is defined by the UNDP as the working-age population (aged 15 and above). Individuals who are retired, in school and/or involved with housekeeping are not included. While the unemployment rates are higher for Roma in all age categories in all countries, the gap levels in the Czech Republic are not consistent with our hypothesis. The gap between unemployed Roma and the majority in the Czech Republic is slightly higher than the Roma/majority gap in Bulgaria and is variably higher than the Roma/majority gaps in Romania. There is virtually no difference in the unemployment rates of the Roma and the majority in Hungary.

A temporal comparison of the self-reported percentage rates of unemployment among the Roma minorities in the Czech Republic, Hungary, Bulgaria, and Romania are listed in Table 3. Based on data from the 2001 and 2004 UNDP surveys between 2001 and 2004, the unemployment rate of the Roma decreased in all countries except Hungary, where it increased by 6 percentage points. The decrease was most pronounced in Romania, slightly less so in Bulgaria, and smaller yet in the Czech Republic.

Looking at the longer term, unemployment rates for the Roma appear to have peaked in the late 1990s—they reportedly reached 76 and 70% in the Czech Republic and Hungary, respectively (Ringold, 2000, 15–16). In Bulgaria, Roma unemployment was reported between 80 and 90% in 1998 (NDI, 2003, 2). Earlier estimates put it at 45% in Romania in 1993 and 46% in Bulgaria in 1996. Because of the active labor policies of the socialist governments prior to 1989, unemployment rates for the Roma (at least for the men) were not dramatically different around 1990 (Ringold, 2000, 15).

Table 2: Unemployment Rates: Percentage of People Unemployed, by Age Category, 2004

	15–24 years		25–54 years		55 years and above	
	Roma/majority (%)	Gap (%)	Roma/majority (%)	Gap (%)	Roma/majority (%)	Gap (%)
Hungary	37/36	1	10/8	2	7/0	7
Czech Republic	40/12	28	27/4	23	27/4	23
Bulgaria	56/32	24	34/12	22	41/19	22
Romania	46/33	13	25/8	17	34/12	22

Table 3:
Change in the Unemployment Rate Among the Roma from 2001 to 2004

	Percent of unemployed respondents over the age of 15		Change in percentage points 2001/2004
	2001	2004	
Czech Republic	31	27	−4
Hungary	26	32	6
Bulgaria	56	49	−7
Romania	60	50	−10

The years coinciding with active preparations to join the EU thus have seen a decrease in the unemployment rates among the Roma in all four countries despite some short-term fluctuations. The drops are also more significant in Hungary and the Czech Republic and seem to have been more delayed in Bulgaria and Romania, in line with our expectations. Compared to the changes in total unemployment in the four countries (Table 4), the Bulgarian and Romanian advances pale even more.

Education

Based on the data we present, the Roma in EU-member countries experience greater equality in education than their fellow Roma in non-member countries(in 2004). The actual percentage of individuals aged 12 and above—Roma and majority—who have attended at least 4 years of primary school is quite high in both member countries at 98.5% (the Czech Republic) and 94.5% (Hungary). The gaps between the percentage of Roma and the majority with at least 4 years of primary education in both countries are relatively small at 1 and 7%. The actual percentages of individuals with at least 4 years of primary school in EU-candidate countries is substantially lower at 79.5 and 66% in Bulgaria and Romania, respectively; the gaps between the Roma and majority are significantly higher in these countries, 33 and 37% respectively.

Table 4: Total Unemployment Rates, by Country, 1997, 2001, and 2004

	1997 (%)	2001 (%)	2004 (%)	Change in percentage points (2001–2004)
Czech Republic	4.7	8.2	8.3	0.1
Hungary	8.7	5.8	6.1	0.3
Bulgaria	13.7	17.9	13.5	−4.4
Romania	6	9.3	6.2	−3.1

The percentages of children still attending school at age 15 reveal a similar pattern. This observation is even more important as this indicator reflects the most recent developments in state policies. Majority children are enrolled at very high rates in all four countries, but there is a clear difference in the values of the gaps. The gaps between Roma and majority children are 14 and 10% in the Czech Republic and Hungary, respectively. The gap in Bulgaria is 41% and in Romania it is 33% (Table 5).

Because measurements vary and the baseline dates are not uniform, it is un-clear how much education and access to education have improved for the Roma in the four countries since the mid-1990s. Looking at the longer term, educa-tional levels seem to have declined since before 1990. For example, average illiteracy rates among the Roma in Bulgaria have increased from about 10% in the early 1990s to 20% in 2005 (Education International, 2006). The mid-term consequences of education policy are particularly difficult to assess due to their delayed nature. However, according to the 2007 *Equal Access to Quality Educa-tion for Roma Report* 'governments in [Bulgaria, Hungary and Romania] have energetically adopted policies and programs to improve education opportunities for Roma' (REI, 2007). While problems of implementation remain and govern-ments are being encouraged to pursue better strategies in this regard, progress has been noted, and seems to be partly accounted for by the EU-supported De-cade of Roma Inclusion initiative.

Table 5: Education Indicators, 2004

	Share of people over the age of 12 with more than 4 years of education		Share of children in school at 15 years of age	
	Roma majority (%)	Gap (%)	Roma majority (%)	Gap (%)
Hungary	90/97	7	81/91	10
Czech Republic	98/99	1	86/100	14
Bulgaria	63/96	33	59/100	41
Romania	46/83	37	55/88	33

Living Conditions

Finally, we turn to the actual physical conditions in which the Roma live. The data pattern of the four indicators measuring living conditions support our accession hypothesis with the exception of accessibility to improved water sources. The data points in the table otherwise fit the pattern we have reported thus far. Smaller gaps between the Roma and majority populations exist in the

EU member countries—the Czech Republic and Hungary—compared to the non-EU member countries, Bulgaria and Romania (Table 6).

The four indicators included are access to essential drugs, secure housing, improved sanitation, and improved water sources. The essential drugs value is the percentage of households responding 'Yes' to the question, 'Were there any periods in the past 12 months when your household could not afford to purchase medicines prescribed to/needed by a member of your household?' The housing values reflect the percentage of people living in what are considered to be 'ruined houses' or 'slums.' The sanitation indicator measures the percentage of households that do not have a toilet or bathroom inside the house. The water indicator measures the number of households that do not have piped water inside their house or garden yard (UNDP, 2005). Based on these four living conditions indicators, the Roma in Bulgaria endure the worst living conditions while the Roma in the Czech Republic experience the best living conditions among the four groups of Roma in this study.

The largest gap in the percentage of Roma who at times cannot afford essential drugs compared to the majority is 43% in Bulgaria. The smallest gap of 19% is in the Czech Republic. The indicators for Hungary and Romania also fit with our expectations. The comparison of 'access to secure housing' in the four countries reveals a similar trend. The largest gap between Roma who do not have access to secure housing compared to the majority is in Bulgaria (29%), while the smallest gap is in the Czech Republic (13%) The remaining two countries follow the expected trend. The largest gap between the percentages of Roma without access to improved sanitation compared to the majority is recorded in Bulgaria (55%). This gap is substantially higher than the lowest gap (4%) reported in the Czech Republic. Romanian Roma are most disadvantaged when it comes to access to improved water. The gap between the Roma and the majority is 35% compared to a low of 3% in the Czech Republic.

Table 6: Living Conditions Indicators

	Share of people without access to essential drugs		Share of people without access to secure housing		Share of people without access to improved sanitation		Share of people without access to improved water	
	Roma/majority (%)	Gap (%)	Roma/majority (%)	Gap (%)	Roma/majority (%)	Gap (%)	Roma/majority (%)	Gap (%)
Hungary	74/50	24	36/19	17	46/24	22	34/9	25
Czech Republic	27/8	19	17/4	13	10/6	4	8/5	3
Bulgaria	75/32	43	33/4	29	81/26	55	10/0.2	8.8
Romania	77/42	35	29/4	25	88/53	35	68/33	35

Table 7 reports data on our final indicator, life satisfaction among the Roma. The question 'Do you believe that over the previous 5 years your life has improved or deteriorated?' was asked of the Roma individuals participating in the survey in 2001–2002. This question helps shed some light on the overall perception among Roma as individuals regarding whether they felt their governments were committed to improving the conditions of the Roma and whether they had experienced any of these improvements. Our expectations are that the proportion of Roma in Hungary and the Czech Republic that report an improvement in their lives will be higher than the corresponding proportions in Bulgaria and Romania.

The data reported support our hypothesis that the EU accession process is effective in improving conditions for the Roma. Nearly 17% of the Roma surveyed in the Czech Republic believed their lives had improved over the previous 5 years. About 12% of the Roma in Hungary believed their lives had improved. The percentage of Roma in Bulgaria and Romania who felt their lives had improved over the previous 5 years was substantially lower at 5 and 7%, respectively. The survey also provides balance to the improvements recorded here and those discussed in previous sections of the article. Improvements should not overshadow the fact that living conditions for the Roma remain far below acceptable levels. In some instances, the case may be that Roma communities continue to experience the fall-out of the post-communist transitional period as indicated in the following statistics asking whether they (Roma) feel that their lives have deteriorated over the last 5 years.

Table 7: Life Satisfaction Among the Roma, 2001–2002

	Percent Roma, who, in 2001–2002, believed that, over the previous 5 years	
	Life had improved (%)	Life had deteriorated (%)
Czech Republic	16.80	29.72
Hungary	11.90	57.20
Bulgaria	4.81	57.77
Romania	6.99	73.43

The percentage of Roma in the Czech Republic who felt their lives had deteriorated was the lowest reported at 29.7%. In Hungary, 57.2% of the Roma surveyed felt their lives had deteriorated over the last 5 years. The percentage of dissatisfied Bulgarian Roma was slightly higher at 57.7%. Nearly 74% of the Roma in Romania felt that their lives were worse in 2001 than in 1996. While the same question was not asked in 2004, preventing a temporal analysis, these attitudes demonstrate that the EU accession process has had some impact—more in member countries—on the situation of the Roma.

CONCLUSIONS

An analysis of the conditions of the Roma and comparable groups among the majority population in four countries has allowed us to draw some conclusions about the differential treatment of the Roma. The gaps between the Roma and the majority of similar socio-economic status are generally higher in Bulgaria and Romania than in Hungary and the Czech Republic. This finding supports our hypotheses that countries closer to EU accession will make greater efforts to improve the situation of the Roma. The EU accession process seems to have narrowed the gap between Roma and the majority as illustrated by the survey data.

Analyzing the conditions of the Roma over time lends additional support to our hypothesis. Poverty rates, unemployment rates, and education statistics for the Roma populations in all four countries improved over time, with larger improvements taking place in the member countries. Perhaps the most dramatic improvement was the narrowing of the unemployment gaps in the member countries of Hungary and the Czech Republic. While all of the indicators are inter-dependent, improved employment opportunities for the Roma will presumably have a significant impact on reducing poverty and improving living conditions.

We believe that this work has shown the value of looking beyond state policies in our attempt to assess the impact of the EU accession process on the minorities in candidate states. However, while countries may have satisfied the Copenhagen criteria and introduced and implemented policies that provide for the protection of minorities, our data indicate that the Roma are still substantially worse off than the majority in all four countries. In addition, the absolute values of some of the indicators discussed here paint a very bleak picture of the conditions in which Roma live in these European countries. Further support from the EU will clearly be needed for the gaps to be narrowed further and the overall conditions of the Roma to be improved. Given the high numbers of Roma people in the post-2007 EU, and the low priority of the Roma issue within the old (pre-2004) member states, the EU general policy towards the Roma might need to be reformulated as well.

Acknowledgments

The authors would like to thank the anonymous reviewers of CEP for their comments and suggestions.

Notes

1. Candidate states for which the Copenhagen criteria have been/are applied include: the Czech Republic, Estonia, Hungary, Poland, Slovenia, Cyprus, Latvia, Lithuania, Malta, and the Slovak Republic (current member states), Bulgaria and Romania (acceding countries), Croatia, Macedonia and Turkey (candidate countries).

2. The survey is available at http://roma.undp.sk/.

3. The surveys and data are available at http://vulnerability.undp.sk/. The authors gratefully acknowledge the help of Andrey Ivanov from UNDP for his help in locating and using the data.

4. This dynamic between the EU and candidate states is not a new phenomenon. The political developments in Greece in the 1960s and 1970s were largely influenced by the political and economic importance of the EC to Greece. The development of democracy in particular was largely shaped by the negotiations with the EC through direct and indirect ways (Tsingos 2001).

5. The protection of minorities has been a 'European' concern since the CSCE Helsinki Final Act of 1975. With its emergence as an actor with increased influence, the EU has coordinated efforts with the CSCE/OSCE and the Council of Europe to promote minority rights as a European idea through joint initiatives (Brusis 2003, 4).

6. Reports for all countries are available at http://ec.europa.eu/enlargement/key_documents/index_en.htm

7. These efforts include attempts by EU administrators to convince candidate governments of the importance of including minority groups in the policy-making process, and advice on how to promote tolerance in candidate societies.

8. For a detailed annual description of the PHARE assistance for the Roma in Central and Eastern Europe, see EC (2002a).

9. See, for example, the extensive publications of the European Roma Rights Center available at: www.errc.org and Ringold *et al.* (2003).

10. Further evidence that the accession process, as opposed to democratization over time, helps to motivate countries toward improving conditions of the Roma is the fact that Roma living in long-time EU member countries in Western Europe often experience living conditions far below those of the general population. According to the *Report on the Situation of the Roma in Select Western European Countries* presented by the International Helsinki Federation for Human Rights, despite the attention focused on the Roma in Eastern and Central Europe, less attention has been directed at the living conditions of Roma in Western Europe. Roma there continued to suffer from great disparities in housing, health care, employment opportunities, and education, as well as a climate of increased intolerance (Mandorff 2005).

11. In 2004, Bulgaria had a GDP per capita of 8,978 USD, Romania—8,480; Hungary—16,814 and the Czech Republic—19,408. Gini coe cients ranged from 25.4 in the Czech Republic (1996), to 26,9 in Hungary, to 29.2 in Bulgaria, and 31.0 in Romania (UNDP 2006, 330–335).

12. PPP expressed in US dollars is a way of expressing the value of GDP or income from different countries through the use of a common denominator allowing international comparisons.

13. For more discussion of the indicators and methodology used by the UNDP, see UNDP (2005) *Introduction: Why These Profiles?* http://vulnerability.undp.sk/DOCUMENTS/introduction.pdf.

14. The Bulgarian measure of poverty was set at two-thirds of mean per capita consumption.

15. The poverty measurement used in Romania was set at 60% of mean consumption, per adult equivalent.

16. 'Long-term poverty' was defined as those households that experienced poverty four or more times during the panel period, with the poverty line set at one-half of mean adult equivalent income.

17. The poverty measurement used by the United Nations was percentage of population living on or below 50% of the country's median income.

18. This percentage is based on the percentage of individuals living on less than 60% of the average median income in the Czech Republic.

REFERENCES

Barany, Z. (2002) *The East European Gypsies: Regime Change, Marginality, and Ethnopolitics*, Cambridge: Cambridge University Press.

Bokulic, S., Bieber, F., Bíró, A.-M. and Cheney, E. (2006) *Minority Rights Advocacy in the European Union: A Guide for NGOs in South-East Europe*, London: Minority Rights Group International.

Brusis, M. (2003) 'The European Union and interethnic power-sharing arrangements in accession countries', *JEMIE* 3(10): 1–23.

Center for International Development and Conflict Management (1995) *Minorities At Risk Project*, University of Maryland. Available at: http://www.bsos.umd.edu/cidcm/mar/tableee.htm

CIA World Factbook (2005) *Country Studies*. Available at: www.cia.gov

Commission of the European Communities (2002) *Regular Report on Romania's Progress Towards Accession*. Available at: http://ec.europa.eu/enlargement/archives/pdf/key_documents/2002/ro_en.pdf

Commission of the European Communities (2003a) *Regular Report on Romania's Progress Towards Accession*. Available at: http://ec.europa.eu/enlargement/archives/pdf/key_documents/2003/rr_ro_final_en.pdf

Commission of the European Communities (2003b) *Regular Report on Bulgaria's Progress Towards Accession*. Available at: http://ec.europa.eu/enlargement/archives/pdf/key_documents/2003/rr_bg_final_en.pdf

Commission of the European Communities (2004a) *Regular Report on Romania's Progress Towards Accession*. Available at: http://ec.europa.eu/enlargement/archives/pdf/key_documents/2004/rr_ro_2004_en.pdf

Commission of the European Communities (2004b) *Regular Report on Bulgaria's Progress Towards Accession*. Available at: http://ec.europa.eu/enlargement/archives/pdf/key_documents/2003/rr_bg_final_en.pdf

Education International (2006) 'A day in the life of . . . Nadia, teacher in a Roma school', available at: http://www.ei-ie.org/efaids/en/article_detail.php?id=32&theme=educationforall&country=bulgaria

European Commission (EC) (1998) 'Composite paper on the Commission Reports 1998, November 4, 1998', available at: http://ec.europa.eu/enlargement/archives/pdf/key_documents/1998/composite_en.pdf

European Commission (EC) (2002a) 'EU support for Roma communities in Central and Eastern Europe', May 2002, Enlargement Information Unit, Brussels. Available at: http://europa.eu.int/comm/enlargement/docs/pdf/brochure_roma_may2002.pdf

European Commission (EC) (2002b) 'Strategy Paper 2002. Towards the enlarged Union—strategy paper and report of the European Commission on the progress towards accession by each of the candidate countries', available at: http://eur-lex.europa.eu/smartapi/cgi/sga_doc?smartapi!celex plus!prod!CELEXnumdoc&lg=en&numdoc=502DC0700

European Commission (EC) (2004) *The Situation of the Roma in an Enlarged European Union*. Available at: http://ec.europa.eu/employment_social/publications/2005/ke6204389_en.pdf

European Council (1993) *Conclusions of the Presidency*. Available at: http://ue.eu.int/ueDocs/cms_Data/docs/pressdata/en/ec/72921.pdf

European Monitoring Center on Racism and Xenophobia (EUMC) (2005) 'The only hope for the European Roma is the European Union', *Equal Voices*, Issue 16. Available at: http://eumc.europa.eu/eumc/index.php?fuseaction=content.dsp_cat_content&catid=42de2076e07d2&contentid=42de226753dd4

European Parliament (EP) (2000) *The Charter of Fundamental Rights of the European Union*. Available at: http://www.europarl.europa.eu/charter/default_en.htm

Guglielmo, R. (2004) 'Human rights in the accession process: Roma and Muslims in an enlarging EU', in Local Government and Public Service Reform Initiative; EURAC Research, Minority protection and the enlarged European Union: the way forward, Budapest, pp. S.37–S.58.

Hughes, J. and Sasse, G. (2003) 'Monitoring the monitors: EU enlargement conditionality and minority protection in the CEECs', *Journal on Ethnopolitics and Minority Issues in Europe*, issue 1. Available at: http://ecmi.de/jemie/download/Focus1-2003_Hughes_Sasse.pdf

Johns, M. (2003) '"Do as I Say, Not As I Do": The European Union, Eastern Europe and Minority Rights', *East European Politics and Societies* 17(4): 682–699.

Kelley, J. (2004) 'International actors on the domestic scene: membership conditionality and socialization by international institutions', *International Organization* 58: 425–457.

Liegeois, J.-P., Gheorghe, N. and Shuinear, S.N. (1995) 'Roma/gypsies: a European minority', 1995 Minority Rights Group Report.

Linden, R.H. (2002) *Norms and Nannies: The Impact of International Organizations on the Central and East European States*, Oxford: Rowman and Littlefield Publishers, pp. 227–244.

Mandorff, A.M. (2005) *Situation of the Roma in Select Western European Countries*, Vienna, Austria: Helsinki Research Foundation.

National Democratic Institute [NDI] (2003) *Roma Political Participation in Bulgaria*. Available at: http://www.accessdemocracy.org/library/1611_romaassess_020803.pdf

Papagianni, K. (2003) 'The Role of European Integration and International Norms on Minority Rights in Estonian and Latvian ethnic Politics in the 1990s', Paper presented at the 99th APSA Meeting; Philadelphia, August 2003.

Pridham, G. (1999) 'Complying with the European Union's democratic conditionality: transnational party linkages and regime change in Slovakia, 1993–1998', *Europe-Asia Studies* 51(7): 1221–1244.

Ram, M. (2003) 'Democratization through European integration: the case of minority rights in the Czech Republic and Romania', *Studies in Comparative International Development* 38(2): 28–56.

Ringold, D. (2000) *Roma and the Transition in Central and Eastern Europe: Trends and Challenges*, Washington, DC: Europe and Central Asia Region, Human Development Unit, World Bank.

Ringold, D., Orenstein, M.A. and Wilkens, E. (2003) *Roma in an Expanding Europe: breaking the Poverty Cycle*, Washington, DC: World Bank.

Roma Education Initiative [REI] (2007) *Equal Access to Quality Education for Roma*. Available at: www.soros.org/initiatives/roma/articles_publications/publications/equal_20070329

Smith, K.E. (2001) 'Western Actors and the Promotion of Democracy', in J. Zellonka and A. Pravda (eds.) *Democratic Consolidation in Eastern Europe*, Oxford: Oxford University Press, Vol. 2, pp. 31–57.

Tsingos, B (2001) 'Underwriting Democracy: the European community and Greece', in P.C. Schmitter (ed.) *The International Dimensions of Democratization: Europe and the Americas*, Oxford: Oxford University Press, pp. 315–347.

Tubbax, C. (2005) 'The Largest Trans-European minority', *Café Babel: the European Magazine*, April 2005.

United Nations Development Program (UNDP) (2001) 'Human development report', available at: http: //hdr.undp.org/en/reports/global/hdr2001/

United Nations Development Program (UNDP) (2002) *Avoiding the Dependency Trap*, Regional Data Set. Available at: http://roma.undp.sk/

United Nations Development Program (UNDP) (2004) *Millennium Development Goals Reducing Poverty and Social Exclusion in Czech Republic*. Available at: http://www.undg.org/archive_does/4438_MDGs_Reducing_Poverty_and_Social_Exclusion_in_Hungary_Slovenia_Slovak_Republic_and_Czech_Republic_Report.pdf

United Nations Development Program (UNDP) (2005) *Faces of Poverty, Faces of Hope*. Available at: http://vulnerability.undp.sk

United Nations Development Program (UNDP) (2006) *Human Development Report 2006*, New York: Palgrave Macmillan.

Vachudova, M. (2001) 'The Leverage of International Institutions on Democratizing States: Eastern Europe and the European Union', Robert Schuman Centre of Advanced Studies Working Paper, Fiesole.

Vermeersch, P. (2003) 'EU enlargement and minority rights policies in Central Europe: explaining policy shifts in the Czech Republic, Hungary and Poland', Paper presented at the 8th Annual World Convention of the Association for the Study of Nationalities; Columbia University, 3–5 April 2003.

***Maria Spirova** is a post-doctoral fellow in the department of political science at Leiden University, the Netherlands. She is the author of *Political Parties in Post-Communist Societies: Formation, Persistence and Change* (Palgrave Macmillan, 2007).

Darlene Budd is an assistant professor in the department of political science at the University of Central Missouri.

Maria Spirova and Darlene Budd, "The EU Accession Process and the Roma Minorities in New and Soon-to-be Member States," *Comparative European Politics* 6 (2008): 81–101. Reproduced with permission of Palgrave Macmillan.

Chapter 4: "Do as I Say, Not as I Do": The European Union, Eastern Europe and Minority Rights

*by Michael Johns**

This article tests the assumption that the European Union has forced the potential new members from Eastern Europe to adhere to standards regarding the treatment of national minorities current member states do not meet. The article examines the treatment of the Russian minorities in Latvia and Estonia and the Roma population in Slovakia compared to the treatment of the Turks in Germany and the Roma in Italy. Using EU accession reports, Organization for Security and Co-operation in Europe (OSCE) recommendations, and the Minorities at Risk data set, a double standard becomes apparent. The newly democratized states of Eastern Europe are being forced to choose between the economic advantages of membership in the EU and legislation designed to protect the language and culture of the majority group. The article concludes with an examination of the histories of Estonia and Latvia to illustrate why being forced into altering laws concerning culture and citizenship is so difficult.

To the degree that the Union and its members do wish to create a community of shared values, some measure of common standards should be identified that constitutes the minimum that membership requires.[1]

In October 2002, the European Union voted to expand its membership by 10 countries by 2004. The majority of the countries that were extended an invitation to join were from Eastern Europe.[2] There were numerous hurdles prospective members had to pass before they received their invitation into the fraternity of Europe, and each of them was set out in the progress reports for each country.[3] Issues such as national debt, farm subsidies, and other economic policies were all open for criticism, and changes were needed to be made to comply with EU standards before final accession could be achieved. Another area where the EU demanded changes by the applicant states concerned human rights in general and the state's treatment of minorities. Laws that were deemed to be discriminatory to minorities or policies that adversely affect their ability to compete politically, economically, or socially were red flagged, and until they were sufficiently amended the targeted country could not become an EU member.

It is these policies concerning minority rights that are the emphasis of this article. Issues of minority nationalism and the rights of minority populations have become increasingly important in Europe.[4] Based on this importance, it would appear that the states of the EU were acting in a responsible manner when they imposed restrictions on the prospective member states in regards to their minority policies. It could be seen as the established democracies of Western Europe providing helpful advice to the newly democratic states of Eastern Europe as they prepare to join the European community. However, this would be the case if the laws that are found to be unacceptable in Eastern European countries are also found to be the same in Western Europe. A recent special edition of *East European Politics and Societies* (Vol. 17, No. 1) was dedicated to the issue of EU enlargement into Eastern Europe. Many of the authors had concerns about the amount of changes the prospective members needed to make to ensure membership. As Cameron states, "the candidate countries will have agreed to adopt the entire *acquis* of the EU with only a few transitional phase-ins."[5] Moravcsik and Vachudova went further, stating that they believe that many of the changes the East has been forced to make do not reflect the laws of the West. They believe that the accession process "imposes something of a double standard in a handful of areas, chiefly the protection of ethnic minority rights, where candidates are asked to meet standards that the EU-15 have never set for themselves."[6] This article will build on this statement and examine more thoroughly the possibility that what the Eastern European nations have been forced to change still exists in Western Europe. Are the laws that were deemed unacceptable in Eastern Europe by the EU still law in countries that are already members? If this is the case, then there is an apparent double standard by the EU. It seems that the EU is holding prospective members to a higher standard than they themselves are willing to meet with their own minority groups.

This article tests the hypothesis that there is a double standard between the western and eastern halves of Europe that obliges the East to choose between legislation they have deemed important to protect their own culture and legislation that complies with EU standards. To accomplish this task, it is first necessary to place the issue in a larger context. Then it is followed by an examination of the recommendations by the various organizations of Europe for the prospective members. This will be juxtaposed with the laws and regulations of countries within the EU. The cases that will be used from prospective EU members will be the Baltic countries of Estonia and Latvia, and the Slovak Republic. Their laws will be compared to EU members Germany and Italy. The history of the Baltic states will be examined in some detail to show why this apparent double standard is of great importance to the newly democratizing states of Eastern Europe.[7]

The states of Eastern Europe currently have two important goals that seem to be in conflict with each other. First, it is imperative for the long-term well-being of the newly democratic states that they are accepted into the EU and the other organizations of Europe. Through accession, they seek the economic and security advantages that membership offers. The second goal is to protect their culture. To ensure the long-term survival of the states' dominant language, culture, and society, it is necessary to enact laws that will protect them. By their nature, laws that protect one culture disadvantage another. The EU has made the elimination of these laws paramount for accession. Therefore, to achieve the first goal, the second must be abandoned and vice versa. Without both of these issues being of such importance to the East, it could be argued that even if a double standard was in effect it is of little consequence and that EU membership is worth any changes to the laws. Finally, the ramifications of this double standard, to incoming states and to the EU itself, will be discussed. This article does not attempt to examine every minority group and their treatment by the state within Europe. Such an analysis would be informative, but it is beyond the scope of this article and is not necessary to prove that the Eastern European states face critical choices that those already with the EU do not.

This article touches on many of the important issues addressed by others. The work of Brubaker is of particular interest. Brubaker's discussion of the concept of a nation in the "new Europe" is of value to this article. The new Europe is defined by the triadic relationship between the new nationalizing state, the nationalism of minority groups, and the nationalism of diasporas.[8] It is clear that this relationship can prompt change in certain laws in Eastern Europe. The national ideals of emerging states, long under foreign control, can be in contrast to those of a national minority who want what the majority now can enjoy. While both of these forces are in play, only the majority group can act on them. This causes the development of the emerging state to be concerned only with the majority; the minority suffers and attempts to respond. As Kymlicka states, "National minorities have typically responded to majority nation-building by fighting to maintain or rebuild their own social culture, by engaging in their own competing nation-building."[9] As a result, there maybe a need for changes to be introduced by an outside party that can restore some balance between these competing claims. This is where this article diverges from the ideas of Brubaker. The author does not account for the role of an outside force (other than a diaspora, which is an interested party), in this case, the EU. It is clear that the new Europe is dominated by the EU, and if it has the power to influence legislation that at its core revolves around identity, then it needs to be accounted for in Brubaker's analysis. If this fourth influence is affecting only some of the countries of Europe and not others, then the ramifications are clear. The balance between the majority and the minority is skewed in some cases and not in others. Keating notes that when there are discrepancies of treatment between states that are both under the influence of international institutions, both states suffer consequences.[10] Herrberg goes further to argue that the EU must influence the identity politics of the member (and prospective member) states for security purposes.[11] This article begins to discuss some of these consequences in Europe.

Institutions such as the EU allowed for a means of conflict prevention because they provide voices for minority groups. This is a second issue that this article is concerned with, the management of ethnic conflict. Many authors have concerned themselves with the study of ethnic conflict, its causes, and potential solutions.[12] The EU has indicated that the reason it has emphasized the rights of minority groups is to prevent the type of violence seen in the former Yugoslavia. What is of importance is that the rules designed to prevent ethnic conflict within the potential members are not being enforced in the West, and therefore there is still the potential for continuing ethnic unrest within EU countries such as Spain and Northern Ireland and future unrest in other EU countries that contain unhappy ethnic groups.

The work of Ted Robert Gurr and his study of ethnopolitical violence and the warning signs that indicate potential problems are a valuable resource for this study. This article uses the Minorities at Risk data set as a main source of information. This data set contains information on 285 ethnic groups across the globe that have been identified as at risk. The majority of the ethnic groups found in Europe are tracked within this database. The database contains information on the types of laws affecting groups, as well as their grievances. This allows for the comparison of policies across states within Europe. If there are cases in which two groups are treated in a similar manner by their state but the EU responds to the two cases differently, this data set will be able to identify them.[13]

This article takes all of these issues and relates them to the policy choices of the EU (the rules they set for accession) and the various states that are affected by them (the decisions they make as they attempt to comply with the rules while maintaining their society). To understand the policy choices of the EU and the apparent double standard it has created, it is necessary to examine the organization in Europe that monitors minority issues most closely and on whose recommendations the rules for accession are based, the Organization for Security and Co-operation in Europe (OSCE).

The OSCE: The Watchdog for Minority Rights?

In 1992, the OSCE (then known as the Conference on Security and Co-operation in Europe) created the position of "high commissioner on national minorities" to deal with the increased level of ethnic tensions and ethnic conflict in Europe and throughout the world. The mandate for the commissioner is to provide

> early warning and as appropriate, early action in regard to tensions involving national minority issues which have not yet developed beyond an early warning stage, but in the judgement of the High Commissioner, have potential to develop conflict within the OSCE area.[14]

The OSCE emphasizes that the post is that of high commissioner *on* national minorities, not *for* national minorities. The post is to promote conflict regulation rather than to act as a voice for national minorities. The position is to "contain and de-escalate tensions" and to be concerned with cases that could potentially "have a bearing on security."[15]

By most accounts, the OSCE and the high commissioner on national minorities has been very successful in achieving their goals, in the countries where they have decided to intervene. Zaagman describes the OSCE as being able to encourage "various forms of *structured dialogue* between the authorities and minority representatives so that these parties would interact and also find solutions on their own."[16] Chigas et al. describe the role of the OSCE as that of an "insider third party"; this allows the OSCE to maintain its distance and neutrality in dealing with issues while being privy to the knowledge and experiences of the various parties within a state.[17] This combination of roles has, in the authors' view, allowed for unprecedented access and influence in the minority group/majority group relationship. While the success of the OSCE has been applauded, as Troebst notes, what can only be accurately said is that no cases of ethnic conflict have broken out since the OSCE became involved in minority issues in 1992; there is nothing to prevent an outbreak in the future.[18]

When the influence of the high commissioner is examined, an interesting pattern emerges. The mandate set out by the OSCE for the commissioner is to identify potential conflict and develop early warning strategies for states and minority groups in the entire OSCE region, not just in Eastern Europe.[19] While the entire region is open for analysis, the Western countries have historically not been examined equally with the East. While some reports are made for the entire region, on general issues such as linguistic rights of national minorities when specific countries are targeted for analysis, all 14 of the recommendations have been countries in Eastern Europe.[20] There are 55 participating states in the OSCE (all of Europe and the United States and Canada), and yet all of the country recommendations are from one area of Europe, the East. How can this be? Is it possibly that only in Eastern Europe there are national minorities that are potentially ready for militant activity and as a result need OSCE recommendations to avoid such conflict? This seems unlikely. Another possibility is that to make recommendations on the relationship between the state and the minority group, particularly as an insider third party, the OSCE needs to have permanent missions on the ground for long periods of time to collect information and survey the situation. These are large operations that are funded mainly by the richer countries of the OSCE (the West); therefore, the commission has avoided criticizing the "hand that feeds it." As a result, according to Chandler, there has been a "qualitatively different level of intrusiveness into the affairs of the states of Eastern Europe."[21] Most likely of all is that the high commissioner knows that any recommendation given to Western countries would be summarily ignored, and therefore it is more productive (both in appearance and in reality) to concentrate on the newly democratic countries of Eastern Europe. It is more productive because the OSCE has influence on these groups compared to the West. The recommendations of the OSCE to the countries of Eastern Europe tend to become the rules for accession to the more important organization in Europe, the EU.

The EU: A Fair Judge?

The proof that the EU accession holds the key to explaining why the states of Eastern Europe allow for OSCE observers in their country, let alone adhere to the recommendations they make, can be seen in the individual accession progress reports for each prospective member.[22] It is in these reports one finds that many of the recommendations made by the OSCE have become hurdles for accession to the EU. The 1999 accession report for Latvia provides a clear example. One of the issues identified specifically by the high commissioner on national minorities is the naturalization process for the numerous Russians living in Latvia who upon Latvian independence lost their citizenship. The Latvian government decided that only Russians who could prove that they or their family had been in the country during its period of independence from 1918 to 1945 (this period will be discussed in more detail below) could claim citizenship.[23] Pressure from the OSCE has changed the process used to obtain citizenship, but the high commissioner still has found faults with the process.[24] From an early stage, the OSCE was involved in trying to alter the relationship that was developing between the Latvian majority (only a slight majority) and the

Russian minority. As Bernier contends, speaking of both Latvia and Estonia, which has similar laws,

> the High Commissioner made it clear, from the beginning of his involvement, that the path taken by both countries to secure the "privileged position" of the core group over minorities not only ran against international norms, but also disrupted internal social cohesion.[25]

At issue is the use of an exam that tests a respondent's knowledge of Latvian society, laws, and government. The OSCE believes that the test is too difficult, and therefore many Russians are being denied citizenship. This was incorporated into the 1999 report. Under the category of "Minority rights and the Protection of Minorities," the Latvian government is congratulated on meeting many of the OSCE recommendations, with statements such as, "the Government took a number of important decisions in order to speed up the citizenship and naturalisation procedures . . . based on assessments by international organisations such as the OSCE."[26] Unfortunately for the Latvians, other OSCE recommendations relating to the citizenship test were not met and remain the final hurdles for accession. Near the end of the 1999 accession report's section on minorities, there is the following statement: "A last issue to be addressed in this context, concerns a further simplification of the citizenship tests on Latvian history, and the constitution in accordance with the recommendations made by the OSCE."[27] To meet the EU's demands, Latvia has a great amount of work to do; as of 2001 there were still more than 550,000 stateless people (the vast majority Russians) in Latvia, comprising approximately 20% of the total population.[28] As mentioned, there is a similar debate occurring in Estonia where the Russian minority faces challenges to citizenship, and as a result Estonia faces challenges to accession.[29]

A similar situation is found in another prospective EU member, Slovakia. Slovakia has two large minority groups within its borders, the Roma and Hungarians. As with the Baltic countries, after the creation of an independent Slovakia, the constitution refers to the state as "the State of the Slovak nation."[30] As Schöphlin notes, this creates a situation that "links citizenship with nationhood and seemingly makes the rights of one conditional on membership of the other."[31] As a result of this situation, growing resentment has developed among both the Roma and Hungarian populations in Slovakia.[32] To try to alleviate some of this tension, the OSCE has tried to persuade the Slovak government to change its policies. In 1998 the high commissioner urged changes to the countries language laws so that the Hungarian and Romani could become more integrated into Slovak society. He suggested that the laws as they stood could be questioned as to "whether a number of provisions are compatible with international standards accepted by Slovakia."[33] Under pressure, the Slovak government changed the laws, but their implementation was slow. The EU accession progress report in 2000 identified the new language law's implementation as a new requirement for Slovakia to attain.[34] The second issue that the EU has put pressure on the Slovak government to improve is the discrimination and violence directed at the Roma population. The Roma will be discussed in greater detail below.

What the Slovak, Latvian, and Estonian cases show is the impact the OSCE has had on the states of Eastern Europe. If a state of Eastern Europe is slow to respond to the recommendations by the high commissioner, the EU adds the recommendations to the accession report. The EU has decided how the states of Eastern Europe should deal with their minority issues and how their laws and constitutions should be structured. Failure to comply has serious repercussions. As Burgess states in regards to the Slovak governments willingness to change its laws concerning the Hungarian minority, "until they are judged to have shown enough willingness in this regard they are likely to remain marginalized. Perceived attentiveness to the wishes of minorities is deciding the fate of states and not simply that of nontitular national minorities."[35] The question must be asked: are the fates of Western states affected the same way?

THE EU MEMBERS AND MINORITY RIGHTS

Since 1992, there has been a tension between the established states of Western Europe and the newly democratized Eastern Europe. The East has felt as though they have been held to a higher standard. According to Chandler, the Western OSCE countries (the vast majority of them members of the EU) "had no conception of how to apply such policies in relation to their own minorities or of accepting such a level of international regulations in the affairs of the state."[36] It appears that the Western states have chosen to ignore the regulations as opposed to adapting to them. Due to a technical loophole, Germany does not include the Turkish minority as a national minority in the country. They claim that they are a new minority and should not count.[37] Other countries, such as Sweden and Denmark, have also specified what minority groups they would provide cultural rights for. Austria has limited protection to citizens, and Luxembourg claims to have no minorities so the treaties do not apply to them. France, Greece, and the Netherlands also have not signed the treaty on minority protection.[38] How the German treatment of the Turkish minority differs from the Latvian or Estonian governments' distinction between the Russian community that arrived prior to annexation and those who came after is unclear. The Russian minority in the Baltic and the German Turks provide a good comparison of treatment by their respective states. Both have faced severe restrictions to gaining citizenship in the past, and both have faced discrimination by the state. The Turks began arriving in what was West Germany in the early 1950s as a solution to Germany's labor shortage. It was expected that when the shortage ended, they would return to Turkey. In reality, many stayed and have continued to arrive. Many have now been in Germany for generations and have little connection with Turkey. They speak German, and feel German, but face restrictive barriers to citizenship and continue to be classified as foreigners. The Turks in Germany face restrictions on voting, access to jobs in the civil service or military, and face expulsion for illegal activities. While the restrictions on citizenship have been loosened, less than 10% of the total Turkish population was able to vote in the 1998 election, and only one member of the Bundestag was Turkish.[39] Some German provincial governments as late as the 1980s banned Turkish children from attending German schools, claiming it was multiculturalism. As Kymlicka notes, "multiculturalism without the offer of citizenship is almost invariably a recipe for, and rationalization of, exclusion."[40] It is clear that the treatment of the Turks in Germany is similar to that of the Russians in the Baltic. Citizenship is based on ethnicity, and while there are procedures in place to gain citizenship, the barriers are so high that few can reach them.

As mentioned above, the EU is concerned with the treatment of the Roma population in Slovakia and has made an end to the discrimination by the Slovaks a key element of accession. While the EU does praise the efforts of the government on the Roma issue, as of 2000 "tangible improvement of the situation of the Roma minority in particular by implementing specific measures, a short term priority of the 1999 Accession Partnership, has . . . not been achieved to a large extent."[41] It is true that the Roma are discriminated against in Slovakia. The European Roma Rights Centre (ERRC), an advocacy group that tracks the treatment of the Roma across Europe, as well as others have raised serious questions about the treatment of the Roma in Slovakia. Beyond the citizenship questions, and discrimination faced by Romani children in education, the Roma face difficulty gaining employment and have been targeted by both the police and right-wing "skinheads."[42] While there is no denying the poor treatment of the Roma in Slovakia, there is evidence that their treatment in other areas of Europe is no better. The Roma in Italy, for example, also face severe discrimination. The ERRC has documented cases of abuse by the police, including torture and sexual assaults on women by police during searches. The Italian Roma have faced restrictions on education, employment both in and out of the public sector, and mobility, with many Roma confined to "camps." The Roma also face the threats of violence by nonstate actors.[43]

Based on this evidence, it appears that the states in Western Europe should face the same recommendations as those put to the states of Eastern Europe. This evidence is further reinforced when the data from the Minorities at Risk database are examined. As discussed above, the Minorities at Risk database tracks the treatment and actions of more than 285 minority groups across the world. Two of the variables tracked in the database concern political discrimination (POLDIS) and economic discrimination (ECDIS). There are five categories for these variables, with 0 indicating no discrimination and 4 indicating exclusion/repressive policies.[44] Table 1 illustrates how the groups discussed above were coded for the year 1998, a year when the EU was making demands for changes in the accession reports.

Table 1. 1998 Political and Economic Discrimination Codes; Minorities at Risk Dataset[45]

Group	POLDIS	ECDIS
Russians in Estonia	1	1
Russians in Latvia	1[a]	3
Turks in Germany	3	1
Roma in Slovakia	3	3
Roma in Italy	3	3

a. In 1997, the POLDIS score was 4.

The table shows that both Eastern and Western European states have discrimination in their societies. Other minority groups in Western states have similar scores, such as the Muslim community in France (POLDIS = 4) and Afro-Caribbeans in the United Kingdom (ECDIS = 3). A double standard is clearly in place, and the states in the East are aware of it, as seen by a letter sent on 4 June 1997 by the Estonian Minister of Foreign Affairs Tomas Ilves to the high commissioner on national minorities. Ilves argued that the laws in Estonia were similar to those of many Western states. He argues that it "can therefore not be argued that Estonian legislation in the present formulation is at variance with international practice or with practice in Council of Europe States."[46]

A DIFFICULT CHOICE

What makes the double standard even more painful for the prospective members of the EU is that they currently have two main goals; the first is to join Europe, and the second is to protect their culture and society. These goals appear to be in conflict with one another. It is important to understand why both of these goals are of equal importance. The importance of joining the EU is obvious. Why then is it so important to protect culture? Why is it so hard to give up the laws that the EU has demanded? A brief look at the history of the Baltic states of Estonia and Latvia holds the answer.

Estonia and Latvia have been ruled by many different countries throughout their history. At different times, Swedes, Germans, Russians, and eventually Soviets tried to replace the Baltic culture and language with their own.[47] After World War I, Estonia and Latvia became independent for the first time in their histories. During that period, minorities were treated well, but the constitutions and other policies were designed to favor the Balts. Democracy eventually failed but was briefly restored in Estonia before the start of World War II. The Balts fell victim to the secret German-Soviet Molotov-Ribbentrop Pact, which gave control of the countries to the Soviet Union. During the period of Soviet annexation (which the West never recognized) the now-Republics of Estonia and Latvia faced both a large influx of Russians and Russian speakers[48] and severe repression and deportations by the Soviet government.[49] Finally, with Perestroika and Glasnost, the Baltic republics were able to begin nationalist movements under the guise of protests over ecological concerns.

The Baltic story, although in some ways unique, is similar to those of other newly democratic nations. Due to this history of invasion and domination, there is an understandable concern for the protection of the majority language and society. This is, for many countries, their first real opportunity for many years to ensure the long-term survival of their ethnic group. As Dawisha and Parrott note, the nationalist feeling in these countries was based on the belief that "their hard-won independence could easily be subverted by political actions of the non-native residents."[50] Smooha describes the society created by the Estonians and Latvians (and could be argued to apply to other Eastern European countries such as Slovakia) as an "ethnic democracy" where democratic principles favor the dominant group.[51] However it is described, it is clear that the protection of the majority group is of key importance to the emerging states, which makes the fact that they must choose between it and joining Europe when other states do not have to even more difficult.

Conclusion: What Happens Now?

Countries in Eastern Europe are trying to protect their culture through discriminatory laws while at the same time join the EU, which they cannot do. The EU, on the other hand, is trying to enforce laws with prospective members while not holding existing members to the same standards. The EU has been able to accomplish it so far because the pull of joining is greater than the pull of nationalistic protectionism. It would appear that Brubaker would need to add the impact of international agents into his current triadic relationship discussed above. The long-term effects of this double standard will need to be examined in the future. Many questions arise now that evidence of the double standard has been documented and the impact on the affected states understood. Will there be a backlash in the states of Eastern Europe against this forced form of democratization, resulting in these countries turning their back on Europe to restore their protectionist legislation? Will a schism form between East and West since the East appears to be aware of the double standard they have been subjected to? Once EU members, will the state revert back to its old habits and policies? Will this pattern of double standards continue after accession is reached and the states of Eastern Europe become, in the words of Holmes, "second-class citizens"?[52] Also, questions arise concerning the minority groups who do not have the advantage of living in states currently trying to gain EU membership. When the states of Eastern Europe become full EU members, will they then have precedents for action? Who do they turn to?[53] These questions currently do not have answers. There does appear to be a realization of a double standard in at least one of the organizations of Europe. The new OSCE high commissioner on national minorities, Rolf Ekeus, has recently begun to call on the EU member states to meet their own standards. In a speech given on 5 November 2002 in Copenhagen to discuss the enlargement of the EU and the application of the Copenhagen criteria on minority rights, Ekeus stated that "the standards on which the Copenhagen criteria are based should be universally applicable within and throughout the EU, in which case they should be equally—and consistently—applied to all Member States."[54] The EU may face problems in the future because it tried to do good deeds now. Improving the rights of minorities is a noble and important goal, and the EU should be commended for deciding to make it a criterion for membership. Unfortunately, the value of that deed may be lost because the EU is unable or unwilling to apply the same standards to itself as it would others. As Ekeus states, "Simply, the EU cannot ignore minority -related issues on its own turf."[55]

NOTES

1. Open Society Institute, *Monitoring the EU Accession Process: Minority Protection Overview* (Budapest: Open Society Institute, 2002), 20.

2. "EU Set for Eastward Expansion," *TorontoStar.Com*, 8 October, 2002. The countries that were offered membership are Poland, the Czech Republic, Slovakia, Hungary, Slovenia, Cyprus, Malta, Latvia, Estonia, and Lithuania.

3. See the European Union Web site at http://www.europa.eu.int for accession reports for all of the current prospective countries from 1999 to the present.

4. See, for example, George Schöpflin, "Nationalism and Ethnicity in Europe, East and West," In Charles A. Kupchan, ed., *Nationalism and Nationalities in the New Europe* (Ithaca, NY: Cornell University Press, 1995); Rogers Brubaker, *Nationalism Reframed* (Cambridge: Cambridge University Press, 1996); Richard Caplan and John Feffer, ed., *Europe's New Nationalism* (Oxford: Oxford University Press, 1996); David Laitin, *Identity in Formation* (Ithaca, NY: Cornell University Press, 1998); Camille C. O'Reilly, ed., *Language, Ethnicity and the State* (New York: Palgrave Press, 2001), vol. 1 and 2; Nenad Miševic, *Nationalism and Beyond* (Budapest: Central European University Press, 2001); and Michael Keating and John McGarry, ed., *Minority Nationalism and the Changing International Order* (Oxford: Oxford University Press, 2001).

5. David R. Cameron, "The Challenges of Accession," *East European Politics and Societies* 17:1(winter 2003): 25.

6. Andrew Moravcsik and Milada Anna Vachudova, "National Interest, State Power, and EU Enlargement," *East European Politics and Societies* 17:1(winter 2003): 46.

7. The case of Lithuania will not be included in the analysis of the Baltic states. Lithuania has been more successful than Estonia and Latvia in incorporating its minorities. This is a result of the much smaller size of the Russian population within Lithuania due to the lack of industrialization during the period of Soviet rule. See Thomas Lane, *Lithuania: Stepping Westward* (London: Routledge, 2001); Walter C. Clemens, *The Baltic Transformed* (Lanham, MD: Rowman and Littlefield, 2001); and Rob Zaagman, *Conflict Prevention in the Baltic States* (Flensburg: European Centre for Minority Issues Monograph #1, 1999).

8. Brubaker, *Nationalism Reframed*, 6.

9. Will Kymlicka, *Politics in the Vernacular* (Oxford: Oxford University Press, 2001), 28.

10. The main consequence is an increase in intrastate ethnic conflict. See John McGarry, "Nationalism without States: The Accommodation of Nationalism in the New State Order," In Keating and McGarry, ed., *Minority Nationalism*.

11. Antje Herrberg, "Which Identity for Which Europe?" In Antje Herrberg, ed., *Which Identity for Which Europe?* (Aalborg: Centre for Languages and Intercultural Studies, 1998).

12. See, for example, Donald L. Horowitz, *Ethnic Groups in Conflict* (Berkeley: University of California Press, 1985); Ted Robert Gurr, *Minorities at Risk* (Washington, DC: U.S. Institute for Peace Press, 1993) and *Peoples versus States* (Washington, DC: U.S. Institute for Peace Press, 2000); Daniel Chirot and Martin E. P. Seligman, ed., *Ethnopolitical Warfare* (Washington, DC: American Psychological Association, 2001).

13. Beyond the quantitative data, the Minorities at Risk project has extensive qualitative analysis on each group and a chronology detailing major events, protests, and international intervention. These will also be used in the analysis for the article.

14. Organization for Security and Co-operation in Europe (OSCE) fact sheet *High Commissioner on National Minorities* taken from the OSCE Web site http://www.osce.org.

15. OSCE fact sheet *High Commissioner on National Minorities*.

16. Zaagman, *Conflict Prevention*, 16.

17. Dennis Chingas et al., "Preventive Diplomacy and the Organization for Security and Cooperation in Europe," In Abram Chayes and Antonia Handler Chayes, eds., *Preventing Conflict in the Post-Communist World* (Washington, DC: Brookings Institute, 1996).

18. Stefan Troebst, *Ethnopolitical Conflict in Eastern Europe and the OSCE* (Flensburg: European Centre for Minority Issues Brief #1, 1998).

19. Troebst, *Ethnopolitical Conflict.*

20. The OSCE Web page http://www.osce.org/henm/documents/recommendations/ contains all of the recommendations produced by the High Commission on National Minorities. The country reports available are for Albania, Croatia, Estonia, the Former Yugoslav Republic of Macedonia, Hungary, Kazakhstan, Kyrgyzstan, Latvia, Lithuania, Moldova, Romania, the Russian Federation, the Slovak Republic, and the Ukraine.

21. David Chandler, "The OSCE and the Internationalisation of National Minority rights," In David P. Forsythe, ed., *Human Rights in the New Europe* (Lincoln: University of Nebraska Press, 1994), 68.

22. All of the more recent EU accession reports are available for each country on the EU Web site at http://www.europa.eu.int.

23. For a description of the citizenship law for Latvia, see Zaagman, *Conflict Prevention*, 39.

24. See the correspondence between the high commissioner and the Latvian government on the OSCE Web site.

25. Julie Bernier, "Nationalism in Transition: Nationalizing Impulses and International Counterweights in Latvia and Estonia," In Keating and McGarry, ed., *Minority Nationalism*, 347.

26. *1999 European Union Accession Progress Report–Latvia* taken from the EU Web site.

27. *1999 European Union Accession Progress Report–Latvia.*

28. Vadim Poleschuk, *Accession to the European Union and National Integration in Estonia and Latvia* (Flensburg: European Centre for Minority Issues Report #8, 2001), 4.

29. See *1999 European Union Accession Progress Report–Estonia* taken from the EU Web site and the high commissioner on national minorities country recommendations for Estonia on the OSCE Web site.

30. Schöpflin, "Nationalism and Ethnicity," 62.

31. Schöpflin, "Nationalism and Ethnicity," 62.

32. Bugajski, "Fate of Minorities in Eastern Europe."

33. Letter sent on 4 November 1998 to the prime minister of Slovakia, Mikuláš Dzurinda by Max van der Stoel, high commissioner on national minorities, found on the OSCE Web site.

34. *European Union Accession Report, 2000–Slovakia* found on the EU Web site.

35. Adam Burgess, "Critical Reflections on the Return of National Minority rights Regulations to East/West European Affairs," In Forsythe, ed., *Human Rights*, 54.

36. Chandler, "OSCE," 66.

37. Chandler, "OSCE," 67.

38. Duncan Wilson, "Minority Rights in Education" report by the *Right to Education Project* 2002, 10.

39. See the analytic summary for the Turks in Germany on the Minorities at Risk Project Web site http://www.cidcm.umd.edu/inscr/mar/data/germturk.htm; also see Michael Ignatieff, *Blood and Belonging* (Toronto: Penguin Press Canada, 1993). The Turks situation had improved

somewhat by 2001 when Turkey and Germany reached an agreement on expanding Turk citizenship.

40. Kymlicka, *Politics*, 171.

41. *European Union Accession Progress Report, Slovakia–2000* from the EU Web site.

42. See European Roma Rights Centre, "Time of the Skinheads: Denial and Exclusion of Roma in Slovakia," *ERRC Country Report Series* 3 (January1997); and the analytic summary for the Roma in Slovakia on the Minorities at Risk Project Web site http://www.cidcm.umd.edu/inscr/mar/data/slvroma.htm.

43. See European Roma Rights Centre, "Campland: Racial Segregation of Roma in Italy," *ERRC Country Report Series* 9 (October 2000); and the analytic summary for the Roma in Italy on the Minorities at Risk Project Web site http://www.cidcm.umd.edu/inscr/mar/data/italroma.htm.

44. Ted Robert Gurr et al., *Minorities at Risk Dataset Users Manual* .899 August 1999 version. The remaining variables indicate the following: 1 = historical discrimination with remedial policies, 2 = historical discrimination with no remedial policies, 3 = social exclusion.

45. *Minorities at Risk Dataset Version* .899, Center for International Development and Conflict Management, University of Maryland–College Park.

46. Letter by Ilves found on the OSCE Web site.

47. See Anatol Lieven, *The Baltic Revolution* (New Haven, CT: Yale University Press, 1993); Graham Smith, *The Baltic States* (New York: St. Martin's Press, 1994); and Clemens, *Baltic Transformed* for a full history of the region.

48. Beyond those of Russian origin, many Belorussians and Ukrainians immigrated to the Baltic region due to its better economy and standard of living.

49. Aksel Kirch et al., "Russians in the Baltic States: To Be or Not To Be?" *Journal of Baltic Studies* 24:2(summer 1993): 173–88; and Peteris Zvidrins, "Changes in the Ethnic Composition of Latvia," *Journal of Baltic Studies* 23:4(1992): 356–68 for statistics of percentage of Russian speakers in the two republics; and Mikhail Gorbachev, *Memoirs* (New York: Doubleday, 1995) for a discussion of the influx of Russians and the repression faced by the Baltic states during the Soviet rule.

50. Karen Dawisha and Bruce Parrott, *Russia and the New States of Eurasia* (Cambridge: Cambridge University Press, 1994), 77.

51. See Pritt Järve, *Ethnic Democracy and Estonia: Application of Smooha's Model* (Flensburg: European Centre for Minority Issues Working Paper #7, 2000); and Sammy Smooha, *The Model of Ethnic Democracy* (Flensburg: European Centre for Minority Issues Working Paper #13, 2001).

52. Stephen Holmes, "A European Doppelstaat?" *East European Politics and Societies* 17:1(winter 2003): 107.

53. A leader of the Muslim community in France hinted at such action when he said, "Muslims are informed about European legislation, but for the time being they do not see the necessity to call upon non-national authorities." Quoted in Open Society Institute, *Monitoring Minority Protection in EU Member States*, 2002, 138.

54. Speech available from the OSCE Web site.

55. Speech available from the OSCE Web site.

***Michael Johns** is assistant professor of political science at Laurentian University, Georgian College in Ontario.

Michael Johns, "'Do as I Say, Not as I Do': The European Union, Eastern Europe and Minority Rights," *East European Politics and Societies* 17 (2003): 682–699. © American Council of Learned Societies.

Section III:
Roma Political Mobilization

The post-1989 debate on Roma integration has, in one way or another, involved questions of Roma political mobilization. While different stakeholders all seem to agree that Roma participation in the decision-making process—particularly involving decisions directly affecting Roma groups—is highly desirable, wide disagreement exists over how this participation should be organized. The initial enthusiasm over the creation of the first Roma political parties after 1989 was short-lived, with a majority of these parties having either disintegrated or fallen into disgrace. Even with affirmative action, the normal political process has afforded Roma leaders few chances to bring their issues to the wider political table and be taken seriously by their fellow citizens. Individual Roma leaders have been able to claim most of their success as a result of personal charisma and dedication as well as the luck of more tolerant constituencies. For the most part, however, the political process appears to have failed Roma leaders. Grassroots actions and activists have oftentimes proven much more effective despite limited access to capital; however, these actions offer only limited and short-lived solutions that are usually unsustainable. This section debates not only the current possibilities for Roma political mobilization but also discusses (through a series of cases studies) the success of different past mobilization platforms, particularly mobilization through the normal political process vs. grassroots mobilization.

Chapter 5: Political Participation of Roma, Traveller and Sinti Communities

*by European Roma Information Office**

INTRODUCTION

Political participation is an essential requirement of functioning democratic systems; it is important that everyone plays an active role as voters, community participants, workers, activists, and political party members. However, ethnic and religious minorities are frequently excluded from political participation, and are unable to exercise their political and civil rights.[1] Political scientists often describe two types of political participation: descriptive (or symbolic) and substantive, according to Dirk Jacobs:

> There is descriptive representation when the composition of a political body reflects the socio-demographic characteristics of the overall population it is supposed to represent. We talk about substantive representation when interests of subgroups of a population are sufficiently voiced and taken into account in political deliberation. It is often assumed that descriptive representation leads to substantive representation—but there is no guaranteed link between the two.[2]

In an ideal world the political establishment would accurately reflect the composition of the society it represents, and the issues facing all communities would be adequately reflected in the mainstream political debate. Thus in a European Union with an estimated Roma population of 10 million,[3] one would expect 2% of political representatives to be from the Roma community. Likewise 16 of the 785 members of the European Parliament should come from the Roma community. However this picture is very far from reality.

Roma in Europe have always been faced with numerous social, political, and economic challenges that prevent them from fully integrating into the larger, majority society and actively taking part in politics. As a result, both the quality and quantity of Roma participation in political affairs is generally low. Racial prejudice, poverty, low education levels, sub-standard living conditions, language barriers, and other social and economic factors increase the communication and policy gap between governments and the majority population on one side, and the Roma population on the other, reinforcing mutual distrust. If Roma are to advocate for better opportunities and effective solutions, they will need to become more active participants in the political processes of their countries and of the European Union. This will require consistent, long-term efforts and assistance.

The aim of this fact sheet is to provide an overview of the key issues and challenges in securing effective political participation of Europe's largest minority, drawing out broader issues of political participation of ethnic and religious minorities. The fact sheet will conclude by outlining examples of good practice initiatives both general and specific to the Roma community, which should serve as a model for promoting the political inclusion of minorities across all EU member states.

OVERVIEW OF POLITICAL PARTICIPATION OF ROMA, TRAVELLERS AND SINTI

Despite their numerical strength in several countries, Roma in Central and Eastern Europe remain to date un- or underrepresented in political life due to the fact that they do not stand equal chances to participate and to exercise their political rights. Romani exclusion is even more pronounced in Western Europe: the total number of public officials in European Union member states who state that they are Romani can literally be counted on the fingers of one hand.[4]

As the process of democratisation in Central and Eastern Europe has continued, the Roma have increasingly been recognised as an ethnic and national minority, and for the first time they have been offered the opportunity to exercise the same rights as other officially recognised minorities. However, the pressing need for transformation in the social and economic structures of post-communist states led to rapid socioeconomic decline and deprivation for many groups, particularly though not exclusively the Roma. After a decade of mobilisation the Roma remain underrepresented in Europe's politics.

The failure of old and new European democracies to include the Roma community is a complex phenomenon, which is not easily accounted for—both structural and individual factors must be taken into account. These include:

- **Prejudice and stereotypes:** Mainstream political actors regularly assume that members of the Roma community are not interested or do not have the capacity to engage. Given the reactions of the majority population, some believe that Roma participation will damage the prospects of mainstream political actors.
- **Lack of political experience and networks:** There is low voter participa-

tion among many Roma communities, who may have become disillusioned by existing power structures. Without exposure to networks and parties, few Roma have been provided the opportunity to participate politically.

• **Institutional discrimination within political systems:** Many political systems are structured in a way that works against Roma participation. For example voting registers may require registration in a particular geographic location long before an upcoming election. Electoral systems can be constituted in a way which is inherently discriminatory against minorities, such as single voting districts; multi-district systems can facilitate more accurate representation between districts.

• **Citizenship and residency:** Like migrants, often Roma face barriers to political participation due to their legal status. Many Roma have no identity cards, either because their births or marriages were never registered with the state, or, in the case of many Roma displaced during the conflicts in the Balkans, because their documents are not recognised by the state in which they now live.

Political Parties

As the key gatekeepers of political participation, political parties have a key role in both facilitating and undermining the political participation of ethnic and religious minorities in Europe.

One of the primary obstacles to Roma political participation is the lack of an open and fair environment that encourages their active involvement in **mainstream parties**. These parties are central to Roma political participation and yet, in most of Europe, they are ill-prepared to engage in this issue. As noted above, there is reluctance among most political parties to advocate Roma interests, appoint Roma candidates, or associate themselves with Roma, as this is generally feared to be politically damaging. Roma candidates who do make their way onto mainstream party lists are often placed so low as to be unelectable.

As a result, Roma views of mainstream parties are generally negative. Typically expressed concerns are that mainstream parties manipulate the Roma vote and are dismissive of Roma community problems. While they generally have little trust in politicians, polling and election results indicate that Roma voters favour mainstream parties over their own.[5]

Given the limited response of many mainstream political parties, new Roma political groupings could provide an effective means to promote Roma identity while articulating and advancing their human rights through political representation. However, no **Roma-based political parties** have achieved measurable success. In addition, as with all forms of identity politics, there is a risk that Roma issues could become marginalised, or that Roma parties would not fully reflect the diversity of views within their community. The Roma parties' failure to attract a substantial percentage of the Roma vote during elections indicates that Roma do not necessarily vote as a bloc, nor do they necessarily support the ethnic-based parties and candidates who claim to represent them. For example in Bulgaria during the 2005 elections, a Roma party, Euroroma, put forward a list of candidates, but none were elected.[6]

Roma Politicians

Despite the barriers and obstacles, some members of Roma communities have successfully participated in the electoral processes at all levels of the political system: local, national and European. Roma politicians have an important role to play, not only in providing leadership and role models, but also in addressing the substantive issues facing Roma communities across the European Union.

In general, due to the barriers described above, Roma tend to have more opportunities to engage at the local rather than national level. In some countries, Roma are exerting increasing influence in local politics, such as for example the Roma municipality Shuto Orizari, in Skopje, Macedonia. Voter turnout records and reports indicate that Roma recognise that their political interests are best represented at the local level.[7]

However Roma who are elected into office often face significant challenges in fulfilling their role. Given their limited numbers it can be extremely difficult to effect any significant change for their community. Incidents of scapegoating and racist attacks, in increasing numbers, have added new and formidable obstacles to addressing Roma problems.

GOOD PRACTICE IN PROMOTING POLITICAL PARTICIPATION

There have been a number of initiatives in recent years aimed at securing enhanced political participation of ethnic and religious minorities in Europe, including a number of specific initiatives aimed at enhancing the representation of the Roma community. Responses range from hard measures such as the use of quotas and party lists, such as those which have been used to promote the political participation of women, to softer initiatives targeted at both the minority and majority populations, aimed at enhancing capacity and opportunities for change.

Examples of recent initiatives include the establishment of Roma self-government in Hungary. While such models are subject to criticism as they fail to ensure participation in mainstream decision making, can have insufficient power and competences, lack appropriate funding, and be too dependent on the support of local government structures, they have proved successful in: promoting cultural identity, highlighting Roma rights, encouraging political mobilisation, stemming assimilation, and addressing legitimacy problems among Roma from the perspective of representative democracy. The Hungarian government passed Act LXXVII on the Rights of National and Ethnic Minorities, the so-called Minorities Act, in 1993. According to this law, local and national self-governments will be elected and established.[8]

The **NGO sector** represents a tremendous asset and resource. NGOs dealing with Roma issues as well as broader anti-racist NGOs undertake empowerment, advocacy, monitoring and anti-discrimination initiatives to increase Roma access to education, jobs, political participation, health care, legal services, etc. There are also specific initiatives by NGOs aimed at increasing voter participation, and enhancing capacity for Roma participation in elections. Roma organisations have achieved success in influencing politics—for example Roma organisations in Bulgaria, together with the Human Rights Project, pushed for the "Framework Programme for Equal Integration for Roma in Bulgaria" in 1999. More recently the Resolution of the Catalonian Parliament on the persecution faced by Roma is the result of intensive advocacy by FAGIC—Federació d'Asociaciones Gitanes de Catalunya (Federation of Roma Associations from Catalonia).

The **round tables**[9] organised in many countries provided a unique opportunity for Roma political activists and representatives of mainstream political parties to meet and engage in dialogue around some of the most pressing issues in their countries concerning Roma political representation. In addition, the round tables served as fora in which Roma groups could consider common issues and possibilities for alliances, as well as their different views on political representation and other matters.

Some political parties have made commitments to increasing their representativeness, and conducting business in a way which does not negatively impact minority communities. For example the **Charter of European Parties for a Non-Racist Society** calls on democratic political parties in the European Union to act responsibly when dealing with issues related to race, ethnic and national origin and religion. It encourages political parties to work towards fair representation of racial, ethnic, national and religious minorities within and at all levels of their party system. The Charter presents a standard to which civil society can hold political parties to account.[10]

CONCLUSION

The problems confronting Roma are many and complex. Essential to their resolution is active, widespread participation by Roma in the political process. This requires first and foremost a more open political, social and economic environment; it also requires individual skills training, enhanced political organisation, and strategies that allow for political diversity among Roma while promoting collective interests. Governments need to implement Roma development strategies in a manner that derives meaningful and measurable benefit to Roma communities in the areas of political representation, economic development, social integration and human rights protection. International organisations need to recognise that political participation is key to Roma development, and then provide the resources and oversight to ensure that progress is made. Mainstream political parties need to incorporate Roma as voters, members, candidates and eventually among their leaders.

Given the breadth and depth of the political, social and economic obstacles facing Roma, a broad, multi-faceted and long-term approach is needed to create meaningful political participation. In terms of enhancing political participation this approach must be informed by:

- A focus on change within existing political systems and institutions in order to create opportunities for engagement;
- Comprehensive strategies which recognise the complexity of initiatives needed to enhance participation, including hiring Roma as public officials;
- Promote strategies in order to foster political participation of Roma communities, including self-government initiatives, as a first step towards mainstream political participation;
- Create the broader socio-economic conditions in order to facilitate political participation;
- A medium to long term view which can create the conditions for participation;
- A focus on women and younger people, as well as other groups who are most marginalised within Roma communities;
- A bottom-up approach which is inclusive of all stakeholders;
- Local and grassroots development;
- Commitment to mainstream and targeted programmes to support and

build capacity amongst Roma communities, as well as to empower Roma voters;

- A desire to build trust through demonstrating integrity and openness;
- International learning and exchange.

KEY DOCUMENTS

- Charter of European Parties for a Non-Racist Society, http://eumc. europa.eu/eumc/index.php?fuseaction=content.dsp_cat_content&catid=3ef 0500f9e0c5&contentid=3ef0568924fa5
- ERRC, Roma Rights 4/2003: Political Rights, available at: http://www. errc.org/cikk.php?cikk=1310
- ENAR Fact Sheet No. 26, Political Rights (April 2006), available at: http://www.enar-eu.org/en/factsheets/index.shtml
- ENARgy, Representation of Minorities (January 2007), available at: http://www.enar-eu.org/en/enargy/enargy.shtml

NOTES

1. For an introduction to political rights see: ENAR Fact Sheet No. 26, Political Rights (April 2006), available at: http://www.enar-eu.org/en/factsheets/index.shtml

2. Jacobs, D (2007) The challenge of representation of minorities, in: ENARgy January 2007, available at: http://www.enar-eu.org/en/enargy/enargy.shtml

3. Estimated population figure in: European Commission (2004), The situation of Roma in an enlarged European Union, p. 11, available at: http://ec.europa.eu/employment_social/publications/2005/ke6204389_en.pdf

4. Russinova, S (2003) Political Rights of Roma, in: Roma Rights 4/2003: Political Rights, available at: http://www.errc.org/cikk.php?cikk=1310

5. For example see: Survey on the Political Participation of Roma in Romania, available at: http://www.accessdemocracy.org/library/2056_ro_survey_080106.pdf

6. Lambert, P (2007) Parliamentary representation of minorities in four European Union member states, in: ENARgy January 2007, available at: http://www.enar-eu.org/en/enargy/enargy.shtml

7. Project on Ethnic Relations (2006) Romani Politics. Present and Future. PER: New Jersey, available at: http://www.per-usa.org/Reports/PER_Romani_Politics.pdf

8. Wallsh, Niahm (2000) Minority Self-Government in Hungary: Legislation and Practice. ECMI: Flensburg, Germany, available at: http://www.ecmi.de/jemie/download/JEMIE04Walsh30-07-01.pdf

9. Project on Ethnic Relations (PER) (1998) Political Participation and the Roma in Hungary and Slovakia, see: http://www.per-usa.org/reports/PoliticalPart99.pdf

10. For the text of the Charter and a list of signatories see: www.eumc.europa.eu

*The European Roma Information Office (ERIO) is an international advocacy organization that promotes political and public discussion on Roma issues by providing factual and in-depth information on a range of policy issues to European Union institutions, Roma civil organizations, government authorities, and intergovernmental bodies.

ERIO, "Factsheet 32: Political Participation of Roma, Traveller and Sinti Communities," May 2007. Available at: http://cms.horus.be/files/99935/MediaArchive/pdf/FS32_roma_political_participation_may2007.pdf.

Used by Permission.

Chapter 6: Limited Opportunities for Political Participation: A Case-study of Roma Local Councillors in Slovenia

by Irena Baclija and Miro Haček*

Throughout the transition period, Roma populations in central and Eastern Europe have been largely left out of economic and policy-making processes. Many Roma communities were marginalised through poverty and physical isolation. When addressing this issue one should consider that if the Roma are to advocate better opportunities and solutions to the problems of their own communities, they will need to strengthen the level of their participation in political processes. Since few Roma have any political experience they will need strategies that address the obstacles to the Roma's political participation and the development of organised Romani political leadership. Such strategies should be implemented in legislation at the national level, considering the specifics and culture of each individual civil society. In Slovenia, legislators recognised this problem and have amended the Law on Local Self-government in 2001, which obliged local communities and political leaders to include the Roma minority in the policy-making process. This led to the first elections of local Romani councillors in 2002 in 19 Slovenian municipalities. The article aims to offer an evaluation of the institution, tasks and function of the Roma local councillor. Another goal is to challenge current practices and solutions and to criticise the method used at the national level for dealing with the problems that the Roma encounter.

1. INTRODUCTION: THE IMPORTANCE OF POLITICAL PARTICIPATION FOR THE ROMA MINORITY

Democracy is defined through citizens and their political actions. Citizens participate through political parties and elected government bodies or other forms of political participation. The term 'participation' means being involved in decision-making and other activities in the area of social life. In most cases, the term relates to the concept of political participation which Nie and Verba (1975: 1) defined as 'those legal activities by private citizens that are more or less directly aimed at influencing the selection of government personnel and/or actions they take.' We can divide forms of public participation into two broad categories: formal and informal. 'Public participation may be formal, meaning its form has been prescribed by a law, or informal, meaning the public decides independently the form of participation it will take' (Bowman et al., in Nagy [and Vrecko] 1994: 65).

Most often, public participation takes the form of participation in elections. There are other forms too, such as participation in referendums, political demonstrations and election campaigns, further political party or pressure group memberships, civil disobedience, etc. In addition to these forms of political participation, other forms exist which are less politically charged, such as participation in public exhibitions and public debates. Due to today's changed circumstances and the rapid development of information technology, new informal forms of public participation have emerged, such as:

- organized groups of citizens (environmentalists, denationalization claimants etc.) forming networks aimed at influencing the development of policies;
- groups of citizens drafting laws or commenting on draft laws;
- grassroots lobbying; and
- the use of new technologies to make suggestions or to participate in debates.

Not having access to the means for improving or even establishing informal forms of public participation, those groups that are in an underprivileged situation or discriminated against in some other way need extra protection of their rights to be able to function in society. Nationally mixed societies or societies with one (and often several) national minorities must provide additional institutionalised forms of political participation for minorities. Especially vulnerable are those minority groups that do not have a motherland to act as their patron, which through mediations and interventions provides a favourable atmosphere for preserving and developing the national culture that links a minority to its motherland. The Roma community is such a minority. Our starting point is the assumption that, to ensure its rights, it is mandatory to provide the Roma minority with an appropriate tool for its political participation. This is necessary in order to enable its adequate representation in local and national decision-making bodies, and to guarantee the implementation of appropriate policies which would bring real benefits to the Roma minority, rather than being just theoretically conceived projects without any tangible results.

In the past thirteen years, the democratic processes underway in central and Eastern Europe have dispelled at least two illusions—or false assumptions—about the representation and participation of the Roma in public life. The first is that Romani concerns can be effectively addressed and their rights promoted within the ordinary political process, through individuals in publicly elected bodies who are not necessarily Roma. The second one is that a token number of Roma in the public administration can make a difference to formation and implementation of policy on the Roma. While it cannot be claimed that the Roma minority is not represented in national or locally elected bodies,[1] it will be argued that, despite the introduction of some forms of so-called 'positive discrimination', inclusion of the Roma minority in the political participation processes is insufficient and ineffective.

According to Sobotka (2002), the involvement of Roma in state structures, as related to the effectiveness of political participation and influence on policy formation, can be identified through two models. Although Sobotka analysed the political involvement of the Roma in the Czech Republic, Poland, Slovakia and Hungary, the models can also be applied to the case of the Roma minority's political involvement in Slovenia. The first is the *policy formation model*, applicable to the Czech Republic, Slovakia and Poland. The second is the *political representation model*, which relates to the duty of representing and advancing interests, through the process of elections that authorise persons to do so; this has been formed in Hungary and, as we will see later, in Slovenia. The *policy formation model* prioritises different Roma governmental advisory bodies. We argue that this model offers limited solutions and is basically just a channel for promoting *some* political opinions. The *political representation model*, on the other hand, has, according to Vermeersch (2000), acted to stifle influence on policy formation, which has downplayed the effectiveness of the Roma's political representation in Hungary. The state only has limited means to secure the representation of minority groups; as in an electoral democracy, it is up to the particular group to enter into deals and political negotiations to secure places on electoral lists with mainstream parties. Transnational advocacy organisations as well as some academics have suggested that racism and the stereotyping of the Romani problem have stood in the way of the electoral success of many Romani politicians.

Although both models have certain limitations, the political representation model is more applicable to Slovenian Roma populations. The main argument here is the existence of two primary areas in Slovenia with a Romani population, namely, the Prekmurje and Dolenjska regions. So far, these two large Romani communities have been dealing with quite separate problems.[2] The biggest differences in the two communities' characteristics renders the formulation of national policies on Roma issues problematic. What is acceptable for the Dolenjska region might be too dated for the Prekmurska region, and vice versa. To form an advisory body at the national level one would presume that:

(1) the representatives of both main communities would have to establish common ground; and (2) that an agreement should be reached that identifies issues which both Roma communities are encountering. On the other hand, the political representation model enables a heterogeneous Roma community to solve their issues within their respective local community. In 2001, Slovenia addressed the lack of a Romani representative through a legislative obligation for local communities and their political leaders to include the Roma minority in policy-making processes. This led to the first elections of local Romani councillors in 2002 in nineteen Slovenian municipalities.

Since Slovenia is not usually included in international comparative surveys and research concerning the status and well-being of Roma populations in central and Eastern Europe, one could wrongly assume either that Romani issues are not addressed in Slovenia at all, or that the percentage of Romani populations is so insignificant that they are overlooked. The Roma population in Slovenia represents approximately 0.5 per cent of the total population (between 6,000 and 10,000 individuals) and so it is by all means significant, although when compared to other countries much smaller.[3] This mainly resulted in Romani issues in Slovenia being unpublicised and a lack of comparative studies in this field. The goal of this article is to fill this void in relation to the Slovenian policies of addressing the Roma minority's political participation. We shall examine the work of Romani local councillors since their election. We will also challenge the solutions that have been provided, and criticise the way in which the problems encountered by the Roma are being dealt with at the national level in Slovenia.

2. POSITIVE DISCRIMINATION: A NEED OR AN OBSTACLE?

In Europe, the Roma are a minority which extends beyond the boundaries and responsibilities of any single country. Especially since the EU's enlargement it has become obvious that the Roma are neither a small population or facing the usual minority problems. Although the actual size of the Roma population in Europe is unknown, it is estimated[4] that it includes as many as 10 million members. The number closest to this was based on an estimation made by eleven European Union countries (in 2002) according to which the number of Roma amounted to between 2.7 and 5.6 million. Since then, the Roma population in Europe has grown considerably since the accession of twelve new member countries (in May 2004, and in January 2007), when the European Roma minority was estimated to have expanded, already representing the biggest ethnic minority in Europe in 2004 (cf. European commission 2004).

Since the beginning of the political transformation in the region, the social status of the Romani communities has been deteriorating, raising a red flag to the whole of civil society. Ironically, the collapse of communism has in many aspects been a bad experience for the Roma community. The safety net of social transfers has gone or been seriously minimised, along with free health security and scholarships and an increased rate of violence against the Roma. In some cases, the new democratic governments have left the Roma out of the decision-making process altogether. The main issues common to almost all marginalised Roma communities may be put into five categories: (1) inadequate housing; (2) inadequate access to education; (3) high unemployment; (4) high dependence on social security; and (5) obstructed participation in policy-making processes. We argue that addressing the latter could gradually result in the Roma themselves resolving all other issues, meaning that policies would be made by the Roma for the Roma.

In solving the problems of enhancing participation in the policy-making process it is necessary to further regulate Roma issues. 'Perhaps no principle is more essential to the success and legitimacy of initiatives to alleviate the concerns of Romani communities than that Roma themselves should be centrally involved in developing, implementing and evaluating policies and programs. The basic democratic principle that individuals should have a say in how they are governed requires nothing less, and pragmatic considerations counsel the same approach. The importance of minority participation in public affairs is specifically provided in paragraph 35 of the Copenhagen Document, which requires participating States to 'respect the right of persons belonging to national minorities to effective participation in public affairs, including participation in the affairs relating to the protection and promotion of the identity of such minorities' (Organisation for Security and Co-operation in Europe 2000).

In addition, the OSCE directives demand that its members strenuously and conscientiously ensure the exercise of the rights of the Roma. In its reports, the OSCE is especially aware of the importance of including the Roma in the policy-making process at the local level. The roles of local government and civil organisations are important in this respect; some of the most impressive programmes launched in recent years have been undertaken at local levels, frequently at the initiative of non-governmental organisations (NGOs). But local governments have also served to block promising initiatives; some have even sought to institutionalise anti-Roma discrimination through exclusionary policies. It falls on national authorities to ensure that the Roma enjoy the fundamental right to equality in both law and in practice, irrespective of the division of jurisdiction within the state. While the principle of equality requires protection against discrimination, it also entails proactive policies and special measures to ensure equality of opportunity. This is especially relevant for the Roma who have been excluded from opportunities and otherwise disadvantaged for so long—indeed, for generations.

To include Roma in policy-making processes, some mechanisms of 'positive discrimination' have to be implemented. The term 'positive discrimination' lacks a common definition but one can generally define it as 'action aimed at favouring access by members of certain categories of people . . . to rights which they are guaranteed to the same extent as members of other categories' (Flander 2004: 99). The goal is to prevent and do away with the consequences of discrimination in the past. However, the goal and means of positive discrimination could be debated, and critics have focused on its contradictory impact: 'Positive discrimination instruments' should prevent indirect discrimination and an unprivilegalised status, on the other hand this is against the basic democratic principle of equality. In the *pro et contra* debate, those in favour of positive discrimination emphasise the importance of the mere realisation of constitutions and laws in which equality is guaranteed. In connection with this, instruments of positive discrimination are a tool in the hands of a written law.

The chief focus of our paper is to analyse the introduction of a 'positive discrimination instrument' which represents the first step towards co-operation between the Roma and decision-makers at the local level, i.e. the introduction of the Roma councillor in certain local councils in Slovenia. Within the framework of the European directives and recommendations, Slovenia has responded to the problems of the deficient or inappropriate inclusion of the Roma in political decision-making in such a way that it has granted the Roma—as a specific ethnic group—representation in the local council. In each local council (but only in those municipalities where there is a substantial number of Romani inhabitants) there is a minimum of one councillor of Romani origin—a Roma councillor. This form of positive discrimination was considered by decision-makers to be the most appropriate in Slovenia.

Nevertheless, this *equal opportunity policy* for the Roma minority in Slovenia came late given that the Slovenian constitution of 1991 obliged the legislative body to pass a special so-called 'Roma law', and that this law has still not been adopted today.[5] The government has also responded poorly to the so-called problem of the 'erased'. The 'erased' are individuals who after Slovenia's independence in 1991 were not granted citizenship. There are approximately 19,000 'erased' people in Slovenia, and many of them could be of Roma origin. The establishing of partly favourable policies in different areas, such as access to education, housing, policy-making and equal employment possibilities, is questionable and the lack of an overall approach at the national level is obvious.

3. Participation at the Local or National Level?

To establish the Roma as an equal partner in the policy-making process one has to bear in mind their incapability to muster sufficient electoral strength for parliamentary presentation at the national level. Their political participation has been limited by society as well as by themselves and, as one anonymous participant at the PER (Project on Ethnic Relations) roundtable in Budapest, put it, 'Roma have always been passive and disunited, often characterized as living day-by-day existence with no perspective. Solutions should be sought within the framework of this character.'

Some research into the political participation of the Romani minority suggests[6] that the Roma's political participation is stronger at the city and town levels where the degree of frustration is high. Voter turnout records and various reports (see UNDP Regional Human Development Report, 2002) indicate that the Roma recognise that their political interests are best represented at the local level. However, regardless of the higher levels of engagement, there is no indication that their political participation is organised, effective or developed to its full potential. At best, it could be estimated that the Roma community's political orientations generally lean to the centre-left. This is especially true among the older, rural and poorer populations who are nostalgic for the days when the government was perceived to provide for their financial needs. Younger, educated and urban Roma, however, have recognised that the system has locked many Roma into a cycle of dependency and poverty. Indeed, government intervention and support are necessary to help solve the institutionalised poverty, discrimination and social ills. However, Roma appeals for governmental and international assistance need to be balanced by a new understanding among the Roma that they can and should address basic needs in their communities through self-help initiatives, something which is critical to fostering political participation (Koulish 2002).

Since 1990 the political participation of the Roma minority in the region at the national level has been in decline.[7] The reasons for the decline vary from country to country, depending on constitutional provisions that allow the Roma parliamentary representation, the development of Roma NGOs and the level of activism among the Roma. The number of deputies in national parliaments in the region has also been declining since 1990. Some have expressed the opinion that this was merely a consequence of the broader political actions at the time and that 'the participation of Romani parties and associations in national elections has played a symbolic role, serving as a political manifestation of Romani identity and an expression of the desire to participate in the electoral process.'[8] However, a number of Romani political parties do exist in central and Eastern Europe.[9] Yet this does not apply to Slovenia which, besides the umbrella NGO organisation *Roma Association of Slovenia*,[10] does not have any other visible organisation nor political party. The Roma Association of Slovenia has 19 members (local Roma associations); the main political and non-political activities are co-ordinated by this umbrella organisation. There are also no Romani deputies (regardless of political party) in the Slovenian National Assembly, in contrast to the representatives of two other Slovenian minorities (Hungarian and Italian) which have a seat each (one for each minority, as codified in the constitution). Since 'the main problem facing the Roma parties is getting Roma to vote for its candidates'[11] one could stipulate that having a seat reserved in the national representative body would be the best mechanism for ensuring the Roma's political participation. However, few legislators have used that option.

In Hungary and Slovakia, Romani representatives[12] stress the importance of local-level governance which would create more realistic possibilities of increasing the political capital of the Roma as a relatively young political nation. At the same time, there is a need to address the wider political climate in order to raise the priority given to Romani-related issues among political parties, recognising that negative attitudes to the Roma among majority populations make this more difficult.

At the local level, a concerted effort to provide basic political organising and leadership training will inject competition that will challenge the traditional political formulas that have poorly served the Roma population. Generally speaking, cities and towns—as opposed to the national political arena—are ideal sites to launch a sustained education, training and organisational effort, provided they have a relatively high Roma density. Although localities will most likely have a clan-like political hierarchy in place, some assessments indicate that these structures can make way for genuine grassroots education, development and the organising of initiatives.

By most accounts, the Roma in Bulgaria are exerting a growing influence in local politics.[13] Yet, among the relatively few local Roma candidates elected to serve in office, almost none is re-elected for a second term. While this reflects a common trend throughout many parts of the region among non-Roma candidates as well, it does suggest that Roma leaders, like many of their non-Roma counterparts, are often unprepared to govern once elected. Based on both the

2001 election results, as well as the consensus of the Roma who were interviewed during the assessment, research by the National Democratic Institute also concluded that, as with most non-Roma politicians in Bulgaria, the Roma politicians and the establishment they represent have been discredited and, to all intents and purposes, have been abandoned by the Roma population.

In Hungary, National Roma Self-government Legal Offices are attached to local minority self-governments and mainly offer legal advice. Minority self-governments are regulated by a law adopted in 1993 which is intended to guarantee cultural autonomy and represent minority interests in Hungary. The first National Roma Self-government was elected in 1995 for a four-year term by minority electors who consist of local government representatives elected to represent minorities, as well as local minority self-government representatives and spokespersons. Each minority is allowed to only create one self-goverment, but several national and ethnic minorities can create a joint national self-government. The law permits the establishment of minority self-governments in all settlements and districts in Budapest. Under the law, a minority self-government has at least half of its members elected as representatives from within the national or ethnic minority. Currently there are 776 Roma self-governments in Hungary (Kállai and Törzsök 2005).

When observing the political participation of the Roma minority at the local level one cannot overlook the absence of literature on this matter relating to Slovenia. In comparison to other mechanisms of enhancing political participation, the Slovenian Roma councillor is one of the most institutionally organised, has the greatest power and is indeed a balanced counterpart to local decision-makers.

4. ENSURING THE ROMA'S POLITICAL PARTICIPATION IN SLOVENIA

It is estimated that between 6,000 and 10,000 members of the Roma community live in Slovenia. The actual number of the Roma has still not been established, mainly due to difficulties in carrying out the census and providing access to all the Roma living in Slovenia, as well as the substantial problem of the so-called 'erased'—those individuals who after Slovenia's independence in 1991 were not granted citizenship. There are approximately 19,000 of these erased people in Slovenia and many of them could well be of Romani origin. The most frequent contact with the Roma is maintained by the centres for Social Work, which in 2003 recorded 6,264 Roma in Slovenia, whereas in the 2002 census only 3,246 people declared themselves to be members of the Roma minority (Perić 2001).

The legal position of the Roma community in Slovenia began to be regulated in 1989 when constitutional amendments contributed to the adoption of a provision that the Roma's legal status should be regulated by law. This laid the legal foundations for regulatory and protective measures and, at the same time, it meant that, due to its specificity, the Roma community could not be equated with the regulation and protection of the country's two other constitutionally acknowledged minorities, the Italian and Hungarian minorities (The Reporter of the National Council 1995). The question remains why the constitution of the Republic of Slovenia defines the Roma as an autochthonous minority, although they are considered a national minority in the opinion of most experts; moreover, they also do not have the position of a national minority but rather the status of a special ethnic community or a minority with special ethnic characteristics (their own language, culture, and other ethnic characteristics). It is because of these so-called special ethnic characteristics that the decision-makers decided on a regulation that is separate from both the Italian and Hungarian minorities in the so-called Roma Act.

The Slovenian constitution distinguishes between the two biggest ethnic minorities, Italian and Hungarian, and the 'autochthonous' Roma minority, granting the latter fewer special minority rights. Their rights are not nearly as protected as the rights of the Italian and Hungarian ethnic groups. A crude but telling comparison is the length of Articles 64 and 65 of the Slovenian constitution: Article 65, addressing the status and rights of the Roma, is one of the shortest in the constitution, simply stating the following: 'The status and the rights of Roma communities living in Slovenia shall be such as determined by statute.' By comparison, Article 64 of the Slovenian constitution recognises a whole range of rights pertaining to the Hungarian and Italian ethnic minorities, regardless of their numbers, including but not limited to the official use of language and education in their mother tongue, and direct representation at both the local level and in the National Assembly (Perić 2001).

As mentioned, Slovenia has followed the European directives and recommendations in its 'search' for the most appropriate vehicle to enhance the political participation of the Roma. Apart from including the Roma in education, social, employment and financial policies, decision-makers have found it most appropriate to include the Roma in the core process of decision-making at the local level. This follows the Recommendation of the European commission, which states the importance of co-operation in the joint formulation of public policies:

> The effective participation of Roma ought to be ensured at the earli-
> est stages of policy formation, programme design, implementation and

evaluation. As has been stressed repeatedly by actors involved both in implementing and developing projects and policies, Roma involvement at all stages is key to the real impact and sustainability of initiatives. (European commission report 2003)

Further, the recommendation by the OSCE—which encompasses legislative, judicial as well as police and security systems, the election system and political participation of the Roma—includes an appeal based on recent analyses to member countries to support the development of the Roma minority by enabling them to participate in decision-making at all levels. Apart from that, the minority should have access to all important information concerning the Roma. The recommendations also refer to the motto 'think globally—act locally' since implementation of national (or even European) strategies at the local level is extremely important. Without effective mechanisms at the local level such strategies are bound to fail. This specifically applies to the Roma issues which are quite specific.[14] Therefore, in Slovenia, too, inclusion in policy-making processes at both national and local levels is extremely important for the provision of equal representation. While some individual members of the Roma community were included in political life decades ago,[15] unlike other countries of the European Union, in Slovenia there is no Romani political party and, according to Jožek Horvat-Muc, the President of the Roma Association of Slovenia,

> it would be unwise to establish one, mainly because politics for Roma is something . . . that is, political parties would cause more damage than positive action. Politics is politics and, as for the European circumstances, even the non-Roma cannot manage it too well, let alone the Roma.

The first step towards ensuring the (more) equal representativeness of the Roma autochthonous minority in Slovenia involved the legally prescribed minimum representativeness of the Roma in local councils. The question of how to further regulate this problem remains open. Who is competent to regulate Roma issues and are they doing their work efficiently? The task of a democratic country is to enable the co-operation of all citizens and modify the existing mechanisms in order to adjust them to their users and facilitate more efficient participation of all citizens. We may conclude here with the thoughts of the OSCE High commissioner on National Minorities 'although governments generally acknowledge the importance of Roma participation, many are unaccustomed to engaging Roma as partners.'

5. AN ANALYSIS OF THE INSTITUTION AND TASKS OF THE SLOVENIAN ROMA COUNCILLOR

After amendments to the Law on Local Self-government and the decision of the constitutional court of the Republic of Slovenia, local Roma councillors finally ran for office for the first time in the local elections of autumn 2002. After the introduction of the Roma councillor institution, publicly acknowledged as a great triumph for the Roma minority, the public alienated themselves from the actions of the Roma minority at the local level. We are interested in an evaluation of the local policy networking, the success of its implementation and its influence on the wellbeing of Roma communities, in order to define the 'success' of this newly established body.

Methodology

In pursuit of answers to this question, a research group at the Faculty of Social Sciences at the University of Ljubljana developed a diagnostic tool—a specially adapted questionnaire[16] and pre-trained field researchers[17] in order to gain relevant data on local Roma councillors, their work and their perception of the problems Roma communities encounter. The analysis took place from June 2004 to March 2005 and the Roma councillors as well as the mayors of those municipalities with local Roma councillors were interviewed between October 2004 and December 2004. Relevant data gained from the Roma councillors and mayors themselves had to be collected to evaluate the current state of affairs regarding how Roma councillors actually work in practice. A diagnostic tool was developed in such a manner that the interviewed persons were always able to express their opinion regardless of whether they were directly asked for it or not. Further, the questions were modified to suit the different backgrounds of the Roma community[18] and linguistic specialities. Nineteen Roma councillors and twenty mayors[19] participated in the interviews,[20] which means that the entire observed population was actually interviewed.

The interview itself was divided into three main parts. In the first part, the field researchers sought to obtain information about the difficulties faced by the Roma community in general.[21] This information was not directly connected to the core of our research but it served as: (1) the introductory 'warm-up' part of the interview where a fragile link between the respondent and the field researcher had to be established; and (2) it served to gather data on the diversity of problems both Roma communities in Slovenia (from the Prekmurje and Dolenjska regions) are facing.

In the second part of the questionnaire we wanted to acquire information on co-operation between the local council and the Roma councillor. The local council is the highest decision-making body for all matters within a municipality. The decision-making process at the local level falls within the sphere of activities of the local council, which adopts decisions at its sessions with a majority vote of all members present. Within its competence it adopts the municipal statute, decrees and other municipal acts, environmental and other plans for development of the municipality, the budget and the annual financial statement. It can also set up working bodies (commissions and committees) which deal with specialised matters within the competence of the local council and give opinions and proposals (potentially also on Roma issues). The Roma councillor is, in their competencies and all other aspects, equal to all the other councillors in the municipal council. Besides a special right to be elected through a 'positive discrimination mechanism' of so-called 'double political' subjectivity,[22] the Roma councillor does not benefit in any other way after the elections have been held. Since there can be 7 to 45 councillors in the local council (depending on the number of residents in the municipality), the power and weight of an individual councillor's opinion may vary somewhat.

Since rivalry and leadership within a Roma community are unlike the traditional leadership seen in democratic systems, the complexity of their characteristics had to be addressed in an intradisciplinary way, bringing some anthropological findings (Sutherland 1986) into the research. In this connection—the third part of the questionnaire—tried to encompass the relationship between the elected Roma councillors (who in most cases are not the actual clan leaders) and their electorate. This also involved adding a few questions about their opinions on how to further improve the situation and what poses the main obstacle to realising improvements.

In order to obtain equally relevant data on the work of the Roma local councillors we had to note the observations of other significant local actors. For the purpose of the research we included interviews with the mayors of the municipalities involved. In Slovenia's local self-government system the mayor represents the executive body of the municipality. He is directly elected through elections and has the right to propose local legislation, the budget, the annual financial statement, ordinances and all other acts within the competence of the local council. The mayor calls and runs local council meetings and is the guardian of legality and can withhold the issuing of an act of the local council if he thinks it is illegal or unconstitutional. The mayor also runs the municipal administration, which is his most important task. The importance of the institute of the mayor, their influence on the work of the municipal administration and on co-operation with the local council underpinned the reason for which struc-tured interviews with all mayors of municipalities which have a Roma council-lor were also carried out. Like the guided interviews with the Roma council-lors, these interviews were also anonymous. The questions posed to the mayors were composed so that they would show their opinion or relationship to the same problems or phenomena as presented in the Roma councillor interviews. This way of collecting information enables insights into the same area from the points of view of both key actors, which allows a further analysis of the opinions.

Relations Between the Roma Councillor, the Mayor and the Local Council

After establishing that certain 'issues' are common to all Roma communities (in the first part of the interviews), the main question was whether these issues are ever put on the agenda of local councils. In the opinion of the Roma coun-cillors, only 69 per cent of observed local councils had discussed issues that the Roma community encounters. The Roma councillors who affirmed that their municipal councils do not discuss problems which the Roma community en-counters specifically stated that (1) their initiatives never make their way on to agendas; (2) the councils do discuss Roma problems but the discussion is off the record; and (3) other councillors have no interest in discussing their problems. At this point, a few Roma councillors revealed a special relationship that they share with the mayor. It is not rare for the Roma councillors to prefer to discuss ideas and problems with the mayor on a one-to-one basis. As one of them said, 'in the council we discuss most of the problems the Roma community is facing, but only after I express them to the mayor first.' Does this indicate the fact that the councillors are not sovereign in their work or that the informal power of the mayor as a formal representative of the municipality prevails over the somewhat weakened status of the Roma councillor?

It is also significant that in at least three municipalities there is a Commis-sion for Roma Questions[23] which discusses Roma issues at meetings held sepa-rately from meetings of the municipal council; the commission then forwards its conclusions to the municipal council for discussion. Some municipalities had introduced the commission and before the Roma councillor institute had been introduced.[24] This form of co-operation was recognised as positive in the interviews and it is possible to conclude that the Roma councillors prefer to dis-cuss things in an informal way and in smaller groups: the commission for Roma Questions seems very appropriate for such a type of discussion. One should have in mind that such commissions have no real power and can only act as a submitting body. Reducing the role of the Roma councillor to a mere actor in a sub-local council body would actually mean a step backwards.

However, even in those local councils where discussions of Roma issues are more or less frequent, according to the Roma councillors, the responsiveness of other councillors is still quite poor. With the use of our open-ended questionnaire we managed to encompass the wider causes of the deficient co-operation between local councillors and the Roma councillor: (1) frequently this depends very much on the party membership of other local councillors (according to the Roma councillors especially non-cooperative are councillors from the right-wing Slovenian National Party); and (2) some councillors clearly have a prejudice against the Roma. As some respondent Roma councillors stated.

> The local council is usually good with words, but when it comes to taking actions, everybody backs out. Their common excuse is that there isn't any money, but I know that the money is—in Europe. Because of this unfulfilled promises I look bad in the eyes of my Roma community. And then I am the guilty one.

> I am pleased with the situation. Well, I have to say that I don't talk much at the local council sessions since I am illiterate and I don't want to say something stupid.

On the other hand, all the mayors' answers to the question 'Do you discuss Roma problems in your municipal council (if yes how often, if not why not)?' were positive, which means that in all local councils Roma issues should more or less be frequently discussed. In municipalities that have a commission for Roma Questions working within the municipal council, these problems are put on the agenda of the municipal council less frequently, however they are regularly discussed at commission meetings. There is a difference in the percentage of affirmative answers to this question. However, there is also a great difference in attitudes expressed concerning communication in the local council, so the conclusion as to who is right and who is wrong could be biased.

In addition, the mayors were asked about the appropriateness of the local council for addressing Roma issues. Almost 70 per cent of the mayors thought that the local council is inappropriate for resolving Roma issues. In this connection, the dominant opinion of the majority is that the state should approach these problems more rigorously with unified programmes at the national level, different intermunicipal forms of co-ordination and additional financial aid. Those mayors who answered that the local council is a body that is partly appropriate for decision-making on Roma issues, think the state should take on the lion's share of responsibility. On the other hand, they agreed with the regulation of matters of local importance in an appropriate and legally appointed body, namely the local council. The ongoing dispute between local communities and the state as to who should be primarily dealing with the special issues of Roma populations in Slovenia leads in itself to the question of whether the local councils are suitable bodies for addressing this problem. The mayors have quite different perspectives on this issue.

I think the local councils are absolutely not an adequate body to address problems that Roma populations encounter. This should be a matter for the state. [. . .] I absolutely expect help from the state.

Of course it is adequate! I don't see any other body or institution that could do this job better and easier.

As presented here, one might conclude that the mayors do have very distinct points of view that are hardly ever similar. This may be (which cannot be firmly established since the interviews involve absolute anonymity) a result of the already mentioned polarisation of Roma populations between the two communities in the Prekmurje and Dolenjska regions. It might be assumed that the more rigorous answers come from the Dolenjska region, where there is tense co-habitation between the Roma minority and the majority population that has also resulted in poor co-operation in the decision-making field.

Regardless of opinions on the (in)appropriateness of the local council for resolving Roma issues, the mayors thought the local council in their municipalities is mostly responsive to resolving the problems encountered by the local Roma community. A considerable number of mayors estimates the responsiveness of the municipal council as neither good nor bad—they claim that the municipal councils respond to Roma problems in the same way as with the many other problems found in every municipality. Two respondents estimated the responsiveness of the local council as being very poor due to the bad relationship between the Roma and other locals and due to the assumption made by other locals that the Roma receive extremely high levels of social aid.

During the interview period, the first four-year mandate of the Roma councillors was underway following and amendment to the Act and the municipal statutes. Therefore, in the structured questionnaire we were also interested in whether during this time the local council had adopted any resolution which would mean a considerable shift towards a solution of to the problems of the Roma communities. Although some Roma councillors did not know the term 'resolution' or were not acquainted with its meaning, we may conclude that in 12 municipalities at least one resolution had been adopted in the presence of a Roma councillor (here the interviewers could detect that many Roma councillors do not attend council meetings or, as they put it, they 'gave up' arguing and not doing anything), which considerably contributed to a solution to the Roma question in a positive direction (no respondent told us they had adopted a conclusion which would mean a marked shift in the negative direction), while in the remaining seven cases there were no such resolutions. This question specifically highlights the problem that the Roma councillors are mostly unfamiliar with the elementary concepts and processes of political participation at the local level such as the basic terms for official acts, adopted conclusions or public policies. Of course, another question that arises here is the potential need for additional education of Roma councillors.[25]

On the other hand, the mayors share the opinion that Roma councillors should not be treated differently from other people and that the institution of the Roma councillor itself is a sufficient form of positive discrimination. Therefore, many councillors see the solution in the periodical meetings of Roma councillors at the national level. The conditions in which Roma councillors work and the engagement of individual Roma councillors are extremely diverse.

We were also interested in the mayors' assessments of the presence of the Roma councillor in their local council. As it turns out, a good half of the mayors see the presence of the Roma councillor in the municipal council as being important or even very important.

> His presence is important, but something should be done about educating Roma councillors. The Roma councillor in our council is barely literate and besides that he is not the representative of all Roma in our community. Some voted for him and some against.

Conversely, one-third of them believed that the presence of the Roma councillor does not mean any essential shift towards a resolution of Roma problems.

> He is quite unimportant for the constructive debate, however because of his physical presence we are aware that there are Roma issues we have to deal with.

Low education, illiteracy, poor knowledge of the basics of the operations of local democratic systems, the inability and even lack of interest of Roma councillors are mentioned as big obstacles to mutual co-operation and the consequent solving of Roma problems. On the other hand, some mayors thought that the implementation needs more time before it can be evaluated:

> this [Roma councillor] is somewhat of a novelty, so the local councillors look at it in a careless way.

Rivalry Between Roma Leaders

Considering the specific relationship of the Roma councillor with his elec-torate (as was perceived in the test interview), one can question the extent to which a Roma councillor actually represents his voters. As it turned out, the level of identification of the Roma community with their own Roma councillor is very questionable. The Roma community is not homogenously distributed across the municipality but is partly dispersed in hamlets and villages. As a result, the Roma are divided into so-called clans or family branches which are often opposed to or even hostile to one another. In such cases, it is very diffi-cult if not impossible to appoint a single representative for all the Roma living within a community. Mirga and Gheorghe (1997) reported similar findings in their analysis when they researched elective patterns of the Roma Minority in Siklósnagyfalu, Hungary.[26]

An informal Romani leader or the *rom baro* (big man) has to have certain important characteristics. According to Sutherland (1986) the *rom baro* has to be physically large, tall, have a big frame, be fat. It is as if their physical size corresponds proportionally with the amount of influence they hold in the com-munity. Another very important leadership factor is wealth. Wealth is displayed in specific ways, primarily in the gold jewellery his wife wears, but also in a large and expensive car. Wealth is also shown by generosity and a leader who is gen-erous is highly respected by all. Another display of power is their relationship with non-Roma officials in power; having informal access (telephone number, address) to some individuals in the police department, health care unit, social care centre or at the municipal administration.

> Well, we Gypsies are a special kind of people, we are together all the time. I can say that lots of things are better now since I am the council-lor. I am there at the core of the decision-making, I can propose many things. For example, I can read the Official Gazette of Republic of Slove-nia and see what tenders we can apply for. In those municipalities where the Roma community got their councillor, you can see the progress in the co-operation of the municipal administration. Before all Roma in the municipality directly addressed the municipal administration, but now I can intervene as a middleman,

was the answer of one Roma councillor to the question, 'How do you see your relations with the local Roma community since you have been elected?'

However, such a positive experience is rare. Statements were also made about threats of violence by the Roma community being made to their elected Roma councillor. Most Roma do not acknowledge local elections as a legitimate way of electing their representative, preferring instead the traditional way of electing an informal leader (through personal assertion, experiences, initiation rituals, etc.) who frequently is not (does not want to be) a candidate at the local elections. According to 17 per cent of the Roma councillors, their relationship with the Roma community deteriorated after the elections, 44 per cent claimed that their relationship had remained unchanged, and 39 per cent said that their relationship had even improved. The statements indicating threats of violence by the Roma community being made to their elected Roma councillor are not rare. As Sutherland (1986: 97) concluded in her observation of Romani life in America, 'one of the most apparent characteristics of the Rom is that they are almost constantly involved in conflict with each other, a factor that masks their equally intense solidarity as a group'.

One Roma councillor stated (about any improvements following his election).

Nothing major, they (the municipality) promise a lot, but do little instead. I am important just because there are eight councillors in opposition and eight in the coalition, so my vote prevails. And, truthfully, nothing has got better. Everybody thinks, 'Let them (Roma) kill each other, they have their representative.' And I stay in the middle because members of the Roma community are threatening me when nothing is done and, on the other hand, I have my hands tied, the state and the municipality are a brick wall.

Other local political actors, too, are aware of this matter. Since traditional democratic principles enable us to recognise elected individuals as our political leaders, our vision of the relationship between political elites and civil society is somehow limited. Thinking 'out of the box' could provide us with some other perspectives. The limitations of our knowledge of Romani culture make it impossible for us to embrace their differences. Or, as one mayor said,

To this moment his [Roma councillor] role as a political leader is still not clear since he has many problems with his electorate. Not all of the Roma community members have supported him so many are actually obstructing his work. The Roma need a leader they formally and informally respect! They [Roma] don't embrace the institution of elections.

The Actors Causing Disturbance

In the second part of the third complex of questions in the interview we were primarily interested in how the Romani councillors would improve their co-operation with the local council in order for Romani issues to be resolved in an easier and quicker way, and we were also interested in their perception of any disturbing actors in the policy-making process for Roma policies as well as in how they estimate the introduction of the Roma councillor mechanism. There was a range of answers to the question 'What would you change to improve the efficiency of operations of the local council in the field of resolving Romani issues?', which mostly called for a boost to informal communications, either with the mayor, councillors or even with other NGOs. The need for additional resources was also expressed. Roma councillors desperately need access to an office, computer, the internet, etc. In addition, (1) there should be a greater number of meetings dealing exclusively with Roma issues; (2) a commission for Roma Questions should be established (in cases where the municipal council rejected this proposal); (3) co-operation with the centres for Social Work should be improved; (4) the mayor's engagement and that of other councillors should be enhanced; and (5) it should be possible to put Roma problems on the agenda independently of the mayor's will.

According to 31 per cent of the respondents, the biggest obstacle to establishing the better co-operation of the Roma community with other locals is the Roma community itself. In their opinion, the reasons lie in criminal, inadaptable behaviour, a lack of education and a poor financial situation reflected mainly in conflicts between the Roma and other locals. According to the Roma councillors the main obstacle to improving co-operation equally involves the state because it is not resolving Romani issues at the national level; the mayors, who according to the Roma councillors, in some municipalities simply do not take into consideration the Roma councillor's opinion; and other locals, who through their prejudices hinder the normal inclusion of the Roma in the local community. Interestingly, according to the Roma, the local councils themselves do not present an obstacle to the improvement of co-operation. However, one Roma councillor pointed himself out as being the biggest obstacle to co-operation, being illiterate and therefore (in his opinion) unfit for the job.

Not surprisingly, the mayors do not identify themselves or the municipal administration they represent as an obstacle to the provision of better co-operation, while at the same time they blame the state which in their opinion does not do enough to resolve Roma problems.

At the end of the questionnaire we wanted the Roma councillors to evaluate their work and what has improved since they were elected. The previous answers more or less defined the current situation of resolving Roma issues as being inappropriate and deficient. But, surprisingly, the majority approved the introduction of the Roma councillor mechanism. The Roma councillors evaluated their work very positively. However, it cannot be established whether some policies (on building infrastructure, land acquisition, education, etc.) were formed as a consequence of their work or were already in the process of formulation before their appointment and would have been implemented irrespective of the Roma councillor mechanism being introduced.

If we summarise both sets of interviews it may be concluded that, in the eyes of local political actors, the Roma councillor mechanism is a tool that is somehow not 'falling into place'. Perhaps a second longitudinal analysis after several mandates of Roma councillors would produce a more varied picture of how this mechanism is being implemented.

6. WHERE DO WE GO FROM HERE?

Perhaps the best starting point for further action is a constructive critique and categorisation of the local actor's opinions. One mayor pointed out that in his perception the biggest obstacle to better co-operation between the Roma community and majority population

> is the state, and then the local community. Why? Because the state
> didn't prepare the grounds before introducing the Roma councillors,
> who were implemented by force, if I may say. Many of those councils had
> never previously had a Roma representative or even committee for Roma
> issues. I believe there should be some existing local initiative before we
> build on that.

Constructive and effective communication and co-operation are the preconditions for mutual respect. That is why extra effort should be made for the purpose of including the Roma minority more actively in decision-making processes, especially if the consequence of policy implementation is important for their lives and work. However, it is possible to achieve this kind of functioning only by including the Roma's elected representatives at all levels of power. Ideally, the mechanisms or institutions which would guarantee such functioning would suit the specifics of the individual country and their Roma community. This would guarantee the optimum inclusion of the underprivileged in the existing system. The effectiveness of the systems introduced could be measured by several criteria: (a) the scope of the early involvement of the Roma in Roma-related policy formation; (b) the extent to which the process is broadly representative; (c) transparency; and (d) the involvement of the Roma in implementing and evaluating Roma-related programmes.

However, in this short period of activity of Roma councillors the need for additional or auxiliary forms of positive discrimination has presented itself. Such further positive discrimination would enable the (even) better co-operation of the Roma councillors with other decision-makers at the local level. One can draw a parallel when comparing the only two countries in central and Eastern Europe (Slovenia and Hungary) that actually enable the political participation of the Roma minority at the local level through positive discrimination mechanisms. Hungary guarantees the 13 'historic' minorities living in Hungary (including the Roma) the right to establish local and national self-government. On this basis, the minority can establish elected bodies that act in the field of education and culture and hold a veto over issues in those fields at the local level. Mostly this self-governing body can request information, submit proposals, initiate measures and file complaints (Kállai and Törzsök 2005). This, however, differs significantly from the institution of the Slovenian local Roma councillor. Both mechanisms provide the much needed framework for Romani political activism, making room for opportunities to modify the current legislation to make the system more effective. In many surveys, Roma leaders have stressed the importance of local governance which would create more realistic possibilities for increasing the political capital of the Roma, as a relatively young political nation.

Five years after the election of the first Roma councillors the initial successes and obstacles have been revealed, as faced by both the Roma councillors and the mayors of the municipalities where the Roma councillor institution was compulsorily introduced by law. The provision of the law which lists those municipalities that have to implement in their statute (the statute of a municipality is in its nature independent) the institution of the Roma councillor has been publicly debated in no small measure. It is highly questionable how the legislators decided which municipalities have the right 'quota' of a Romani population in order to be obliged to implement such a decision. The main arguments were: (1) the Roma are nomadic in their nature and often move; (2) the exact number of the Roma population in Slovenia is unknown; and (3) there should be a census (for example 15 per cent of all municipal populations should be Roma) as a threshold for obliging the municipality to introduce a Roma councillor. In the future this anomaly should be further addressed.

Since we have demonstrated in the article that this form of the institutionalised political participation of the Roma minority in Slovenia is limited at best, the main recommendations for a further improvement within the boundaries of this particular policy are (1) the need to emphasise the development of new skills in political leaders/activists; (2) to develop and enhance a political culture among Roma communities; and (3) to introduce and promote democracy at both functional and institutional levels. Although it seems that these recommendations would burden the Roma community, one could argue that 'training to build capacity' is the most appropriate way for addressing the underrepresentativeness of the Roma minority in political bodies. As Jožek Horvat-Muc, the President of the Roma Association of Slovenia said in his interview,[27]

> The constitutional court stated that we have to appoint our councillors. This is the first step, the first procedure on the road to the appointment of our Member of Parliament. I think it will take time, years, for us to be able to organise ourselves in order to have our own MP. Not to have representatives at the municipal level and appoint an MP right away, I do not see any logic in this, considering the present circumstances.

NOTES

1. In most parliaments of Central and Eastern Europe, at least one Romani representative has been elected on the party list of a mainstream party. In some instances, such as in Romania, the Roma have a single reserved seat. In local politics, the Roma have secured even more representatives.

2. The ancestors of the Roma in the Prekmurje region inhabited this territory earlier than those in the Dolenjska region, which resulted in a higher social status, better integration in society and to some extent better living and housing conditions. Longer co-habitation with the majority population has also brought fewer tensions in everyday life as well as a better arranged status (especially citizenship-wise). On the other hand, the Roma community in the Dolenjska region has not had the necessary time or resources to establish itself as a homogenous pressure group. There is a general assumption that the Roma in the Dolenjska region came and are still coming (fleeing) from ex-Yugoslav republics, therefore they have a lower financial and educational status, which often results in the taking of other measures to survive.

3. In the national census at the start of the 1990s, the number of Roma was recorded at almost 150,000 in Hungary (1.4% of the total population), more than 30,000 in the Czech Republic (0.3%) and more than 75,000 in Slovakia (1.4%). However, other official surveys have estimated their numbers at around 450,000 in Hungary (close to 4.5%) and 250,000 in Slovakia (4.8%) (Open Society Institute/EU Accession Monitoring Program 2001: 488; also see European Roma Rights Centre 1999; and United Nations 1999: 6).

4. An accurate or at least a more precise estimate of the size of the Roma population is needed for the further regulation of socio-economic and legislative fields to ensure Roma protection that is comparable to that provided to other minorities. For the Roma minority this is especially important because, due to differences in history and historical conditions, there are extreme differences between individual Roma communities resulting from their traditions, specific ways of life and the level of their socialisation and integration in the environment. This makes implementing common policies at the European and national levels very difficult, in turn supporting the tendency to regulate the Roma question at the local level.

5. The 'Roma Act' raised a lot of public discussion in Slovenia in 2006 since the government announced it would soon be published. However, so far the contents of the act are still unknown to the public and the speculation is that it does not bring any additional rights to the Roma minority. One might expect that the act will merely bring together all provisions

concerning the Roma minority from other legal documents and that the government will thereby basically realise the constitutional provision.

6. In February and March 2003, the National Democratic Institute (NDI) conducted assessments in Bulgaria, Romania and Slovakia to analyse the salient challenges and opportunities to increase the Roma's political participation. Funded by and conducted in co-operation with the Open Society Institute (OSI), this project reflects the interest of both the NDI and the OSI to raise the issue of the Roma's political participation with relevant international organisations and to take the first steps toward initiating strategic blueprints for Roma communities to enhance their political participation, representation and influence. Three separate reports have offered the key findings and recommendations of the NDI assessment team in each country. During the two-month assessment period, the NDI teams travelled to the three countries to meet with a wide range of Roma and non-Roma political and NGO leaders, elected and appointed government officials, as well as policy- and opinion-makers, researchers, journalists, educators, project leaders, analysts and ordinary citizens. The group also met with representatives of international organisations active in relation to Roma-related issues.

7. PER (Project on Ethnic Relations Report), 1999, Budapest, available at http://www.per-usa.org/reports/PoliticalPart99.pdf.

8. PER (Project on Ethnic Relations Report), 1999, Budapest, available at http://www.per-usa.org/reports/PoliticalPart99.pdf.

9. Sobotka, Eva. Roma in Politics in the Czech Republic, Slovakia and Poland, available at http://www.errc.org/cikk.php?cikk=1354&archiv=1, March, 2007.

10. The Roma Association of Slovenia; http://www.zveza-romov.si/predstavitev/clani.htm.

11. PER (Project on Ethnic Relations Report), 1999, Budapest, available at http://www.per-usa.org/reports/PoliticalPart99.pdf.

12. Those who participated at the PER—Project on Ethnic Relations roundtable, Budapest in 1998.

13. National Democratic Institute for International Affairs. Roma Political Participation in Bulgaria Assessment Mission 1–8 Febr. 2003, available at http://www.ndi.org/search/site_search.asp?keywords=roma&submit1=Search%21, February, 2007.

14. With the term 'Roma issues' that is used later in the article, the authors refer to the specific problems of low education levels, high unemployment rates, poor housing conditions, etc., which affect the Roma minority in Slovenia and at the same time do not affect, with all the stated elements, any other marginalised group or minority in Slovenia. The term is not used with a negative connotation.

15. In 1996 the Roma founded the Association of Roma Societies of Slovenia which is today called the Association of the Roma of Slovenia, that is, it not only brings together the Roma societies but all Roma. With the foundation of the Association of the Roma of Slovenia, the political power of the Roma minority has also grown.

16. The questionnaire was specially adapted linguistically-wise—many of our interviewed subjects spoke Slovenian poorly and did not understand the more complex questions.

17. The field researchers were thoroughly acquainted with problems that the Roma encounter in both of the main communities (Dolenjska and Prekmurje regions) as well as with the institutional mechanism of the Roma councillor and past actions connected to its implementation. The field researchers were also trained to recognise potential problems that the basic interview questions did not cover, and consequently asked additional questions.

18. See n. 2—there are two different Roma communities in Slovenia.

19. Twenty mayors and nineteen Roma councillors were interviewed. This discrepancy occurred after the Municipality of Grosuplje did not comply with the Law on Local Self-government and the Rule of constitutional court and did not accept the required amendments to the municipal statute.

20. Structured interviews were carried out in the following municipalities: Cankova, Kuzma, Crensovci, Murska Sobota, Crnomelj, Dobrovnik, Turnisce, Kocevje, Krsko, Novo mesto, Lendava, Puconci, Metlika, Semic, Rogasovci, Tisina, Trebnje, Sentjernej and Beltinci.

21. Since the problem is very different when looked at by the Romani councillors as well as part of the Roma community than when considered by experts from the field, in the first complex of the structured questionnaire we asked about the most important problems individual Roma communities are facing and which may represent specific problems of individual Roma communities. The most frequently stated problem was the inadequate public utilities infrastructure and the non-regulated acquisition of land on which the Roma live. Moreover, many Roma councillors highlighted the problems of electricity, roads and drinking water. As we can see, all of these most common problems are closely interconnected and represent both the cause and the effect. For example, the regulation of public utilities would only be possible through the regulation of land ownership. Because of the consistent indications of all the problem fields mentioned in all the interviews it can be concluded that the problems are not partial but exist in virtually all Roma communities in Slovenia. In another complex of answers to the first question, the problem of the low education level of the Roma population is revealed, along with the poor employment possibilities and lack of interest of communities in the problems faced by Roma communities.

22. Double political subjectivity means that every Romani voter in the municipality has a right to vote for any candidate and to vote for a special Romani candidate. So each Romani voter can cast two ballots at once.

23. As mentioned, the local council can set up working bodies (commissions and committees) that deal with specialised matters within the competence of the local council and give opinions and proposals. In these commissions there are usually up to three councillors who pre-discuss certain issues and then present resolutions to the local council.

24. Such a municipality is Murska Sobota, where the pressure of the organised Roma local initiative was so great that the local Roma representative in the local council was elected in 1998, two years before the law was amended.

25. In 2007 such a request was announced by the Forum of Roma councillors.

26. 'The Roma are a traditional people, whose leadership has typically been vested in informal, but powerful, extended family structures. [. . .] [T]he relative absence of formal structures in the Romani community has been an obstacle to participation in the modern bureaucratic structures that increasingly characterise government and public administration. Thus, the community faces the challenge of building formal structures of representation and participation. The present generation of Romani leaders comes from contrasting backgrounds. [. . .] On one side are those who have little or no formal education or training but have risen within traditional communities by virtue of their everyday struggles on behalf of their people. On the other side is a handful of mostly younger activists who are products of the majority education system and have emerged as successful professionals or politicians but at the same time have retained or rediscovered their Romani identity' (Mirga and George 1997).

27. Interview with V. Pirc in the weekly magazine *Mladina*, 28 May 2001.

REFERENCES

1995. The reporter of the National council of Slovenia. National Council of the Republic of Slovenia no. 18.

European Commission Report. 2003. Recommendations to the OSCE Participating States: Session 1: combating Discrimination against Roma and Sinti in the OSCE Participating States.

European Commission Report. 2004. The situation of Roma in an enlarged European Union. Directorate-General for Employment and Social Affairs.

European Union network of experts in fundamental rights. 2004. Report on the situation of fundamental rights in the European Union for 2003. Available at http://europa.eu.int/comm/justice_home/index_en.htm (January 2005).

European Union accession monitoring program. 2002. Monitoring the EU accession process: Minority protection, case studies in selected member states. Budapest: Open Society Institute.

Flander, Benjamin. 2004. Pozitivna diskriminacija [Positive discrimination]. Ljubljana. Fakulteta za družbene vede.

Kaldor, Mary and Kavan, Zdenek. 2001. Democracy and civil society in central and Eastern Europe. In: Balancing democracy. Roland Axtmann, ed. Pp. 239–54. London and New York. Continuum.

Kállai, E., and E. Törzsök (eds). 2005. A Roma's life in Hungary. Budapest: Public Foundation for European comparative Minority Research.

Koulish, Robert Edwin. 2002. Opportunity lost? The social (dis)integration of Roma minority rights in post-transition Hungary. Nationalism & ethnic politics 8 (1): 81–104.

Mirga, A. and Gheorghe, N. 1997. The Roma in the twenty-first century: A policy paper. Project on Ethnic Relations. New Jersey: Princeton Press.

Nagy, M. Toth, and Barbara Vrecko (eds). 1994. Prirocnik o udelezbi javnosti v postopkih sprejemanja odlocitev. [Handbook of public participation in decisionmaking]. Ljubljana: Slovensko predstavnistvo regionalnega okoljskega centra za srednjo in vzhodno Evropo.

Nie, H. Norman and Sidney Verba. 1975. Political participation. In: Handbook of political science, vol. 4. Fred I. Greenstein and NelsonW. Polsby, eds. Pp. 1–74. Reading, Mass.: Addison-Wesley.

Organisation for Security and Co-operation in Europe. 2000. Report on the situation of the Roma and Sinti in the OSCE Area. High Commissioner on National Minorities.

Perić, Tanja. 2001. Insufficient: Governmental programmes for Roma in Slovenia. Roma Rights 4. Available at http://www.errc.org/Romarights_index.php (Febr. 2007).

Sobotka, Eva. 2002. The limits of the state: Political participation and representation of Roma in the Czech Republic, Hungary, Poland and Slovakia. Lancaster: Richardson Institute for Peace Research, Lancaster University.

Sutherland, Anne. 1986. Gipsies: The hidden Americans. Prospect Heights, Ill.: Waveland Press.

UNDP Regional Human Development Report. 2002. Available at http://roma.undp.sk/(September 2005).

Vermeersch, Peter. 2000. Romani political participation and racism: Reflections on recent developments in Hungary and Slovakia. Roma Rights 4. Available at http://errc.org/rr_nr4_2000/noteb4.shtml (September 2005).

*Irena Baclija is research assistant in the faculty of social sciences, University of Ljubljana.

Miro Haček is researcher at the Centre for Political Science Research and assistant professor at the faculty of social sciences, University of Ljubljana.

Irena Baclija and Miro Haček, "Limited Opportunities for Political Participation: A Case-study of Roma Local Councillors in Slovenia," *Romani Studies* 17 (2007): 155–180.

Chapter 7: Roma Rights on the World Wide Web: The Role of Internet Technologies in Shaping Minority and Human Rights Discourses in Post-Socialist Central and Eastern Europe

by Neda Atanasoski*

Abstract

This article addresses contemporary Roma rights issues in Central and Eastern Europe by exploring the relationship between internet technologies and the discourses surrounding human rights and the post-socialist transition. Because the Roma are a transnational European minority ethnic group, they have been used as a 'test case' by western human rights groups to evaluate minority rights in post-socialist nations. The article highlights the role of new media technologies in redirecting concerns about the lack of human rights in Europe as a whole to the former Eastern bloc countries. It draws attention to the limits of western liberal discourses and new media technologies to redress racial and material discrimination against the Roma.

On 2 February 2005, the prime ministers of nine formerly socialist central and southeastern European nations signed the Declaration of the Decade of Roma Inclusion in Sofia, Bulgaria. The Declaration, which was endorsed 13 years after the fall of communism in Central and Eastern Europe, followed years of efforts on the part of non-governmental organizations (NGOs) and Roma groups to raise public awareness about discrimination. A transnational European minority without a nation state, the Roma have faced violence, expulsion and legal disenfranchisement since their migration to Europe around the 12th century, the best known of which was the Nazi program of mass killings of the Roma and Sinti during the Holocaust (Hancock, 1987). Since the end of the Cold War, global attention to prejudice against the Roma in Europe has turned largely to instances of violence and discrimination in Central and Eastern Europe.

The Decade of Roma Inclusion (www.romadecade.org) aims 'to improve the socio-economic status and social inclusion of Roma within a regional framework' in Bulgaria, Croatia, the Czech Republic, Hungary, Macedonia, Montenegro, Romania, Serbia and Slovakia. According to the project's website, 'all of these countries have significant Roma minorities and the Roma minority has been rather disadvantaged, both economically and socially'. That the Decade uses a regional focus to frame the struggle for Roma inclusion raises important questions about how discrimination against ethnic minorities is made unevenly legible in an enlarged Europe. Funded by financial institutions such as the World Bank and the Council of Europe Development Bank, as well as by socially oriented foundations such as the Open Society Institute (www.soros.org/about) and the European Roma Rights Centre (www.errc.org), this project of Roma inclusion suggests a need to explore the connections between Central and Eastern European economic liberalization, ethnic identity formations and human rights discourses after communism. This article responds to this need by focusing on how internet technologies have been central to making Roma rights struggles visible as a human rights issue during the Central and Eastern European post-socialist transition.

After the collapse of socialism, the West regarded the possibility of ethnic conflict to be one of the greatest challenges to Central and Eastern European transition. For example, western media and politicians explained the violent disintegration of Yugoslavia as an instance of `ancient' ethnic hatreds resurfacing after decades of communist repression (Kaplan, 1994). Rather than considering how the difficulties of economic and social upheaval after communism produced new and, at times, violent manifestations of ethnic and nationalist identity, such discourses supposed that ethnic conflict was inherent to the region itself (Woodward, 1995). Against the backdrop of ethnic and nationalist wars, the West became concerned with the general status of minority civil rights in Central and Eastern Europe. Indeed, granting and promoting juridical and political rights became one of the major conditions, along with economic reform, for the admittance of post-socialist nations into the European Union (EU).

Because the Roma are a transnational minority ethnic group which lives in every European nation, western human rights groups and NGOs have used them as a 'test case' to evaluate minority rights in post-socialist nations. Using the figure of the 'Gypsy' as a metaphor for democratic transition, Václav Havel famously stated that the Roma have become a 'litmus test for civil society' in Central and Eastern Europe (in O'Nions, 2007: 1). Ironically, as western governments focused attention on Central and Eastern European prejudice against the Roma and used this as evidence for how much work the 'democratizing' nations must undergo to become liberal democracies, discrimination against them persisted in western Europe. For example, since 1990, Roma groups in Germany and Austria have experienced a tenfold increase in violent attacks (O'Nions, 2007), and immigrants have been subject to ongoing neo-Nazi violence (Rose,

2007). In 2002, France and Switzerland attempted to expel Roma migrants and to block the migration of Romanian Roma, and as recently as 2008, pogroms against Roma migrants took place in Italy (Wilkinson, 2008).

In light of ongoing western discrimination against the Roma, it is not surprising that western European concerns about Central and Eastern European Roma stemmed from a desire to prevent Eastern European Roma migrants and asylum-seekers from entering the West (Dediu, 2007; Sobotka, 2007; Tamas, 2007). During the 1990s, western governments re-articulated what had been regarded initially as a security threat posed by unwanted Roma migrants as a human rights concern and as a matter of EU policy toward accession countries (Sobotka, 2007). According to Marcel Dediu (2007), in the process of recognizing discrimination against the Roma, the EU developed a 'double language'. While post-socialist nations were 'asked to respect minority rights' as a 'conditionality' mechanism for inclusion in the EU, the EU itself had 'no specific policy promoting the rights of minorities', let alone of the Roma (Dediu, 2007: 114). Human and minority rights conditions were framed in such a way as to apply only to accession countries (Dediu, 2007). In other words, only after the fall of communism did the EU form a policy about the Roma as a vulnerable minority ethnic group and even then, the legal and political status of the Roma only came under scrutiny in Central and Eastern Europe.

Beginning in the mid-1990s, the spread of internet technologies facilitated the discursive production of the Roma as the foremost figure around which to formulate, debate and evaluate the status of minority and human rights in Central and Eastern Europe. My contention is that the rhetoric about democratization after socialism and the utopian hopes for the internet as a democratizing medium enabling the free flow of information and networking across national boundaries—two distinct discourses that coalesced in the 1990s—have been co-constitutive of human rights discourses about the Roma of Central and Eastern Europe. Although an ethnographic study of how Roma groups themselves view and utilize internet technologies to effect policy changes in an enlarged Europe would be important for understanding the nuances of post-socialist media practices, it is beyond the scope of this article. Instead, my focus is on how the twin discourses about technological progress and post-socialist transition not only have masked the fact that economic liberalization often has exacerbated ethnic tensions, discrimination and poverty for minority ethnic groups in the region, but also have redirected concerns about minority and human rights in the West to the former Eastern bloc countries.

The first section of the article explores how the language of human rights has been deployed to conceptualize Roma rights in Central and Eastern Europe as a crucial issue for the post-socialist transition. These discourses conceive of discrimination against the Roma as a problem for democratizing nations while foreclosing discussions about western racism and discrimination. The second section critiques the hopeful discourses about the internet as a tool for promoting human rights by addressing the digital divide that persists in Central and Eastern Europe, and which prevents many Roma from accessing the internet. I argue that sites about Roma rights risk producing the Roma as a 'virtual' subject of rights that metaphorizes Central and Eastern Europe's liberalization. The final section analyses the Kosovar Roma Oral Histories Project website, which reframes dominant discourses about internet technologies and human rights by using an online forum to give voice to displaced Roma. I conclude that there is a need for a broader understanding of human rights in the EU that connects the forms of discrimination in the West to those in the East and makes both legible.

ROMA RIGHTS AS HUMAN RIGHTS IN THE POST-SOCIALIST CONTEXT

Throughout the Cold War, state socialist ideologies were understood to be incompatible with human rights ideals of protecting individual civil and political rights (Thomas, 2005). According to Jacques Ranciere, after the fall of the USSR, the West thought that the human rights movement there would usher in a 'new landscape of humanity freed from totalitarianism' (2004: 297). However, instead it

> became the stage of new outbursts of ethnic conflicts and slaughters, religious fundamentalisms or racial and xenophobic movements. The territory of 'post-historical' and peaceful humanity proved to be the territory of the new figures of the Inhuman. (2004: 297)

This troubling figuration of Central and Eastern Europe as a landscape of inhumanity implicitly positions the West, which evaluates the post-socialist nations' progress towards the standards of European liberal democracy, as the landscape of humanity (which in turn it defines). Although, as I have noted, violence, prejudice and discrimination against the Roma occur in both Western and Eastern Europe, for the most part EU policy debates have suggested that Roma rights violations are a problem of the post-socialist transition. The result is that in Central and Eastern Europe, the issue of human rights has been linked with capitalist development. For example, in a 2002 enlargement briefing about the status of the Roma in Central and Eastern Europe, minority rights are understood as complementary to the development of 'functioning market economies' (European Union Enlargement Information Unit, 2002: 4).

Enshrined in the Universal Declaration of Human Rights, signed by the 208 UN General Assembly in 1948, contemporary conceptions of human rights have their origins in the global community's responses to fascism and the Holocaust. The Declaration internationalized the concept of rights by uncoupling individual human rights from the institution of citizenship that is subject to the jurisdiction of individual nations (Savic 1999: 4). Nevertheless, since the second half of the 20th century, respect for human rights has 'become a standard criteria [sic] for the legitimization of modern nations' (Savic, 1999: 5). As with the Jews, who were a stateless minority until the end of the Second World War, the statelessness of the Roma has made them vulnerable to prejudice in every European nation (Stauber and Vago, 2007). While international human rights law continues to be firmly grounded in Enlightenment ideals about the individual subject of rights (Balfour and Cadava, 2004), discrimination against the Roma demonstrates that the individualist emphasis 'cannot meet the demands of this universally marginalized group' (O'Nions, 2007: 25). For this reason, recent European debates about human rights have conceded the need to address the group rights of the Roma as a European racial minority (O'Nions, 2007). Thus recognizing the group rights of the Roma and legislating against racism have been important aspects of the way in which post-socialist regimes have attempted to legitimize themselves as liberal democracies prepared to join the EU.

In spite of the fact that liberal democracies and non-liberal regimes differ in their interpretation of human rights, almost all states agree that racial discrimination is one of the gravest human rights breaches (Cassese, 1999). However, definitions of racism are complex and varied. As Barnor Hesse has shown, contemporary Euro-American conceptions of racism privilege 'the anti-fascist critiques of the Jewish Holocaust while foreclosing . . . critiques centered on western Imperialism' (2004: 14), so that the racism manifest in nationalist movements is made visible, while the racism inherent in western liberalism is rendered invisible.

Because historically European Roma and Jews have faced similar kinds of prejudices, discrimination against the Roma as a minority group fits this privileged conception of racism. Furthermore, because nationalist sentiment has accompanied the processes of liberalization in Central and Eastern Europe, racism against the Roma in the post-socialist region has been made visible in human rights discourses in a way that discrimination and prejudice against the Roma and other minorities, immigrants and migrants in the West has not. This has reproduced a structure of power in an enlarged Europe that privileges the West as space of minority rights, liberalism and democracy. For example, the Organization for Security and Cooperation in Europe appointed a High Commissioner on National Minorities, whose power is limited to monitoring only those conflicts that could lead to outbreak of war. Implicitly, this limits the commissioner's supervision to the nationalist ethnic conflicts in Central and Eastern Europe, and disregards ethnic and racial tensions in the western liberal democracies (Aukerman, 2000).

THE ROMA MINORITY AS A 'VIRTUAL' SUBJECT OF RIGHTS IN POST-SOCIALIST CENTRAL AND EASTERN EUROPE

At the same time as post-socialist human rights discourses imagine the Roma as a 'litmus test' of the juridical and economic status of minority and human rights in the post-socialist nations, beginning with the spread of email and the world wide web in the early to mid-1990s, the internet seemed to provide a uniquely suited forum for Romani ethnic mobilization. Valery Novoselsky has argued that the internet fosters 'virtual communities' and transnational ethnic identification among the Roma (2007: 143; see also Vermeersch, 2006). Novoselsky (2007) suggests that the internet can transform the way in which the Roma interact, share information, develop civil society and construct social alliances and political movements. In this way, they can develop a 'virtual nation', using the internet as a forum (2007: 148). However, as Novoselsky acknowledges, due to high levels of poverty among the Roma, the task of developing this kind of virtual society will be up to their elites. Indeed, illiteracy, unemployment and homelessness rates are significantly higher for the Roma than for any other minority group in Europe (Ringold et al., 2005).

Novoselsky's view of the internet as an 'emancipatory tool' for the Roma is limited by its top-down vision of the elites' role in the internet-based Romani 'imagined community'. Envisioning the internet as a transnational and democratic public sphere depends upon a distinction between the virtual and the physical that excludes the material realities of the impoverished or uneducated (Slane, 2007). For example, this is why Novoselsky's (2007) hopeful argument that the internet can facilitate the formation of a virtual Romani nation homogenizes different Romani groups' experiences with discrimination across Europe in order to be able to imagine a coherent virtual nation. While the sites he looks to for evidence of the nascent virtual community are chiefly informational websites and Roma discussion forums, the top-down limitation of the internet as a medium for Romani mobilization also applies to human rights websites.

In its early years of broad usage in the mid-1990s, the internet was heralded uncritically as a medium that facilitates democratic development and rights.

According to the Center for Democracy and Technology (2008), the internet is a unique medium of communication:

> Like no other medium before, it allows individuals to express their ideas and opinions directly to a world audience and easily to each other, while allowing access to many more ideas, opinions and information than previous media have allowed. Consequently, there is a vital connection between the internet and human rights. (Center for Democracy and Technology, 2008)

As the social and economic situation of the Roma makes clear, this overly optimistic view of the internet's unique relationship to human rights activism must be critiqued. First, it assumes that as an inexpensive tool for communication, the internet allows groups to seamlessly 'coordinate actions and make contacts', 'expose human rights violations' through the spread of information, and have ready access to online documents and human rights research available through sites such as the one maintained by the United Nations High Commissioner on Human Rights (Center for Democracy and Technology, 2008; Metzl, 1996). However, the fact that a digital divide persists in many regions of the world problematizes these hopes for a 'world audience' with unrestricted access to information. In fact, western telecommunications companies carving markets in nonwestern nations make access to the internet prohibitively expensive. This continues to be the case, for example, for many people living in Bosnia, Serbia and Macedonia.

Ironically, many discussions about the relationship between internet technologies and human rights *a priori* align 'democracy' with the West, whose modernity is signalled by technology, while non-democratic regimes are imagined as exclusively non-western because they do not possess the communications technologies essential for promoting liberal forms of civil society. Michael Hegener's argument is one example of this kind of thinking:

> There is compelling evidence suggesting that dictatorial regimes can survive only in countries with fewer than 20 telephone lines per 100 inhabitants and most western countries now have well above 40 lines per 100 inhabitants. Of course, the internet—e-mail in particular—must have a similar if not a stronger beneficial influence on the most basic human rights. (Hegener, 1999)

Hegener's statements point to the disparity in the extent to which the internet and email are available in western and non-western nations, while leaving unproblematized the geopolitical and structural causes for that technological disparity. When the internet is imagined uncritically to be a tool for human rights, the very same informational technologies to which many poor and disadvantaged peoples lack access are equated with humanitarian action. Thus wealthier nations in which access to internet and communications technologies is commonplace come to symbolize and define the scope of human rights activism.

The uneven production and circulation of human rights discourses within and about Central, Western and Eastern Europe, which is brought on in part by the digital divide, affects how discrimination and minority rights in the post-socialist region have been publicized on the internet. For example, the European Roma Rights Centre, a public interest organization, has used the internet to create the most prominent website focusing exclusively on the topic of Roma human rights. The Centre's website downplays instances of human rights violations against the Roma in Western Europe, thus creating the misperception that Roma human rights is an issue emerging out of the problems of post-socialist liberal development. As an organization, the Centre specializes in 'strategic litigation, international advocacy, research and policy development and training of Romani activists' (see www.errc.org). Since 1996, it has focused on matters of Romani education, health, housing and legal enfranchisement. Its most visible campaigns have included:

- school desegregation in Bulgaria, Croatia, the Czech Republic and Hungary;
- implementation of anti-discrimination laws that accord with the standards set by the EU and the Council of Europe in Bulgaria, Hungary, Romania and Slovakia;
- justice for victims of coercive sterilization in the Czech Republic, Hungary and Slovakia; and
- justice for the victims of ethnic cleansing in Kosovo.

Even though the Centre publishes a quarterly journal and individual country reports, produces cassette tapes for broadcast on Roma radio stations and prints Romani language brochures to promote activist training and to inform Roma of their rights, the primary tool for publicizing its actions is the organization's website. The site archives all of the print materials, news and litigation and is available in English, Romani and Russian.

While the Centre claims to monitor, report and litigate cases of anti-Roma discrimination throughout the enlarged EU, the Balkans, the former Soviet Union and Turkey, the vast majority of violations against the Roma exposed through the website pertain to their socio-economic, political and legal situation in post-socialist nations. For example, in a summary of cases brought up by the Centre in 2005, 42 were in Bulgaria, 21 in Serbia and Montenegro and Ukraine, 20 in Slovakia and 18 in Hungary. The only western nation cited for more than one violation is Greece, with six cases. The Centre's choice of which forms of anti-Roma discrimination to publicize and litigate mirrors the asymmetrical human and civil rights standards for nations embedded in the EU. In addition to focusing almost exclusively on the forms of discrimination that occur in Central and Eastern Europe, the major financial sponsors for the work of the Centre are western embassies to post-socialist nations, western foundations and NGOs. The funding and governing structures of the Centre provide further evidence that the organization's priority is to monitor those states that have joined the EU recently, or that hope to join it.

Just as within the EU Central and Eastern European human rights violations have been monitored through a policy of 'naming and shaming' as part of accession criteria (Dediu, 2007: 119), the Centre's website aims to increase public attention to Roma rights abuses by 'expos[ing] and condemn[ing]' such abuses in European nations and influencing and developing policy and rights standards in an enlarged Europe (European Roma Rights Centre, 2008). However, by highlighting predominantly Central and Eastern European violations, the site reproduces the western role of 'naming' the abuse and 'shaming' the Central and Eastern European nations for it. Because exposure is at the heart of how human rights activists mobilize shame (Keenan, 2004), the Centre has utilized the internet as a medium for public exposure in the hope that this will facilitate post-socialist transformation. Furthermore, due to discrimination, poverty or lack of education, most Roma cannot be involved centrally in the online formulations and calls for their human rights. They become, in a sense, 'virtual' subjects of rights. Physically excluded as refugees from western nations such as France, Italy and Switzerland, in this case the internet functions to redirect Roma disenfranchisement symbolically throughout Europe to the post-socialist nations.

FRAMING THE DISPLACED: THE KOSOVAR ROMA ORAL HISTORIES PROJECT

Replicating the regional focus of the Decade of Roma Inclusion, the European Roma Rights Centre's online archive chiefly constitutes Roma rights as a Central and East European problem. In 2006, the United Nations Development Programme (UNDP) proposed a different framework for addressing the problems faced by the Roma—a 'Decade of the Displaced' (UNDP, 2006: 110). Although the UNDP's proposal focuses on south-east Europe, a policy approach which accounts for the displaced has the potential to hold Western European nations as accountable for Roma human rights as the Central and Eastern European ones. First, as I pointed out at the beginning of this article, many of the Roma who encounter discrimination and violence in the West are migrants or displaced persons. Foregrounding the rights of the displaced across Europe potentially could account for the targeted exclusion of Romani migrants from western nations as a form of discrimination, and highlight the violence experienced by the Roma displaced to the West. Second, as I will elaborate, upon examining the causes of Romani displacement from post-socialist Central and Eastern European nations, it becomes clear that western (military or economic) intervention can contribute to discrimination against the Roma in the post-socialist region.

A focus on Romani displacement also reframes the relationship between Roma rights and internet and communications technologies. As the UNDP (2006) report notes, the mass displacement of the Roma from and within multiple post-socialist nations makes their access to information about their rights, including that found on the internet, and their political participation extremely sporadic. By way of conclusion, I turn to the Kosovar Roma Oral Histories Project (www.balkanproject.org/roma/index.shtml) as an example of a non-traditional website about anti-Roma discrimination, which redeploys internet technologies to give voice to the Roma who have been displaced from their homes in Kosovo, and who otherwise would not have access to digital media. Framing the mass displacement of the Roma in Kosovo in a non-nationalist way, the site suggests that the causes of anti-Roma discrimination stem from Serbian and Albanian ethnic nationalism and from misguided western policy in the region. The site's transnational approach to the causes of anti-Roma discrimination and Roma displacement holds both the West and the East liable for the lack of Roma human rights.

The Kosovar Roma Oral Histories Project was undertaken in 2003 as an online project responding to the failure of the international media and politicians to publicize the mass displacement of the Roma from Kosovo. After NATO's 1999 bombing of Serbia and Kosovo, ethnic Albanians who had been driven out of their homes violently by Serbs sought revenge by expelling and killing Serbs, and along with them many Roma from Kosovo. Although the Oral Histories Project does not address Roma rights in juridical and political terms, it documents the discrimination against the Roma from the perspective of the displaced and gives an online voice to Romani non-elites in a way that produces a more multivalent depiction of the Roma as subjects in need of basic human rights. As with the European Roma Rights Centre, the Oral Histories Project is funded mostly by western non-profit organizations. However, the site's projects are directed by the local Kosovo-based organization, Communication for Social Development (www.balkanproject.org), whose staff includes Albanians, Roma and Serbs. Unlike the Centre, which reproduces the perspective that Roma rights are chiefly a Central and Eastern European problem, the Oral Histories project connects the Kosovar Roma's experiences with minorities in the post-socialist region and the rest of Europe, presumably including the West:

Kosovo's Roma are on the same downward spiral that smaller and poorer national minorities across Europe are in. The Kosovo Roma situation is exacerbated by the 1999 war and the poverty that affects the entire province. (Balkan project, 2005)

The Oral Histories Project deploys internet technologies to archive Roma community members' individual memories of the past and the present in Kosovo, including recent experiences with displacement. The site includes 52 individual interviews with Kosovar Roma, all of which are translated and transcribed into English from Albanian, Romani and Serbian, depending on the primary language of the respondent. Although this presumes that the website's audience will be an English-speaking one, there are video and mp3 clips of the interviews which are not subtitled. For audiences to be able to see the respondents and hear their voices contributes to the archive's feel that it is an oral history. This format provides a forum for Roma non-elites to be heard, which allows a more varied picture of different Roma communities to emerge. For example, the respondents are from different parts of Kosovo and include members of the established Roma community in Pristina, Kosovo's capital, as well as the more persecuted Roma groups in rural areas who have renamed themselves Egyptians to avoid violence (Balkan Project, 2005; Jashari, 2007).

One of the most important topics in the interviews is 1999 NATO bombing of Kosovo. Many of the Roma who were interviewed for the site consider the western military intervention to be the cause of ongoing displacement from their homes. As the project's creators explain, although at the time of the interviews the NATO bombing was long over, most of the respondents still referred to it in the present tense, since the long-term consequences of the bombing were more significant in their lives than the military action itself (Balkan Project, 2005). Ardita, a 19-year-old internally displaced person who fled the small town of Obilic after someone threw a hand grenade at her family's home, remembers that the Roma got along with both the Albanians and Serbs in her town until the 1999 bombing. For Ardita, the shift in the meaning and significance of ethnic difference within her local community occurred only after western intervention (Balkan Project, 2005). Her discussion of why she is displaced suggests that international policy shapes local identity formations. As with Ardita, many of the Kosovar Roma who were interviewed saw ethnic tensions not as inherent to their region, but rather as a more complex experience of ethnic discrimination that includes the effects of western intervention as well as those of the post-socialist transformation.

CONCLUSION

By concluding with a discussion of the Oral Histories Project I do not mean to imply that these Kosovar Roma voices present a more authentic understanding of ethnicity than the more official voices of the Roma elites and NGOs operating within the frame of EU human rights policy. Instead, I put forth this web project as a starting point from which to theorize how internet technologies can be used as a online forum, giving a voice to those who otherwise do not have access to the medium. Furthermore, by foregrounding the way in which the site frames displacement as the result of western intervention as much as local ethnic differences, I suggest that, within an enlarged Europe, the question of minority and ethnic rights should be rearticulated so as to assert that the problem of human rights is as much a problem of western liberalism as it is of the post-socialist transition. In fact, as I have been arguing, the two are connected. Thus the Oral Histories Project represents an opening in the discussion of human rights and the internet, making it possible to begin to theorize alternative forms of inclusion which also account for displacement in transnational human rights discourses and on the web.

REFERENCES

Aukerman, M. (2000) 'Definitions and Justifications: Minority and Indigenous Rights in Central/East European Context', *Human Rights Quarterly* 22(4): 1011–50.

Balfour, I. and E. Cadava (2004) 'The Claims of Human Rights: An Introduction', *South Atlantic Quarterly* 103(2–3): 277–96.

Balkan Project (2005) 'Who We Were, Who We Are: Kosovar Roma Oral Histories'. [Accessed 22 April 2008: http://www.balkanproject.org/roma/ index.shtml]

Cassese, A. (1999) 'Are Human Rights Truly Universal?', in Belgrade Circle (eds) *The Politics of Human Rights*, pp. 149–65. New York: Verso.

Dediu, M. (2007) 'The European Union: A Promoter of Roma Diplomacy', in V. Nicolae and H. Slavik (eds) *Roma Diplomacy*, pp. 115–50. New York: Idebate Press.

European Union Enlargement Information Unit (2002) 'EU Support for Roma Communities in Central and Eastern Europe'. [Accessed 20 June 2008: http://www. legislationline.org/upload/old/ 2e18726aO345b7O7f8df92c8dO642e94.pdf]

Hancock, I. (1987) *Pariah Syndrome: An Account of Gypsy Slavery and Persecution*. Ann Arbor, MI: Karoma Publishers.

Hegener, M. (1999) 'The Internet, Satellites and Human Rights', *On the Internet*, March/April. [Accessed 20 June 2008: http://www.isoc.org/oti/ articles/0399/hegener.html]

Hesse, B. (2004) 'Im/Plausible Deniability: Racism's Conceptual Double Bind', *Social Identities* 10(1): 9–29.

Jashari, S. (2007) 'Together in Alliance—The Roma Ashkali Egyptians of Kosovo: The Challenges of a United Political Party', in V. Nicolae and H. Slavik (eds) *Roma Diplomacy*, pp. 219–29. New York: Idebate Press.

Kaplan, R.D. (1994) *Balkan Ghosts: A Journey through History*. New York: Vintage.

Keenan, T. (2004) 'Mobilizing Shame', *South Atlantic Quarterly* 103(2–5): 455–49.

Metzl, J. F. (1996) 'Information Technology and Human Rights', *Human Rights Quarterly* 18(4): 705–46.

Novoselsky, V. (2007) 'The Internet and Public Diplomacy in the Formation of a Non-territorial Roma Nation', in V. Nicolae and H. Slavik (eds) *Roma Diplomacy*, pp. 145–56. New York: Idebate Press.

O'Nions, H. (2007) *Minority Rights Protection in International Law: The Roma of Europe*. Aldershot: Ashgate.

Rancière, J. (2004) 'Who Is the Subject of the Rights of Man?', *South Atlantic Quarterly* 103(2–3): 297–310.

Ringold, D., M. Orenstein and E. Wilkens (2005) *Roma in an Expanding Europe: Breaking the Poverty Cycle*. Washington, DC: The World Bank.

Rose, R. (2007), *Roma and Sinti: Human Rights for Europe's Largest Minority*. Heidelberg: Documentation and Cultural Centre of German Sinti and Roma.

Savic, 0. (1999) 'The Global and the Local in Human Rights: The Case of the Federal Republic of Yugoslavia', in Belgrade Circle (eds) *The Politics of Human Rights*, pp. 5–15. New York: Verso.

Slane, A. (2007) 'Democracy, Social Space and the Internet', *University of Toronto Law Journal* 57(1): 81–105.

Sobotka, E. (2007) 'Human Rights and Roma Policy Formations in the Czech Republic, Slovakia and Poland', in R. Stauber and R. Vago (eds.) *The Roma: A Minority in Europe*, pp. 155–62. Budapest: Central European University Press.

Stauber, R. and Vago, R. (2007) 'The Politics of Memory: Jews and Roma Commemorate Their Persecution' in R. Stauber and R. Vago (eds) *The Roma: A Minority in Europe*, pp. 117–34. Budapest: Central European University Press.

Tamas, P. (2007) 'Central European Roma Policy: National Minority Elites, National States and the EU', in R. Stauber and R. Vago (eds) *The Roma: A Minority in Europe*, pp. 163–76. Budapest: Central European University Press.

Thomas, D.C. (2005) 'Human Rights Ideas, the Demise of Communism and the End of the Cold War', *Journal of Cold War Studies* 7(2): 110–41.

United Nations Development Programme (UNDP) (2006) *At Risk: Roma and the Displaced in Southeast Europe*. Bratislava: Regional Bureau for Europe and the Commonwealth of Independent States.

Vermeersch, P. (2006) *The Romani Movement: Minority Politics and Ethnic Mobilization in Central Europe*. New York: Berghahn Books.

Wilkinson, T. (2008) 'Italy's Right Targets Gypsies, Migrants', *Los Angeles Times* (24 May). [Accessed 20 June 2008: http://www.latimes.com/news/la-fg-right24-2008may24,0,7905479.story]

Woodward, S. (1995) *Balkan Tragedy. Chaos and Dissolution after the Cold War*. Washington, DC: Brookings Institution Press.

*Neda Atanasoski is an assistant professor in the department of feminist studies at the University of California, Santa Cruz.

Neda Atanasoski, "Roma Rights on the World Wide Web: The Role of Internet Technologies in Shaping Minority and Human Rights Discourses in Post-Socialist Central and Eastern Europe," *European Journal of Cultural Studies* 12 (2009): 205–218. © American Council of Learned Societies.

Section IV:
Proposed Solutions

The four major targeted areas for Roma integration are education, housing, health care, and employment, corresponding to the four main areas of welfare provision across Europe and the EU. While legislation has been introduced in most EU countries to ensure equal access to each of these services, in practice, the Roma remain a highly discriminated against group. The search for successful models for targeting discrimination in each of these areas and ensuring equal access has resulted in at least two main approaches to the issue: 1) the search for models that could be replicated with similar expectations for success across-the-board, and 2) the search for unique solutions that target individual communities and take into account individual contexts. While many funders of Roma initiatives prefer the first, researchers in this volume point to the success of the latter, underlining the extent to which the practicalities surrounding solutions are often disconnected from the broader moral, legal, and political incentives that dictate the need for equality in the first place. The case studies presented in this section point to the wide variation in the needs of different Roma communities, the importance as well as difficulty of involving them in the decision-making process, and the often unacceptable compromises that must be made for solutions to be at least partially implemented.

Chapter 8: Good Practices Addressing School Integration of Roma/Gypsy Children in Hungary

*by Vera Messing**

Our recent project[1] has a comparative perspective: it compares selected good practices of integration of ethnic minority children among three European countries (Italy, Switzerland and Hungary). The project examines several key areas of integration: governmental policies, NGO practices and most importantly good practices that might be transferable, irrespective of differences regarding national environment and ethnic group. We focus here on Hungary and aim to identify key elements of good practices of integrating Roma/Gypsy[2] children such as creative pedagogical methods, differentiated personal treatment of children with learning problems, a multicultural curriculum, teacher training, extracurricular activities, community building and family involvement. This paper describes an innovative and transferable practice that promotes inclusion and addresses low school-performance and high dropout rates among low status Roma children. The 'Learnery' project is an after-school programme run by the minority community with the professional assistance of the public school. Results of the innovative practice are convincing: improved school performance, significant decrease in dropout rates, improved community relationships, and decrease of interethnic conflicts within the school.

INTRODUCTION: THE CONTEXT OF INTERETHNIC RELATIONS IN HUNGARY

As the main ethnically, culturally and—partly—linguistically diverse group in Hungary, the Roma, who have lived in Hungary for centuries, constitute about 6 to 7% of the population. Most settled in the nineteenth century, giving up their traditional travelling lifestyle. Although there are significant differences between Roma subgroups, the various groups continue to be characterized by social and economic marginalization. During the years of state socialism, their overall level of education and employment improved significantly, which implied that the majority of Roma finished primary education and were engaged in low-skilled or unskilled work. The changes after 1989 had a major impact on the Roma: most of the formerly employed Roma workers—employed typically in the 'socialist' heavy industry and agriculture—lost their jobs. Statistics show the dramatic consequences: the employment rate of Roma decreased from 77% in 1984 to 29% by 2003 (Kemény, Janky and Lengyel 2004). In addition to labour market exclusion, increasing residential segregation has also taken place: Roma move (or stay) in low status (slum) districts of larger towns or in settlements with little or no economic activity. Simultaneously, anti-Gypsy attitudes have risen significantly in the past decade: approximately half of Hungarian citizens are overtly prejudiced against Gypsies. In very simple but obvious terms: the vast majority of the Roma population have become the major 'loser' of the political and economic transition that took place during the 1990s. In contrast, the immigrant population of Hungary is small (less than 1% of the population) and the vast majority of them (over 70%) are of Hungarian descent.

It is difficult to compare the school integration of Roma children with migrant children in Europe. If migration is understood in a narrow sense—referring to people who have migrated from one country to another with the hope of building a better life—Hungarian Roma do not fit the definition. But if we consider the social and personal consequences of migration—i.e. being 'othered', being the subject of prejudice and neglect, being discriminated against, being segregated and finally becoming 'outcasts' in society—then problems related to the integration of Roma children do, to a great extent, resemble the situation of immigrants in older member states of the EU. Let me refer to Szalai here:

> It is not an exaggeration to state that, given the rather homogeneous national/ethnic composition of its dominant population,[3] and also the traditionally low rates of inward migration,[4] it is Hungary's only domestic ethnic/racial minority—its Roma citizenry—that embodies 'otherness' and that 'takes up' the position of deprived and marginalized groupings labelled as 'culturally alien' migrants in most other European societies. (Szalai 2007)

CONTEXT OF THE EDUCATIONAL SYSTEM AND PRESENT PROCESSES OF SCHOOLING FOR ETHNIC GROUPS IN HUNGARY

Educational attainment of Roma has increased significantly since the 1970s. In contrast to the 1971 national Roma survey, when only 27% of the 20–24 year olds completed eight grades of primary education, by 1993 this rate had increased to 78%, and by 2003 to 83% (Kemény et al. 2004). Still, due to an overall increase in the educational level of the population as a whole, the educational gap between Roma and non-Roma population has grown considerably: completed primary education—a compulsory minimum—is not sufficient for successful labour market participation any more. Consequently, even with higher educational levels, Roma have become more excluded from the labour market when compared with the 1970s. According to the PISA research data, Hungarian public education is highly selective with regard to parents' education. Public education provides extremely unequal opportunities for the different social strata and these differences multiply by the time children leave school. Regarding outcome,[5] ethnic background is one of the most prevalent selection variables in primary and secondary schools. On the one hand, Roma children are highly affected by selectivity based on social status, as 80% of them are socially disadvantaged. On the other hand, discrimination and prejudice play an important role in selectivity: non-Roma parents tend to transfer their children if the ethnic composition of the class/school reaches a certain ratio (20–40% Roma) (Messing and Molnár 2008). Consequently, a great deal of stress is placed on schools to segregate Roma children in order to retain non-Roma middle class children. Complex processes, including segregation, differentiated quality of primary education, lack of information among parents, necessity of compliance with prejudiced attitudes of non-Roma parents by the school, all lead to the fact that the vast majority of Roma attend low quality primary schools. Simultaneously, due to frequent dropout during the early years of secondary schooling and the low quality and non-adoptability of vocational training system to industrial needs, very few Roma manage to gain qualifications that are valuable on the labour market. Havas, Kemény and Liskó (2002) have pointed to the huge ethnic gap in school careers after primary school: 15% of Roma children stop studying after primary school, while 66% continue in vocational training schools that do not provide a graduation exam, and less than one fifth of Roma children (19% in 1998/99) continue on to secondary schools that provide a graduation exam. For their non-Roma peers this latter percentage is 57%. Liskó (2002) found that only a small number (less than 25%) of Roma children manage to complete any kind of secondary schooling (including vocational training schools that do not provide a graduation exam). Early dropout and school failure of Roma children is especially pronounced in vocational training schools (36% drop out during the first, and 29% during the second year). Most of these schools provide low quality education that does not prepare students adequately for the labour market. Kertesi and Kézdi (2005) have argued that the widening educational gap may be attributed to the exclusion of Roma working age men from the labour market: when fathers are laid off, younger children are likely to discontinue schooling and stop studying after the 8th grade of primary school (education is mandatory until this age).

GOVERNMENTAL POLICIES AND MEASURES AIMED AT THE EDUCATIONAL INTEGRATION OF THE SOCIALLY DISADVANTAGED AND ROMA CHILDREN

Governmental policies in Hungary have resulted in structurally new and long-term education strategies and programmes aimed at providing equal treatment of different ethnic groups and minorities in Hungary. Since the most recent government came into power in 2002 (and was re-elected in 2006), it has been an explicit and strong priority of the Ministry of Education to address practices which have resulted in extensive segregation and exclusion from quality education. Within the scope of these policies, a number of measures have been taken that include changes in legislation and the system of subsidies, as well as a number of direct programmes that have been introduced to intervene into the spontaneous processes that have increasingly resulted in segregation in the past decade. A recent regulation,[6] which developed a list of priorities in the admittance procedures of primary schools, aimed to curb the, until then, total freedom of choice parents had in their school choice, and to stop the rapidly growing ethnic segregation created by the present system. The afore-mentioned regulation limits the selective procedures carried out by schools: it puts an end to the practice of 'elite-schools' picking the most talented children and those coming from families with the highest status.

An extensive governmental programme—the National Network of Integrating School (NNIS)—was introduced in 2002. NNIS promoted integrated education, introducing various parallel elements:

(a) additional funding ('integration quota') for schools that take initiative to integrate socially disadvantaged children and participate in the programme;

(b) methodological assistance for teachers—schools and teachers taking part in NNIS were provided substantial professional support through regular training, special curriculum and teaching materials;

(c) institutional background—the NNIS provided professional, infrastructural and financial support for participating schools.

The effects of school integration efforts such as these are as yet unclear, since 3 years of practice is too short to draw definitive conclusions. Nevertheless, the first results of the effect study (Kézdi and Surányi 2008) provide some evidence that integration favours all children (Roma and non-Roma, socially disadvantaged and middle class) with respect to changes in cognitive and non-cognitive skills and self-consciousness, confidence and tolerance.

The Ministry of Education has introduced a number of further measures to stop segregation and reintegrate excluded children into public education[7] and decrease high dropout rates,[8] the description of which exceeds the scope of this paper.

INNOVATIVE PRACTICE

Methodology

A number of non-governmental initiatives in Hungarian education have become models for the formal education system during the last few years. Some of these initiatives have provided extracurricular activities (i.e. Learneries), some run special student dormitories (Collegium Martineum), while others led to the founding of alternative secondary schools (Gandhi Gimnasium; Kis Tigris Grammar School, Gilvánfa; Ambedkar Grammar School, Sajókaza), similar to charter schools in the United States. It appears that these initiatives might modify the educational prospects of Roma students, locally or regionally. Interestingly, most of these initiatives dissolved or failed as soon as they were integrated into the regular education system (Arany János Kollégiumi Programme, many of the 'Learneries'). Further research should identify the reasons for why such initiatives have failed in the course of transformation from the individual/local to the general/national level.

One of the main challenges of the present research project was to define how to identify successful innovative practices. A first step was to conduct interviews and engage in discussions with ministry officials, the NNIS and NGOs active in the field of Roma education. Based on information collected from professionals and policy-makers, I selected two primary schools—both participating in the NNIS—one in a poor district of the capital Budapest, the second in a small village in a region of Hungary characterized by economic and social depression. Both schools educated a relatively large number of Roma students. The Budapest school also had a significant number of migrant students, while the village school's student population consisted of Roma children who belonged to two different and rival Roma communities. I conducted field visits, interviewed school directors, teachers, special education teachers, people in charge of family relations and also made classroom observations. The criteria for selecting a practice were comparability with other countries' cases, the involvement of national scope programme and the study of a primary school. After the preliminary research, taking also into consideration comparability with the Swiss and Italian situations, the project team decided to select the village school case, as it involved both the national scope integration programme (NNIS) and a local ethnic NGO initiative, the 'Learnery', an after-school programme organized and run by the Roma minority community. The selection of this particular school and practice was also legitimized by the fact that there are very few successful cases of integrating Roma children in primary schools operating in economically highly depressed small settlements. The case of Turna[9] seemed one of them, and the reason for the success was at least partly due to the integration of a national, public school programme (NNIS) and a local NGO initiative (Learnery), the lack of any of which would have most probably not provided a successful outcome.

In the course of the research, interviews were conducted with the headmaster, the deputy headmaster, five teachers, the headmaster of the pre-school, eight students in the 8th grade, the founder and manager of the Learnery (who is the president of Local Gypsy Self Government). Focus group discussions were conducted with Roma parents as well as a few class-room observations were conducted as well.

THE CASE STUDY

The Turna primary school is a small public school serving 90 children from two neighbouring villages (Turna and Satu) and employs 11 teachers[10] in an economically highly depressed region in the north of Hungary. Roma children compose approximately 60% of the school population. The ethnic composition of the two villages and the school is special: Turna is inhabited by Hungarians, Hungarian and Carpathian Gypsies,[11] while neighbouring Satu is inhabited by Boyash (Romanian) Gypsies,[12] who moved here from the south of Hungary in the 1950s with the intention of getting a stable job in the socialist-state heavy industry. Problems in this region are typical: manifold and overlapping pressure of poverty, low levels of education (a majority of Satu's population did not graduate from primary school), lack of work. According to our interviews, only a few men hold stable jobs, while the vast majority do irregular seasonal work or are unemployed. Almost all women work in the household.

The school hosts children from three ethnic groups, speaking different languages at home and having a distinct identity and cultural traditions. Ethnic boundaries are very strong. Parents, for example, often asked teachers not to seat their children next to a child from another ethnic group in the 1990s.

It is obvious that the school faces enormous problems relating to poverty, low educational levels of the parents and lack of motivation among the children to learn. Despite these facts, the school has been able to have an impact on the educational careers of the children: all the children finish primary school and all are accepted into secondary school. Later results remain ambiguous though: a majority of children graduating from the village school in Turna drop out of secondary education due to a number of reasons related to commuting:[13] i.e. inability to pay for food at school and transport, intolerant, prejudiced attitudes among the majority and rigidity of teaching methods in vocational training schools.[14] Our interviews with parents revealed that most of the Roma parents fear that their children will be verbally intimidated or even physically insulted by their peers because of their ethnicity in the secondary school.

The good practice presented here consists of two complementary elements: the public school's integration programme and the 'Learnery', both of which have an impact. Dropout is non-existent and attendance is good. This result might seem minor in different social settings, but represents a tremendous success in Turna and Satu. Prior to 2003, a large number of children dropped out of school, families were not interested in education and there was often friction between the school and the community. According to the headmaster and leading teachers of the primary school, by the end of the 1990s the situation was so bad that not only students but also the teachers were reluctant to go to school. They started to investigate new methods of teaching and teaching–learning practices at a point 'when the situation could not become worse' (headmaster).

THE FIRST ELEMENT: INTEGRATION PROGRAMME IN THE PUBLIC SCHOOL

Turna public school has been a member of the NNIS since 2003. It has since implemented the integration programme, which provides extra funding, on the one hand, and a number of pedagogical-methodological assistance measures, on the other hand. These include educating teachers how to teach in ethnically and socially heterogeneous classes. In addition, neighbouring Satu's Gypsy Self Government (GSG) initiated an after-school programme ('Learnery') in the village for children from primary and secondary schools in 2005.

The school has started to perform well because of these interventions: the children attended school regularly at the time of the research and teachers were proud to report that no dropouts had been recorded during the two preceding years. All the children graduating from the 8th grade were being accepted to secondary schools. The head teacher was of the opinion that one key factor for the improvement had been the breaking with the traditional concept of frontal teaching and the classroom concept of one-way communication based on the hierarchy between powerful teachers and recipient students. The traditional frontal teaching technique is still widespread in Hungarian schools in general, however. The Turna school introduced a new approach to teaching children with different social and ethnic backgrounds in 2003. The practice incorporates a number of innovative pedagogical methods, a more tolerant ideology, greater emphasis on family outreach and cooperation with families, as well as continuous teacher education. Major elements are:

• First and foremost, *differentiated teaching* conforming to the abilities of individual students was introduced instead of the formerly applied idea of treating all students similarly. Children with learning or behavioural problems were integrated into normal classes, but teachers prepared individual tasks for these students, according to individual skills, needs and motivation. The introduction of differentiated teaching eased the burden on the teacher to keep discipline in the classroom since each child's interests and attention was addressed. Support teachers, specialized in dealing with learning difficulties, assisted the students, especially those with serious lags. In certain cases, depending on the problem and skills to be developed, such assistance took place during regular classes, while there were also instances of individual or small group support outside the classroom.

• *Co-operative teaching* methods were mentioned as an important approach that enabled students to solve problems in cooperation with others. The following benefits of this method were identified by the teachers: (i) it helped to decrease conflicts rooted in ethnic, cultural and age differences because children of various ethnic backgrounds were forced to work together and get to know each other. As a result they became able to see each other free of deeply rooted stereotypes and prejudice. (ii) Teachers stressed that a great advantage of cooperative learning methods was that they encouraged the integration of children with different skills into the same classroom activity. Children involved in a co-operative group became useful and appreciated other members of the classroom community. Consequently, co-operative methodology, if applied correctly, proved to be extremely advantageous for students with low self-esteem and identity conflicts. The disadvantage of co-operative methodologies, according to the teachers, was their time-consuming nature and the problems that might arise from insufficient preparation and inadequate distribution of roles and tasks.

• Another pedagogical method mentioned by many teachers was *drama*. This proved to be especially effective for students who had limited abilities or who feared to engage in classroom processes because of language/cultural barriers or low self-esteem. Drama also proved to be advantageous for those who suffered from psychological or personality problems related to serious social or cultural deprivation.

• *Project-based learning* was mentioned as a useful pedagogical tool for those students whose family background encouraged a great deal of autonomy at a very early age. One example are the Boyash Roma children from Satu. This community views 12-year-old boys as adults: they are given extensive autonomy in the family, have responsibility towards the family and are treated as sovereign members of the community. At the same time, majority society and its institutions, including schools, treat the same age group as minors. Students over the age of 12 were given tasks that demanded autonomy and the skill to manage time. The teacher assigned projects and the children had to complete these tasks according to a jointly agreed time schedule, including deadlines, scope of work and means of completing the project. As a consequence, teachers were able to keep these students in school who otherwise would have dropped out due to being frequently absent, because of the necessity of contributing to the income of the family at a very early age (often by working in the fields). In addition, according to both teacher and student accounts, students enjoyed these tasks, which helped them to develop problem solving skills, independent work and skills related to researching, identifying, processing and applying new information.

• Effective methods of comprehension for children's behavioural and learning problems was mentioned by teachers as a very useful tool, provided by the training received from the NNIS. Teachers took part in workshops that prepared them to identify and comprehend children's behavioural and learning difficulties and treat the real causes of such problems, instead of fighting continuously and fruitlessly for better discipline. All the teachers interviewed mentioned that they became more competent in identifying reasons behind such problems and became more effective in treating them.

In addition to the innovative methods acquired and utilized in the school, a key breakthrough was the recognition of the importance of building partnerships with families and providing a more tolerant atmosphere in the school. The school identified as an important reason for earlier failure the lack of effective communication and functional relationships with the families. Parents avoided going to the school to discuss issues facing their children. This was due to the rigid and hierarchical nature of the relationship between schools and families, due to the enormous social and cultural gap between teachers and Roma parents, most of whom did not finish elementary education and were functionally illiterate. The school realized that they had to take the first steps towards the families in order to gain their partnership in the education of their children.

One separate 'good practice' is the extracurricular after-school programme—'Learnery'—in the village of Satu. The Learnery is a project dedicated to provide means and infrastructure to spend after-school time. More than 30 Learneries operate in the country, usually run by the Gypsy Self Government of a given settlement. Learneries are typically successful in small settlements with a large Roma community, where there is no infrastructure for young people to spend their time after school (cinema, cafeterias, sports clubs).

THE SECOND ELEMENT: THE LEARNERY IN SATU

The Learnery in Satu is an extracurricular after-school activity organized by the minority community, with the assistance of 'Amrita' a Roma NGO network and the public school of Satu. Children aged 6 to 18, irrespective of their ethnicity or school of enrolment (primary or secondary) may take part in the activities of the Learnery. Most importantly, the Learnery is a place where children may enjoy themselves and is not a continuation of the school in the afternoon. Still, the key aim of the Learnery is to assist children in their efforts to finish primary school successfully and proceed to secondary school by providing them with an environment that they often lack at home, and activities that can compensate for social deprivation.

In order to better understand the importance and the role of the Learnery let us examine the reality of life for young people in Satu: children arrive from the Turna school at 1 p.m. and have nothing to do. Extreme poverty is characteristic both within the families and in the settlement. There is no public or private infrastructure where school children can spend their time, they do not have a room or even a table at home, do not have a playground in the village, and nowhere to spend time in the afternoon. Children roam the streets in the afternoons doing nothing. Consequently, the principal aim of the Learnery initiative was to provide time and space for children where they could become involved in age-appropriate activities. The Learnery was established in a house renovated by the local community, furnished and equipped with computers, toys, and tools essential for children's psychological and cognitive development. The Learnery, open from 3 p.m. until 6 p.m., is free and accessible to all children enrolled in school, irrespective of their ethnic or social background or age (3 to 16 years old). Activities in the Learnery are led by one or two teachers from Turna, who organize activities and look after the children. The Gypsy Self Government initiated fund-raising necessary to establish the Learnery and equip it with necessary tools, and was successful in applying for Structural Fund[15] managed by the Ministry of Education in 2005.

The Learnery has become more substantial in recent years: it has developed its own pedagogical programme focusing on identity strengthening, community building, development of cognitive skills, career consultation, and many other elements essential for a child's physical and mental well-being.

The following elements—described in the pedagogical programme of the Learnery—highlight the ideas behind the effective functioning of the Learnery.

Activities That Promote the Strengthening of One's Personality

The majority of children in the village suffer both from multiple social disadvantages and various levels of psychological distress as a consequence of ethnic stigma and social deprivation. One of the Learnery's aims has been to strengthen children's personality and self-esteem in order to enable children to fulfil their potential. The aim of the Learnery has been to combat the psychological pain felt by many, to support children in the forming of their sense of responsibility, autonomy and self-support. In order to achieve this goal the Learnery uses the following tools:

• Each student, together with an adult (most commonly the teacher in the Learnery), develops an individual development programme, which includes a description of the present situation as perceived by the child: results, skills, problems as well as an assessment of her/his strengths and weaknesses, description of her/his motivations and conceptions about the following year's activities, and intended short- and long-term targets. They also formulate means by which they envisage achieving the described goals. Such planning serves to guide the student throughout the following year. The student and the teacher together evaluate performance and success on the basis of this commonly agreed plan.

• The Learnery provides a space for self-promoting peer groups. These peer groups can play an important role in the planning and decisions regarding one's future career. Children need references from their own peer group: they will put greater emphasis on career planning if they see successful role models. This is a key dimension of the Learnery: research shows (see, for example, Liskó 2002), that many Roma students do not aspire to a secondary school education since they lack role models in their direct environment, while many primary school teachers also tend to dissuade them from applying to those secondary schools which provide a graduation exam. It is crucial that Roma children, deprived of middle class wealth and ideals, have role models in the peer-group who can demonstrate that it is indeed possible to attend a secondary school and be successful. Another key goal of the peer groups is to help resolve personal crises: children who have already gone through conflict situations typical of adolescents—i.e. conflicts with adults, family, teachers, love, etc.—help their peers in overcoming these issues.

Activities Related to Identity Development and the Social Environment of Students

• Another key aim of the Learnery has been to promote the development of positive ethnic identity. The Learnery, initiated and managed by the Gypsy Self Government, aims to fight the negative perception of Roma and provide Roma children with the opportunity to identify positively with their ethnicity. Most Roma face stereotypes, prejudice and ethnic hatred by Hungarians on a daily basis and in a variety of situations (on the street, in shops, in public institutions) and encounter negative perceptions of Roma-ness as well as discrimination at a very early age. A recent study by Neményi (2007) has provided evidence along these lines, revealing how Roma school children at an early age suffer from a distorted identity and self-esteem as a consequence of ethnic stigma. The study also shows how negative ethnic identity hinders school performance and limits the career goals of these children. The Learnery recognizes the importance of encouraging positive ethnic identity and offers Roma children knowledge and the means by which they can resist negative influences coming from the majority environment. The Learnery, established in Satu, a majority Boyash Gypsy community, also offers formalized classes in Boyash culture and language. In addition, non-Roma schoolteachers receive assistance in gaining knowledge about Gypsy culture and history in order to enable them to incorporate this knowledge into the regular school curriculum.

• In addition to fighting the consequences of negative perceptions on the part of the majority society, most children also face disadvantages related to poverty and deprivation. The Learnery has dedicated activities to balancing social disadvantages and the consequences of material and mental deprivation. The Learnery regularly organizes excursions and cultural programmes to cities and the capital. It has also taken children to summer holiday camps, where they spend a week with Roma peers who come from various parts of the country. The extreme poverty in the village needs to be re-emphasized: most of the children have never visited other parts of the country and have never been on holiday or travelled with their families.

Activities That Promote Successful School Performance

• A number of activities have promoted successful school performance, including free cramming, free computer and internet access, and parts of an essential infrastructure for learning that is otherwise unavailable in the village. An important activity in the Learnery relates to the fact that teachers have initiated activities that have raised children's interest in topics about to be addressed in the school. Such activities have included drama, games, cultural excursions, or field trips. The Learnery has also aimed to introduce the cultural context of the topics discussed later in school.

• There have been two activities in the Learnery that have been directly related to the school: (i) teachers have provided assistance in preparing for the next day if requested; (ii) personal cramming sessions were provided during the summer for those children who did not finish the school year successfully and thus had to prepare for an exam in September.

Activities That Directly Promote the Continuation of Schooling

• The Learnery has provided career counselling to children and families. Most of the families, lacking a person with more than a primary school education, tend not to have basic information about secondary schools, their accessibility, their function and career opportunities provided by different school types. Furthermore, Roma children are frequently directed automatically to vocational training schools irrespective of their interest, abilities and skills. Interviews with teachers and parents revealed that the majority of Roma children from the village attended the same vocational school, despite the fact that it was of very low quality and experienced extremely high dropout rates. The Learnery, in contrast, has attempted to show the various choices available and also tried to identify the most appropriate educational option for each child. The Learnery has organized excursions to the neighbouring towns' secondary schools, where families and children could see for themselves what school choices they had. These activities were quite effective. The Learnery has also assisted children in their preparation for the secondary school entrance exams.

• There are two problems that have limited the success of Learneries:

1. The prevailing funding system is based on tenders: Learneries are run mainly by the Local Roma Self Governments, which lack resources,[16] and have to re-apply for financing every term (1- or 2-year-terms). The funding system is replete with inappropriate administrative obstacles, while serious payment delays are common due to complicated administration. As

a consequence, most of the Learneries in the country (over 30 altogether) have gone bankrupt. There is an urgent need for the structural financing of Learneries.

2. No professional or pedagogical support is provided for teachers working in the Learneries, despite the fact that Learneries treat underprivileged children with learning and behavioural problems: a target group which is typically in need of creative and innovative pedagogical methods. It is obvious that Learneries can function well, when assistance is provided by teachers involved in the NNIS.

CONCLUSIONS

There is no single formula for good practice when it comes to integrating children of ethnic minority background into schools. There are a number of variables that promote integration or are indispensable for integrated education. Obviously, the professionally prepared and empathetic teacher is a key factor: no programme, project or pedagogical method can replace or even compensate for this. We have identified some of the innovative methods and techniques that can serve to promote the integration of children with language, cultural or social differences when applied by dedicated teachers. Some of these elements focus on how the consequences of distorted ethnic identity may be overcome, others concentrate on the management of consequences relating to mental and social deprivation, and still others assist in escaping routines of career choices deeply embedded in the hierarchical perception of deprived Roma and non-Roma children. The most useful pedagogical methods proved to be co-operative learning, drama, differentiated teaching and project-based learning.

It is of major importance that schools extend their pursuits beyond the teaching that happens during school hours and in the school building. Other buildings in the community have a role to play and the development of ties with families is essential when communities distrust the school (or any other majority institutions) and see it as an 'alien' institution. Extra-curricular programmes proved to be helpful in integrating children with various ethnic, cultural and language backgrounds: excursions, parties, summer camps, and cultural visits have all been programmes that promote acceptance and integration by the peer-group.

The provision of activities after school seems also to be effective where poverty and social and ethnic segregation are profound: the Learnery is good practice in this respect. Organized and managed by the minority community, with the professional assistance of teachers from the local public school, the Learnery can become a bridge between ethnic minority communities and majority institutions. Such co-operation provides a safeguard for children and families and illustrates how ethnic identity and community is not only accepted in such programmes, but strengthened, while positively affecting school performance and progress.

The cases analysed in this paper provide examples of good practice that help primary school students stay in school and perform better. They do not, however, offer a sufficient solution to address early dropout from secondary schools by girls, who tend to become mothers at a very early age, or by boys, who have to contribute to the family income—major schooling challenges for Roma children in today's Hungary.

NOTES

1. The project is entitled 'Good practice in practice. Innovative practices of school integration of children of ethnic and migrant background in three countries of Europe'. The project, conducted in 2006, was led by FIERI (International and European Forum of Migration Research) in collaboration with the Swiss Forum for Migration in Switzerland and the Institute of Sociology, Hungarian Academy of Sciences, in Hungary. The project was funded by NEF (Network of European Foundations).

2. I will use the Roma denomination for Roma and Gypsy because there is no consensus among the ethnic minority regarding the appropriate nomenclature. Some groups prefer Gypsy, while others are reluctant to use it because of the negative connotations attached to the term. Roma is the self-identification of one specific subgroup (Vlah Roma). In certain cases I will use Gypsy because officially it is the denomination (Gypsy Self Government) or if this is the evident denomination (in case of Boyash, or Musician Gypsies).

3. Responding to the questionnaire of the last census of 2001, 94% of the population indicated exclusive 'Hungarian' nationality.

4. The yearly rate of inward migration has remained at 0.5–0.7% during the past 15 years.

5. Results of children, career aspirations and opportunities.

6. Modification of the Public Education Act in 2006, CXLVIII/2005 amended Law LXXIX on Public Education.

7. To limit the frequent practice of segregating Roma children through assessing them as slightly mentally handicapped and directing them to special schools (or classes) three measures were taken: (i) the notion of 'special educational needs' was introduced, (ii) the system of assessing a child to be mentally handicapped was reconsidered and supervised and (iii) the programme 'From the last desk' was introduced. This programme includes methodology and additional financial and professional support for schools, which strive to integrate children coming from remediate schools.

8. Introduction of afternoon schools 'tanoda' (Learnery) for children with special needs (described later in detail). Introduction of programmes and scholarships: 'Path to secondary school', 'Path to graduation', 'Path to profession', 'Path to higher education'. A number of scholarships aiming at supporting Roma and socially disadvantaged children were introduced (Arany János scholarship, Útravaló scholarship, Cinka Panna scholarship). Meals and books

at school became free for children from socially disadvantaged backgrounds. Changes in the public educational law made it compulsory to accept children from disadvantaged backgrounds into nursery schools, boarding schools, and dormitories.

9. The names of the settlements have been changed in order to ensure anonymity.

10. All teachers at the school are non-Roma although returning to the school 6 months later I noticed that the school employed a Roma teaching assistant.

11. A subgroup of Hungarian Gypsies (Romungro).

12. A separate ethnic subgroup of Roma/Gypsies, with its own Boyash ethnic identity, distinct language and traditions.

13. Secondary schools are 25–50 km away from the village.

14. Drug and alcohol problems of adolescents and, as a consequence also physical harassment, become frequent after children leave the small village and commute to the neighbouring town.

15. The Learnery was applying for a sub-programme of the Structural Funds announced under the framework of Human Resource Operative Programme (HEFOP).

16. Leaders of the Roma Self Governments are typically lower educated Roma who are appreciated within the community, but who lack skills, knowledge and resources necessary for applying for such tenders. In addition, very often they are unpaid, voluntary representatives elected by the community.

REFERENCES
Bernát, Anikó. 2006. A magyarországi romák helyzete nemzetközi összehasonlításban [The situation of Hungarian Roma in an international comparative perspective]. Társadalmi Riport. Budapest: TÁRKI.

Havas, Gábor, István Kemény, and Ilona Liskó. 2002. Cigány gyerekek az általános iskolában [Roma children at school]. Budapest: OKI-Új Mandátum.

Kemény, István, B. Janky, and G. Lengyel. 2004. A magyarországi cigányság 1971–2003 [The Hungarian Gypsy 1971–2003]. Budapest: MTAKI.

Kemény, István, ed. 2005. Roma of Hungary. Social Science Monographs, Boulder, CO: Atlantic Research and Publications, Highland Lakes, New Jersey, New York. http://www.mtaki.hu/kiadvanyok/isvtan_kemeny_ed_roma_of_hungary_main.html

Kertesi, Gábor, and Gábor Kézdi. 2005. A foglalkoztatási válság gyermekei [Children of transition crisis]. In A társadalom peremén [On the margins of the society], ed. G. Kertesi. Budapest: Osiris.

———. 2006. Expected long term budgetary benefits to Roma education in Hungary. Budapest: Roma Education Fund. www.romaeducationfund.hu

Kézdi, Gábor, and Éva Surányi. 2008. A hátrányos helyzetű tanulók oktatási integrációs programjának hatásvizsgálata 2005–2007 [Effect study of the integration program aiming at socially disadvantaged children 2005–2007]. Manuscript.

Kováts, András, and Anna Medjesi. 2006. Magyarajkú, nem-magyar állampolgárságú tanulók nevelésének, oktatásának helyzete a magyar közoktatásban [Public education of immigrant ethnic Hungarians in Hungary]. Budapest: Ministry of Culture and Education. http://www.okm.gov.hu/doc/upload/200703/hatarontuli_magyarok_tanulmany_070320.pdf

Liskó, Ilona. 2002. Cigány tanulók a középfokú iskolákban [Gypsy children in secondary schools]. Új Pedagógiai Szemle [Journal of New Pedagogy] 6, no. 11.

Messing, Vera, and Emilia Molnár. 2008. '...több odafigyelés kellett volna' A roma gyerekek iskolai sikerességének korlátairól ['...more attention would have been needed' Study on the barriers to school success for Roma children]. Budapest: Esély, 4–5.

Neményi, Mária. 2007. *Identitásstratégiák*. [Identity strategies]. Budapest: ÉS, no. 7.

O'Higgins, Neil, and A. Ivanov. 2006. Education and employment opportunities for the Roma. *Comparative Economic Studies* 48, 6–19.

Szalai, Júlia. 2007. 'Cultural otherness' or the ethnicisation of poverty? Some considerations on how postcommunist welfare reforms affect Hungary's Roma minority. Manuscript.

Zolnay, János. 2006. *Kényszerek és választások. Oktatáspolitika és etnikai szegregáció Miskolc és Nyíregyháza általános iskoláiban* [Coercions and limitations. Education policy and ethnic segregation in schools of Miskolc and Nyíregyháza.] Budapest: Esély, 4.

*Vera Messing is a research fellow at the Center for Policy Studies at Central European University as well as a research associate of the Institute of Sociology at the Hungarian Academy of Sciences.

Vera Messing, "Good Practices Addressing School Integration of Roma/Gypsy Children in Hungary," *Intercultural Education* 19 (2008): 461–473.

Chapter 9: Roma Housing Projects in Small Communities, Slovakia

by European Union Agency for Fundamental Rights*

INTRODUCTION

This case study[1] is part of a series of case studies on specific housing initiatives for Roma and Travellers. It is intended to contribute to a deeper understanding of lessons learned within the context of the larger research project on housing conditions of Roma and Travellers in the EU.[2]

The focus of this study is the development and implementation of housing policy at municipal level to address the needs of Roma in two rural communities, Val'kovňa and Nálepkovo, using the existing legal and financial tools provided by the national government. The leadership taken within an environment of public opinion unfavourable toward initiatives aimed at Roma inclusion was crucial for the positive outcome of these housing initiatives.

The case study is based on qualitative information from a wide range of sources, including semi-structured interviews undertaken with 15 respondents in March 2009. Those interviewed included three representatives of local governments of Val'kovňa and Nálepkovo, a representative of a regional Roma NGO,[3] three community social workers and nine Roma beneficiaries of the described initiatives. The sample of interviewees contained ten Roma and five non-Roma, ten women and five men. Beyond the respondents with whom the semi-structured interviews were conducted, several other individuals in both municipalities were consulted on particular issues.

The first research stage included a desk review of existing legislation, reports and analysis of data related to the overall housing conditions of Roma in Slovakia. This was followed by a review of specific data related to the Roma communities living in the municipalities concerned and government grants aimed at housing projects for Roma in those municipalities. New primary data was gathered through two three-day study visits to Val'kovňa and Nálepkovo in March 2009 which involved face to face interviews with respondents.

1. Background Information

1.1. Historical and Social Background

In Czechoslovakia under the communist regime, housing was seen as a social service guaranteed by the state. Between 1945 and 1990 about 3,700,000 new dwellings were built (i.e. two thirds of the existing dwelling stock). At the same time, the maintenance of the older housing was neglected.[4] The flats in old residential houses built during the interwar period or earlier were considered to be inferior (because of a lack of modern amenities and poor conditions or old-fashioned architecture) and were predominantly allocated to Roma.[5]

In some cases, Roma from underdeveloped rural settlements were moved to newly-built apartment blocks by the communist authorities. The state carried out this policy without preparing the Roma for living in this new type of urban dwelling.[6] As a consequence, these new flats were sometimes damaged because of inappropriate use, which fed existing negative stereotypes and myths about systematic destruction of new dwellings by Roma inhabitants. Since then, the public perception of any initiative aiming to improve housing conditions of Roma is extremely negative. Thus, such initiatives are seen as politically risky.

The social and economic transition after the fall of the communist regime in 1989 strongly affected Roma. The negative consequences of the economic transformation and subsequent reduction of social welfare had a greater impact on them than any of the new opportunities brought about by economic and political freedom.[7] Roma were among the first to lose their jobs due to their low level of education; the shift in the economy away from the low-qualified labour force; and also racial discrimination.[8]

The transformation in the area of housing after 1989 brought important changes in financing of housing and the state's housing policy.[9] Easily accessible loans and repayable subsidies for the development of housing were abolished. Suddenly, housing was no longer a right guaranteed by a "paternalistic" state (through policies of 'allocated housing') and acquiring it became a personal responsibility, like for any market commodity. State-owned housing was transferred to municipalities and subsequently privatised. Tenants were given the right to buy their dwellings at a low price set by the state. An overwhelming majority of tenants took advantage of that right by the end of 1990s[10] and in most cases, only the housing occupied by socially and economically disadvantaged households remained under the ownership of municipalities. This was the case of many apartments inhabited by Roma in the historical town centres. As these centres developed, such properties became attractive leading to efforts to expel their Roma tenants.[11]

Within the process of decentralisation of public policy-making at the turn of the century, the responsibility for housing policy was transferred to municipalities. They became the competent authority to decide on urban and rural planning, housing development methods and procedures, development of infrastructure facilities, management and maintenance of municipal dwellings, etc. According to the new decentralisation legislation, a municipality shall 'carry out its own investment and business activities in order to satisfy the needs of its inhabitants and its municipal development'.[12] The central government kept only normative powers related to technical and health protection regulations and control over financial support instruments, namely government grants for municipalities.

The communist centrally controlled system was replaced by a set of supportive instruments which aimed at empowering and stimulating individuals and legal entities (mainly municipalities) to acquire accommodation through purchasing or renting housing. These supportive instruments include loans, credits, tax relief, forms of guarantees, saving bonus and other tools. The *Štátny fond rozvoja bývania (ŠFRB) [State Housing Development Fund (SHDF)]*, established in 1996[13] and currently governed according to new legislation from 2003,[14] offers low-interest loans and limited contributions for construction or purchase of new dwellings and interest subsidies (grants to cover a portion of interest on commercial loans provided by banks).[15] Special grants (covering 30 to 80 per cent of the provision costs) are available for municipalities' rental housing projects.

The Slovak welfare reform in 2003 and 2004 brought radical cuts in social benefits which made many unable to pay rent and utilities. The new social aid system introduced a flat-rate housing benefit regardless of the real costs of housing, which often substantially exceeded the amount of the benefit (even in some cases in social housing). As of the beginning of 2009, the amount of housing benefit was 52.12 EUR per month for a single person household and 83.32 EUR per month for a household of more than one person.

However, only about a half of poor households in Slovakia is actually entitled to housing benefits[16] as a result of the provisions of the Law on Assistance in Material Need,[17] which requires firstly, a legal lease for a dwelling and, secondly, evidence of regular payment of the rent and utilities or having a debt repayment schedule agreed with the owner of the dwelling. The first condition excludes the inhabitants of informal Roma settlements from entitlement to housing benefit. The second condition excludes families that have accumulated large debts.[18] As there are no social services to help tenants clear their unpaid rent debts or other housing-related services, Roma are often forcibly evicted because of their debts.

In the case of misuse of cash benefits intended to cover basic needs, including housing, by recipients a *osobitný príjemca* [special receiver][19] can be assigned to collect and spend the cash on behalf of the beneficiary by the *Úrad práce, sociálnych vecí a rodiny (ÚPSVaR)* [Office of Labour, Social Affairs and Family (OLSAF)] upon request by a municipality (and in particular cases even individuals or other legal entities) to a recipient person or family. OLSAF can appoint the municipality (or any individual or other legal entity) as special receiver without the consent of the social aid recipient.

The special receiver is an effective remedy for settling debts and ensuring regular future payments where tenants have accumulated debts or are overdue with payments. It enables an agreement to be reached whereby payments by instalment are made to clear debt, it halts eviction and it enables the receiver to collect the housing allowance directly in order to secure regular future payment of rent. But many municipalities are unwilling to adopt the special receiver instrument, because they see this as an additional administrative burden. Evictions are regularly initiated by the municipalities without resorting to the special receiver option.

1.2. Housing Situation of Roma

A large-scale socio-graphic mapping study of Roma communities was conducted in 2003–2004.[20] The following information on the housing situation of Roma is based on the findings of this study, published in the *Atlas of Roma Communities*.[21] The study discovered that approximately 60 per cent of Roma live integrated/dispersed among the general population. The remaining 40 per cent live in urban or rural concentrations (170 communities), in settlements located on the edge of municipalities (338 communities) or in settlements separated from the general population by a distance or a natural or artificial barrier (284 communities).[22]

Only 19 per cent of the settlements have a sewage system, 41 per cent have gas, 63 per cent have a running water distribution system and 91 per cent have access to electricity. These figures only reflect access, as in settlements with access to relevant infrastructure not all the households are actually connected to them. Only 13 per cent of dwellings in Roma settlements are connected to a sewage system, 15 per cent to gas, 39 per cent to water and 89 per cent to electricity (both legally and illegally). 20 per cent of Roma settlements lack standard road access. According to the study the quality of life in settlements distanced from residential centres of the majority population is lower.

The *Atlas of Roma Communities* defines a segregated Roma settlement as being situated on the edge of a municipality or at a distance from a municipality without access to a water supply network, in which more than 20 per cent of the housing is informal. The mapping identified 149 such settlements; more than 80 per cent of them are located in rural areas. Forty-six settlements were found to have practically no infrastructure (no water, sewage or gas system and no road access). Of these 46 settlement units, 12 do not even have electricity. Most of these settlements are located in the regions of Košice and Prešov (eastern Slovakia), which are the poorest regions of Slovakia with the highest percentage of Roma population. These settlements have 4,460 permanent residents.

Concerning housing types, 55.5 per cent of Roma in non-integrated settlements occupy standard brick family houses, 26.1 per cent in dwellings in residential buildings, 14.1 per cent in makeshift accommodation, 2.4 per cent in wooden houses and the rest in non-standard shelters (including tents, greenhouses, caravans and others). In settlements located out of municipalities up to 21 per cent of the inhabitants live in makeshift accommodation.

About one third of the households in non-integrated settlements live in informal housing, including a wide range of housing types: from standard brick family houses, wooden houses and inhabited non-residential buildings to makeshift accommodation, caravans, tents or other non-standard housing. The highest ratio (45.4 per cent) of informal housing is in settlements located beyond the boundaries of municipalities. An informal dwelling cannot be legally connected to running water, gas, sewage or electricity and inhabitants of such dwellings are not entitled to housing benefits.

1.3. Institutional Response to the Situation

Many socially excluded Roma do not have sufficient income to either build, buy or rent adequate housing. Their income consists mostly of social welfare benefits, occasionally this is supplemented by cash or rewards for odd jobs. Most Roma in need—young families or people who lost their previous housing—find shelter with their families in overcrowded dwellings. Others build housing themselves, from any materials available on any ground available. Such illegal constructions, often on private property do not meet any technical or safety standards. The majority of such makeshift accommodation in Roma settlements was constructed after the fall of the communist regime.

The main government initiative to improve housing for lower-income families is the *Program rozvoja bývania* [Housing Development Program], first adopted in 2001,[23] and administered by the *Ministerstvo výstavby a regionálneho rozvoja Slovenskej republiky (MVRR SR)* [Ministry of Construction and Regional Development of the Slovak Republic (MCRD SR)]. It includes several grants, including a scheme for the procurement of municipal rental housing and another for the construction of infrastructure. Only municipalities (or non-for-profit organisations established by municipalities) can receive these grants and their involvement is optional. The Housing Development Program is an example of affirmative action, as part of its annual budget is allocated to improve the housing of marginalised Roma communities. Eligible costs for the construction of infrastructure in Roma settlements are higher than for other projects (due to their remote location). For example, in 2007 the MCDR SR funded the construction of 374 dwellings in 21 municipalities with a total budget of 5,546,306 EUR and the construction of technical infrastructure in 11 Roma settlements with a total budget of 380,668 EUR.[24]

The Housing Development Program supports the development of two types of municipal rental housing.[25] The first type is the *common-standard housing* (up to 80 m² with better fixtures and fittings). Construction grants cover up to 30 per cent of costs[26] with the remainder covered by the municipality, either from its budget or through a loan. The second, (more usual) type is the *lower-standard housing* with a higher share of financial contribution by the MCRD SR and a lower construction cost. The grant for dwellings up to 40m² (where costs do not exceed 496 EUR per m²) covers 80 per cent of the cost. For dwellings between 40 and 60 m² (with a cost per m2 not exceeding 473 EUR) the grant covers 75 per cent of the cost. The remaining 20 or 25 per cent of the building cost is covered by the municipality. The original intention of the MCRD SR was for future tenants themselves to help in the construction of their housing, thus acquiring a sense of ownership. However for several reasons this does not fully work in practice, as will be seen in the cases of Val'kovňa and Nálepkovo.

The second *lower-standard housing*[27] type has considerably more modest fixtures and fittings than the first type. Until 2006, to qualify as *lower-standard housing* a dwelling had to contain at least the following elements: cement floor, plastering and painting of walls, washbowl, oil paint around washbowl, hot water boiler, shower/bath, flush toilets, local heating system and outlets for kitchen installation. After 2006, some of these elements, such as the shower/bath, flush toilets, local heating system were not included. The MCRD SR justified this by citing alleged damages by their Roma occupants, though this was not verified through independent monitoring.[28] In 2007, the Bratislava-based *Nadácia Milana Šimečku (NMŠ)* [Milan Simecka Foundation (MSF)] conducted independent systematic monitoring of almost all municipal housing projects in Roma settlements implemented between 2001 and 2007 through government grants (83 projects in 68 municipalities).[29] This showed that damages occurred only in certain individual cases. For example, of 39 cases examined, the washbowl and shower-bath were removed only in 3 cases, the windows in one case and the local heating system in 7 cases. However, it also showed problems with the quality of the new housing. In many cases the new dwellings were defective or did not contain the required equipment, for example missing boilers, shower-baths, heating system, washbowls, and even toilets. The poor construction quality seems to have had a stronger effect on the technical condition of the new housing than careless use. The MSF study raises a number of questions and shows the need for systematic independent quality control of construction and delivery of new housing, as well as independent monitoring of tenants' treatment of the accommodation.

The 2005 MCRD SR strategy concerning the housing of vulnerable groups, *Dlhodobá koncepcia bývania marginalizovaných skupín obyvatel'stva a model jej financovania* [Long-term Concept of Housing for Marginalised Population Groups and Its Funding Model] states that the 'selection of locality for the building may not deepen segregation and has to be a tool for the integration of the concerned community; [t]his can be measured through spatial distance and access to public services used jointly by the majority and minority populations of the municipality'.[30] Yet, in reality, this important principle is not translated into adequately specific evaluation criteria for awarding Housing Development Program grants.

According to MSF, in more than 90 per cent of cases of construction of new housing for Roma the degree of segregation was maintained or even aggravated. The MSF concluded that while the Housing Development Program in general improves the life conditions of Roma, it does not foster integration of Roma and non-Roma, because it retains or even deepens spatial segregation.[31]

2. THE CASE OF VAL'KOVŇA

2.1. Project Description

Title of the project is *Construction of social housing in Val'kovňa*.

The **organisation leading implementation** was *Obecný úrad Val'kovňa* [Municipality of Val'kovňa].

The government support provided by the MCRD SR within the Housing Development Program is a **type of initiative** focused on the development of municipal rental housing for low-income families; the grants are aimed at the construction of new housing and the local technical infrastructure for those dwellings. The **rationale for this project** was to address the necessity of new housing for Roma living in overcrowded private family houses or substandard housing conditions.

The **objective of the project** at the time it was initiated (early 2000) was to construct 17 dwellings for Roma and the relevant technical infrastructure for those dwellings. Later, after discussions in the municipal council, the project's scope was reduced to 10 dwellings in two flat-blocks: one composed of 4 dwellings and the other composed of 6 dwellings.

The project included several **main activities**: the selection of construction placement and purchase of the lot by the municipality, the preparation of technical documentation, the construction of the housing and technical infrastructure for the housing and the selection of tenants.

With regards to the **time frame** of the project, the MCRD SR approved the grant for construction in 2000 and construction started in 2001 and was completed in 2002; the occupants moved in on 1st January 2009. The technical infrastructure was built simultaneously with the housing.

The **location** was near the municipal office, between the centre of the hamlet of Val'kovňa and four Roma family houses.

The project's **target group** was defined as young families living with their parents in overcrowded family houses and specifically the occupants of a 19th century brick house and a barn in the village of Val'kovňa, a small municipality of approximately 360 inhabitants, more than half of them Roma. Most Roma lived in four standard brick family houses built during the communist regime, when they were employed in nearby factories. As the children of the original owners started their own families, the houses became overcrowded. One Roma family lived in an brick house from the 19th century in the centre of Val'kovňa, which was in a bad state of repair and several related nuclear families lived in an old wooden barn each occupying one room or one of the new annexes to the house with their children. The building had not been maintained and faced imminent risk of collapse, while lacking a supply of potable water, which had to be carried from nearby wells.

The **budget** of the original project of 17 dwellings was 12 million SKK (398,327 EUR); half of which was granted by the SHDF and the other half was sourced through a bank loan. As the municipality reduced the scope of the project, the budget was reduced to six million Slovak koruna (199,163 EUR). The construction was funded by the grant at the beginning and by a bank loan to the municipality from April 2002. The repayment plan is set at

30 years, payable in monthly instalments of 14,500 SKK (481 EUR). Together with the housing, the existing municipal public utilities infrastructure was extended to reach the dwellings. The total budget for the construction of a new sewage plant and connections to the water and electricity supply system was approximately two million SKK (66,388 EUR). The municipality received a grant of 980,000 SKK (32,530 EUR) and the remainder had to be provided by the municipality.

2.2. Main Elements

Initially the majority of the village and the municipal council strongly opposed the construction of new housing for Roma. **Co-operation with others** was thus crucial for the implementation of the project. The former mayor managed to overcome initial opposition in the municipal council with the help of OPGRC[32] officials, the regional government and human rights activists who attended several meetings of the municipal council and also spoke with Roma. During the final vote, the former mayor requested the Roma to be present. Describing the event, the former mayor said that the Roma: 'were in the room and the others were in front of the municipal office. Each councillor had to vote individually. And then all the councillors had to sign the resolution so that they would not impeach the decision later. That helped.'[33]

Elements of innovation and creativity: Unlike the majority of municipalities in Slovakia, Va kov a selected the higher *common-standard housing* type, even though this required higher (50 per cent) co-funding by the municipality. The former mayor explained: 'From other mayors in Eastern Slovakia, who had experiences in this kind of project, I knew that the future tenants would not be able to work off the 20 per cent of the construction costs as expected by the government. So in the end the municipality would have to apply for a loan to cover these costs anyway. Thus I decided to ask for a higher loan in order to build it properly. And the instalments of the municipality's credit are included in the rent.'

Loan repayments amounting to 1,450 SKK—48.10 EUR are included in the rent of the ten dwellings, as well as an advance payment for the water supply (200 SKK—6.64 EUR), sewage plant (150 SKK—4.98 EUR) and contribution to a maintenance fund (250 SKK—8.30 EUR) for repairs. Thus, monthly payment totals 2,050 SKK (68.02 EUR) excluding electricity bills.

Applicants for the new housing had to pay *an advance rent* of 4,500 SKK (149.37 EUR) to allow the municipality to start paying loan instalments in

April 2002, before they could move in. 'The municipality had a bad cash flow, so I needed some money from the future tenants. Those who gave me 4,500 SKK immediately got the rent lease. Maybe it was not conforming to law, but I needed it, because I did not have the money for the loan instalments,' explained the former mayor.

Although the project was about the construction of new housing, a **multifaceted approach** can be identified in the broader engagement of the municipality with the local Roma community: 'It is a long-term process. We have established a community centre, a kindergarten and the children who go there are much more successful in school; teachers acknowledge it. Thanks to all this, no child was placed in a special school,[34] all of them were prepared to go to standard school,' added the former mayor.

Others echo the view that better housing conditions have a positive impact on education and health: 'The conditions are healthier; family members have more privacy, everyone can find their own place. We see the difference in school. It is silly to concentrate solely on education itself and ignore other spheres [of life]. A child cannot learn in a kennel with trodden earth floor, where it is freezing cold and where rats will eat the school-books.'[35]

The local **Roma community was involved** in project implementation during the phases of flat allocation, housing and infrastructure construction. In order to cope with the compulsory co-funding of the infrastructure construction, the municipality prepared a public works project and submitted it to OLSAF. Using project funds the municipality employed one person on a full time basis from each future family of tenants for the minimal monthly wage of 6,600 SKK (219 EUR) to provide labour for infrastructure construction.

The new housing was intended for two groups: those living in the old wooden barn and some of the young families from the brick family houses belonged to the same extended family, while the inhabitants of the old house in the village were not related to the first group. The two groups have different lifestyles and this was taken into account in their placement as one group lives in the six-dwelling block and the other in the four-dwelling block.

Interaction between tenants and the municipality is facilitated by community workers, who intervene in case of problems with paying the rent or other housing costs, but, reportedly, not always effectively: 'The mayor put the community workers in charge of negotiating with the tenants in order to recover the debts and set up repayment timetables. But the problem is that the tenants do not respect them in these matters, because they know that the dwellings are owned by the municipality and it is up to the mayor to make the decisions. And the mayor does not want to get involved in conflicts with tenants, because they are either his relatives, or potential voters in the election.'[36]

There has been no **specific focus on providing special support to women**: 'We do not really have any women living alone, they live together with their relatives. The solidarity within the families is very strong.'[37]

The project took into account **disability** incorporating a special design for one flat and providing a specially designed bathroom for an elderly man with a physical disability, who unfortunately died before he could move into the new housing.

There was no particular focus on **old age**. Professionals working with Roma and the Roma themselves told us that the older generation is not a specially disadvantaged group in these Roma communities, as they have a regular income. In contrast to the younger generation, where unemployment is high, they worked and paid social insurance contributions under the communist regime, so they receive pensions: 'The elderly have their old-age pensions and disabled persons often have disability pensions. Thus, low income single parents are the most vulnerable group. If there is any selection of tenants for housing, income is taken into consideration in order to ensure that the tenant will be able to pay the rent.'[38]

The **main difficulties** the project faced related to the negative reactions of local non-Roma, as the former mayor explained: 'The whole municipality was against me, it nearly cost me my post, and there were rumours that they wanted to physically eliminate me. Nobody gave me support except my family. Also the councillors were asking "Why housing?" Yet all this was happening only because the housing was intended for Roma.' The project was proposed by the former mayor and was originally approved by the municipal council. 'They have done so only because they wanted to have rest from Roma. They wanted to be out of it and make me responsible,' she said. When the project was approved by MCRD SR in 2000, the council cancelled the project. Finally, after some turbulent discussions, the council approved a more limited plan for the construction of ten dwellings.

The former mayor believes that her attempt to help the Roma cost her the electoral support of non-Roma residents.[39] 'The entire street was alarmed, there was a petition against [the housing]. They were not interested what kind of Roma had to move in; in fact decent people live there,' agreed another respondent.[40] When the construction works started, several cases of sabotage were recorded. 'Construction machines were damaged, cars' tires intentionally punctured, material stolen at night, the police had to watch the site.'[41]

No formal **impact assessment or other evaluation** of the project has been conducted by local authorities or by the MCRD SR. The essential element for the success of a housing project for Roma is, according to the former mayor, close contact with the Roma community throughout the design, promotion and implementation stages.

There is no evidence that lessons learned from this project had any direct **impact on law and policy** at national or regional level, although the case of Va kov a is often cited by the MCRD SR as an example of good practice of local policy of housing for Roma and evidence of efficiency and effectiveness of the national Roma inclusion policy.[42]

A key element for the **sustainability** of the project was the prevention of problems with the payment of rent and the other housing costs. This was achieved by ensuring that rent is lower than the housing benefit, which is paid by the state welfare system. In this way if a household qualifies for the benefit, it will be able to pay the rent without depending too much on its own income. Together with the 'special receiver' procedure, which is applied when tenants have problems paying the rent regularly, this ensures that the municipality can repay the loan it took for the new housing.

The former mayor solved problems with irregular rent payments by applying the special receiver procedure: 'If somebody stopped paying, the municipality became the special receiver and got the whole amount of the welfare benefit. When the debt was settled, or if it would soon be settled, the person was again entitled to get the housing benefit too, which covered the rent.'[43]

The main features of the present initiative which are worthy to serve as an example for other similar initiatives aimed at housing of Roma or other vulnerable groups represent the project's **transferability** potential. Interviewees identified these as: the choice of a location within the mainstream population, which prevented the creation of a ghetto and enabled access to public services; the use of the *common-standard housing* design rather than the *lower-standard housing*; and an ingenious use of the diverse tools available (government grants, bank loan, public interest works project, special receiver mechanism), which enabled the achievement of positive results through quality materials and good construction.

When speaking about the **most important lessons learnt** within the present project, the interviewees pointed out the importance of the strong personal effort of the former mayor who was the motivating force behind the whole project.[44] She was able to undertake such a project because of her strong position as she had been in this post for a long time and could rely on several other persons.

But ultimately, it would seem that the initiative cost her the post of mayor. It is possible that the problems which occurred could have been avoided through more intensive dialogue with the non-Roma.[45]

Additionally, families grew and the dwellings were at risk of becoming over-crowded. Each family was given a flat, yet in the meanwhile, in two households the second generation of tenants started their own families, while living with their parents. Before long, the new housing will be insufficient again and the problem of the lack of housing capacity in the village will resurface.

2.3. Reflections

The example of Val'kovňa is not a typical case. It demonstrates the crucial role of the **personal commitment** of a local leader and the **strategic use of existing tools**. The system of social assistance in the area of housing in Slovakia is based on the initiative of local government to ensure that action corresponds to actual local needs. However, this entails the risk that local political leaders might avoid engaging in 'unpopular' initiatives, such as improving Roma housing.

In the case of Val'kovňa the former mayor met with **resistance from the non Roma majority**, but managed to get support from government agencies and a Bratislava-based NGO *Liga aktivistov pre ľudské práva* [League of Activists for Human Rights] using their influence and pressure from the beneficiaries to promote the project at the municipal council.

Three particularly positive aspects of this project can be highlighted. The decision to treat Roma equally by providing **higher quality housing**, the choice of a location within the **central zone of the municipality** to avoid segregation, and setting the **rent below the level of the housing benefit** to make this type of housing affordable by poorer families.

The application of **clear rules and sanctions** for non payment, such as applying the special receiver procedure and/or the non-renewal of the lease supports the **sustainability of the project** provided that these rules are rigorously applied.

In the long term the need to provide subsidised housing capacity will rise again, as the majority of local Roma are unemployed. Regional economic development leading to increased employment opportunities is therefore necessary for a long term sustainable solution to the housing problems.

3. The Case of Nálepkovo

3.1. Project Description

The **title of the project** is *Rómska osada Nálepkovo* [Roma Settlement Nálep-kovo]—phases I to III.

The **organisation leading implementation** was *Obecný úrad Nálepkovo* [Municipality of Nálepkovo].[46]

The **type of initiative** is the development of municipal rental housing for low-income families with government support provided by the MCRD SR within the Housing Development Program; the grants are aimed at the construction of new housing and local technical infrastructure to those dwellings. The **rationale of the present project** was the necessity of new housing for the Roma living in overcrowded private family houses or substandard housing conditions. Nálepkovo has approximately 3,000 residents, more than 45 per cent Roma, who live in the core zone of the village in old houses, often very overcrowded and in three segregated settlements. The place of residence is important , as it contributes to the determination of social status within the Roma community.

The **objective of the initiative** was to provide Roma in need with adequate new housing by constructing housing in three phases: The first phase included 16 new detached and semi-detached houses in Grün; the second 28 flats in seven blocks in the same location; and the third phase 20 flats in five blocks in Píla.

The **main activities** of the first phase included the construction of a water supply system, sewerage system and plant, and road access, as well as the construction of a community centre in Grün, which now serves as a kindergarten. An important element of the project was the establishment of a micro-loan scheme for home improvement or furniture.

According to the information provided by a municipal officer, in 1938 there were no Roma living in the village. According to the land registry at the time they lived in makeshift accommodation in the area called then *Cigánska osada* ('Gypsy Colony'), two kilometres away from the village. This area is today called *Grün*. During the communist period, almost all its inhabitants moved either to the village or to the other municipalities where they worked, or into a 24-unit apartment block built by the government in the 1970s, halfway between the *Grün* and the village. After the fall of the communist regime, ownership of the block of flats was transferred to the municipality, which transformed it into municipal rental housing. Next to it some Roma families built four brick family houses by themselves, and during the 1990s several makeshift homes appeared.

The 16 new dwellings built in Grün were intended for some of the inhabitants of the overcrowded flats in the old communist era building.

The first phase started in 1994 and was completed in 1998. In the second phase, 1997–2004, another 28 dwellings were constructed there. In the third phase, 2004–2006, the municipality built 20 new dwellings in Píla located by the main road between Nálepkovo and Gelnica, approximately 1,5 kilometres from the municipality. This new housing, consisting of five blocks with four flats each, was constructed between an old wooden house next to a stream, occupied by about 80 Roma, and an old farm owned by a non-Roma, who eventually sold it and moved to the village.

In the winter of 2008 the stream flooded the old wooden house and the municipality accommodated its Roma occupants temporarily in army tents behind the new buildings at Píla and demolished the old house. The Roma spent the winter in tents using small iron stoves for heating and shared one cold water hydrant and one latrine between about 80 people. This situation attracted media attention and the municipality moved some to four mobile wooden cabins. Now the municipality is considering undertaking the fourth phase of the construction of new housing for Roma to address the urgent cases of those living in tents and cabins.[47]

When the first phase of the initiative started in 1994, the SHDF[48] had not yet been set up and the municipality ensured **funding** for the project through joint grants from the former *Ministerstvo výstavby a verejných prác Slovenskej republiky (MVVP SR)* [Ministry of Construction and Public Works (MCPW SR)], the EU pre-accession fund PHARE-PALMIF (Pro-Active Labour Market Intervention Fund) and the municipality's own budget. In order to make the project eligible for the PHARE-PALMIF, the municipality created 20 jobs for a period of two years; those workers were trained and participated in the construction of the new settlement. The overall budget of the activities in Grün between 1994 and 1998 (first phase) exceeded 18 million SKK (597,490 EUR), where the direct investment of the municipality amounted to ten million (331,939 EUR) and the government grants to 7.5 million SKK (248,954 EUR). The second phase was funded from SHDF grants to the amount of 20.5 million SKK (680,475 EUR) and co-funded by the municipality. Within the third phase the SHDF provided a grant of more than 10.3 million SKK (341,897 EUR).

3.2. Main Elements

The municipality engaged in **cross-sectoral co-operation** with the *Fakulta architektúry Slovenskej technickej univerzity (FA STU)* [Faculty of Architecture of the Slovak University of Technology (FA SUT)], which elaborated a study of the new settlement in Grün in 1995. Later, in 2005 the municipality co-operated with an NGO in a microcredit project provided for both Roma and non-Roma residents, aiming at the improvement of their housing. This project *Skvalitnenie bývania rodín s nízkymi príjmami v Nálepkove* [Improvement of housing conditions of low-income families in Nálepkovo] was introduced in 2005 by the Košice-based non-governmental organisation ETP Slovakia and funded by Habitat for Humanity and the Open Society Institute.[49] The project benefits both Roma and non-Roma inhabitants of the village and provides accessible interest-free micro-loans of up to 40,000 SKK (1,327.76 EUR) to furnish or renovate housing. The loan contracts are signed between three subjects—ETP Slovakia, the receiver and the municipality which guarantees the repayment of the loan. Another option provided by the project for Roma families is a saving scheme for a specific aim determined in advance. Families save between 300 SKK (9.96 EUR) and 1,500 SKK (49.73 EUR) monthly and after an agreed period receive a 100 per cent bonus to the aggregated sum of money thus stimulating a "saving behaviour" and improving the management of personal or family resources.

According to a local authority representative, the loans helped to build **mutual trust** between the Roma and the municipality: 'There were no cases in which the receiver intentionally quit repaying the loan, although sometimes he/she did not receive the benefit and was delayed.'[50] In the case of problems with the repayment of the loan, the municipality applied the special receiver procedure.

Some tenants in Píla, however, were not happy that the municipality used part of the loan to equip the homes. A Roma respondent argued: 'They told me that I got a loan of 38,000 SKK (1,261.37 EUR), but only gave me 19,500 SKK (647.28 EUR). They said that for the rest we got the cooking range and the fitting in the bathroom; that they had bought it for us. But sometimes we were not happy with the equipment. We were forced to accept it. Those who wanted to live in these houses had to do so.'[51]

In its efforts to provide **innovative and creative solutions**, a FA SUT[52] team prepared several alternative designs for the new settlement, including a circle-shaped cluster of houses with a common fireplace in the centre and blacksmith hearths in the individual houses. The architects designed a wooden house project, which was intended to reflect Roma needs and cultural traditions, based, arguably, more on romantic stereotypes rather than knowledge of current needs of Roma: 'They wanted to adopt it to the Roma culture. It is all nice, but it does not work like this anymore.'[53]

Only one wooden house was built according to the innovative design of the FA SUT, and according to respondents it is not functional: 'The inhabitants of the wooden house are desperate, all the rooms in the house are triangular, so they are unable to furnish it properly; they would have to buy made-to-measure furniture, but they do not have money for that.'[54] After that experience, the municipality continued building using more conventional design.[55] Some were later published by the MCRD SR and used in many other municipalities. The municipality also tested new construction technologies within the first phase.

A **multifaceted approach** was not designed as an integral part of the housing project and was applied only after the first and second phase of the construction had been completed and tenants had moved in. Since 2004, the ETP Slovakia also operated a community centre at Grün: 'They helped establish informal groups, taught people how to prepare projects. Together with people living in the village, they prepared a project for the embellishment of their streets, with benches and greenery.'[56] Now the community centre is closed and in its place a kindergarten operates at Grün. The ETP Slovakia's micro-credit project also offered household financial management courses.

The principle of **non-discrimination and equality is not evident in the selection of the location and the Roma community was not involved in this process.** Although the remote location was arguably chosen as there were no other available sites closer to the centre of the village, the municipality built two *common-standard* rental housing blocks occupied only by non-Roma, one in the very centre of the village and the other at the edge of the village in the direction of Píla. The Roma community became involved in the allocation of housing: A Roma respondent confirmed this: 'People had to indicate where they wanted to live, to choose their neighbours in order to avoid conflicts among them. We are all relatives living in these flats next to each other.'[57]

Regular interaction with the municipal Commission on Housing and Social Affairs takes the form of regular inspections of Roma families living in new municipal rental units. According to a respondent, 'The committee inspects the condition of the flats, because after the first phase was completed, some families removed and sold some of the equipment. Now we want to keep watching, so that something similar does not happen again.'[58] Roma inhabitants complain that these inspections do not help them to resolve problems: 'If something breaks down or if there is mould on the walls, we indicate it to the committee. They record it in their papers, but nothing happens.'[59] There is no information on similar inspection visits to non-Roma tenants in municipal dwellings.

The project did not include any **specific focus on vulnerable subgroups** of Roma. Within the selection of the future tenants, the condition of financial capacity implicitly excluded single-parent households who live only from the parental benefits or low social benefits: 'Such people live together with their parents; they would not have enough money to live on their own. If they got new housing, they got it together with their parents.'[60] For persons with disabilities, one of the conditions for the SHDF grants is to reserve at least one per cent of the new dwellings (or at least one dwelling) for the disabled and to make it accessible. As there is no such tenant today, the barrier-free dwelling is occupied by a non-disabled tenant. 'Within each of the three phases, there was one barrier-free flat. The leases are for a limited period of time, for one year. If there is a disabled applicant, we will have to accommodate him/her and the tenant in the barrier-free flat will have to leave. According to a respondent, 'There was no request by elderly Roma for special assistance from the municipality, probably because of the strong family solidarity among Roma where relatives always take care of the elderly.'[61] No special attention was given to gender aspects.

The **main difficulty** in the implementation of the housing project relates to the conditions of government grants requiring that future tenants work off a portion of the construction costs. Some respondents expressed doubts if this would be feasible: 'It is impossible for them to cover 20 per cent of the costs. As they are generally unskilled workers, there were no qualified workers for the necessary tasks; they can only dig foundations for the housing and move materials. This work can represent ten per cent of costs at most. So the municipality paid the difference in cash. The situation is different with the infrastructure. There the grant is only up to 70 per cent, but Roma are able to work off the remaining 30 per cent of the costs.'[62]

No formal **impact assessment or other evaluation** of the project has been conducted either by local authorities or the MCRD SR who provided the grant. However, the tenants of all Roma settlements were critical of the long distance to the village. As Píla is located on the main road, there is a bus connection to the centre of the village, but those living in Prvý hámor or Grün, including school children, have to walk. 'I am afraid that children might trip up over the scrap next to the road when they go to or from school. I used to accompany my children, but now I cannot so they have to go alone,' complained a Romani woman.[63] Another Roma respondent said, 'It is too far. You cannot just walk to the village when you need something. A woman cannot go alone for shopping. ... [A]t least there should be a sidewalk; now we must walk on the main road, where there are cars. Four or five months ago a car killed a boy there.'[64] Roma tenants also highlighted the inferior construction quality, especially mould, which appears in the walls of many dwellings.

The municipality of Nálepkovo was among the first in Slovakia to design and implement a Roma housing project; at the time national housing policy did not systematically deal with this issue. Thus the Nálepkovo experience had an **impact on the formation of a specific national policy** on Roma housing. Tools, such as the SHDF grant scheme for municipalities, were inspired by this pioneering project. According to a local authority representative, 'When we started the first phase, the building authority did not want to give us the authorisation for construction, because they said the dwellings were too small and cannot be considered as housing; in 1992 the concept of social housing was unknown. So we built them without authorisation and made them legal post facto. Then the legislation changed and the second phase was already built in line with the regulations of MCDR SR.'[65] On the other hand, the new support system did not favour individual houses, which, according to the respondent, are more suitable for Roma: 'SHDF grants have strict limits and everything exceeding them must be paid by the municipality. We started with individual houses, but then had to continue with blocks of several dwellings, because it is cheaper.'[66]

Some of the projects used in Nálepkovo were **mainstreamed** by the MCRR SR, which published a catalogue of model plans for low-cost housing, to be used by other municipalities taking into consideration the financial constraints of the grant scheme.

The municipality is aware of the **limited sustainability** of the initiative due to the demographic growth of the local population and its limited capacity to afford to use their own funds to buy or build houses by themselves: 'If they do not have sufficient income, they are wholly dependent on the help of authorities. In the local Roma community, only four persons are employed.'[67] Another related issue is the high demand for maintenance.[68]

On the other hand, some respondents believe that the experience and interaction between the Roma and the municipality, especially concerning the micro-credit scheme, had a **positive effect in developing mutual trust**: 'They really got to know each other. The municipality doesn't perceive the clients who regularly repay the loan as before. He or she starts to be considered more reliable by the municipality.'[69]

Some of the innovations tested in Nálepkovo were **transferred** to other municipalities. Besides the project documentation, which was published in the MCRD SR catalogue, the micro-credit scheme was implemented by the ETP Slovakia in other places (e. g. Svinia, Moldava nad Bodvou, Šimonovce).[70] But, according to a former ETP staff member, the other municipalities were afraid to act as guarantors in loan contracts. They were concerned that if Roma tenants stopped repaying the loans, the municipality would be responsible for it.

Perhaps the most **important lesson** learnt from the Nálepkovo experience is the crucial role of micro-grants: 'Municipalities must build housing for Roma. But it is extremely challenging for the municipal budget. The intensity of the SHDF support was reduced to 75 per cent of the costs and people are not able to work off the rest. For that money you can only build empty rooms, without equipment, without any fittings. So the tenants have to participate, either they have to save money or take out a loan.'[71]

3.3. Reflections

The case of Nálepkovo is a rare example of a **proactive and innovative approach** implemented with a **long-term perspective** by a relatively small municipality. The municipality has invested a considerable amount of money from its **own municipal resources** into the housing projects and did not rely entirely on the financial assistance from the central government. This is quite an exception, as the majority of municipalities in Slovakia usually consent to be involved in projects focused on Roma only under the condition that it will not cost them anything and that the whole initiative is in the hands of another agent, typically NGOs. The municipality of Nálepkovo was able to combine a range of existing funding sources in order to achieve its objective.

The experience of **co-operation between the municipality and an NGO** active in the area of housing improvements was particularly positive. The principle of multi-source solutions was transferred to the individual level, when the tenants of the new dwellings were provided with basic equipment, which they can complete with the help of accessible micro-loans and savings programmes. This idea, concerning minimum government standards and the personal engagement of tenants to make improvements, merits being transferred to other municipalities. The implementation of the micro-loan project would be much more risky without the municipality's guarantee.

The main drawback of this project is that it failed to address the problem of **segregation**. Whether intentional or not it does not contribute to integration and Roma inclusion.

The **low quality of housing** is another issue. While some of these problems could be due to testing new technologies, the municipality should have taken corrective action. The well-intentioned co-operation with experts from the FA

SUT in the planning phase should have relied more on consultation with future tenants to better inform them of the real needs of the Roma and allow them to develop realistic and innovative solutions, such as, for example, modular housing models, which can be extended as a household grows.

Similarly as in the case of Val'kovňa the **sustainability** of the project's effects is doubtful, because of the rapid rate of population growth. Thus, a sustainable housing policy needs to be supplemented by policies fostering economic growth that led to more employment opportunities and anti-discrimination measures to ensure that Roma are not excluded.

4. Lessons Learned

Given the structural disadvantages facing a large number of Roma persist assistance in housing from public authorities will be necessary. The experience from the implementation of housing projects, such as these presented here, could provide important insights regarding improvements to the existing grant system, for example the need to include Roma more actively in the design and implementation of housing projects, to empower and facilitate local government to overcome local prejudice and opposition and to stimulate social inclusion and desegregation.

Strong leadership can overcome popular disagreement, but it is also necessary to include the mainstream population in the activities and benefits of the project, or at least to balance the activities focused on Roma and non-Roma. A unilateral focus on one group can provoke a counter-reaction from the other. Furthermore, it is important to remember that what may appear as one Roma community can in reality be several diverse communities, each with different social solidarities, norms and controls and internal relationships.

Municipalities often lack the necessary knowledge or experience to develop effective and sustainable housing projects that can facilitate Roma inclusion. They therefore need support in developing a local housing policy with a clear desegregation and inclusion dimension. The high financial cost of such projects may also discourage local authorities and technical assistance in the form of applying innovative financing methods, such as public-private partnerships would be useful.

Finally, it is important to note that the outcome of housing projects can only provide useful guidance for the future, if it is independently evaluated through standardised formal monitoring and evaluation instruments.

Notes

1. This case study financed and edited by the FRA was developed by Mr Marek Hojsík and Ms Tatjana Peric on behalf of the European Roma Rights Centre (ERRC), Budapest, and Pavee Point Travellers Centre, Dublin.

2. Additional information on the housing situation of Roma in Slovakia gathered within this project can be found in the RAXEN National Focal Point 'Thematic Study on Housing Conditions of Roma and Travellers: Slovakia' available on http://fra.europa.eu.

3. There are no local NGOs operating in either municipality.

4. E. Havelková, B. Valentová (1998) 'Komparatívna analýza bytovej politiky v Slovenskej a Českej republike v rokoch 1990–1996', in: M. Potůček, I. Radičová (eds.) *Sociální politika v Čechách a na Slovensku po roce 1989*, Praha: Karolinum, p. 234.

5. A. Mušinka (2003) 'Roma Housing', in: M. Vašečka, M. Jurásková, T. Nicholson (eds.) *Čačipen pal o Roma: A Global report on Roma in Slovakia*, Bratislava: Inštitút pre verejné otázky, p. 385.

6. A. Mušinka (2003) 'Roma Housing', in: M. Vašečka, M. Jurásková, T. Nicholson (eds.) *Čačipen pal o Roma: A Global report on Roma in Slovakia*, Bratislava: Inštitút pre verejnéotázky, p. 379.

7. I. Radičová (2001) *Hic sunt Romales*, Bratislava: S.P.A.C.E., p. 103.

8. See for example: Council of Europe: European Commission Against Racism and Intolerance (ECRI)/*Third Report on Slovakia, Adopted on 27 June 2003*, (CRI(2004)4), available at: http://www.unhcr.org/refworld/docid/46efa2e53d1.html (24.05.2009).

9. E. Havelková, B. Valentová (1998) 'Komparatívna analýza bytovej politiky v Slovenskej a Českej republike v rokoch 1990–1996', in: M. Potůček, I. Radičová (eds.) *Sociální politika v Čechách a na Slovensku po roce 1989*, Praha: Karolinum, p. 237.

10. See: J. Zapletalova, M. Antalikova, E. Smatanova (2003) 'The Role of Self-government in Housing Development in Slovakia: Local Government and Housing in Slovakia', in: M. Lux (ed.) *Housing Policy: An End or a New Beginning?*, Budapest: LGI Books, pp. 293–351.

11. M. Hojsík et al. (2007) *Forced Evictions in Slovakia—2006 (Executive Summary)*, Bratislava: Nadácia Milana Šimečku, available at: http://www.nadaciamilanasimecku.sk/fileadmin/user_upload/dokumenty/Evictions_ENG_-_Web_version_22_Jan.pdf (22.03.2009).

12. Slovakia/Zákon č. 453/2001 Z. z. ktorým sa mení a dopĺňa zákon č. 369/1990 Zb. o obecnom zriadení v znení neskorších predpisov a menia a dopĺňajú sa niektoré ďalšie zákony (02.10.2001).

13. Slovakia/Zákon č. 124/1996 Z. z. o Štátnom fonde rozvoja bývania (27.03.1996).

14. lovakia/Zákon č. 607/2003 Z.z. o Štátnom fonde rozvoja bývania (06.11.2003).

15. J. Zapletalova, M. Antalikova, E. Smatanova (2003) 'The Role of Self-government in Housing Development in Slovakia: Local Government and Housing in Slovakia', in: M. Lux (ed.) *Housing Policy: An End or a New Beginning?*, Budapest: LGI Books, pp. 306–307.

16. By the end of 2008, only 92,082 households were entitled to receive housing benefits, compared to the total number of 153,516 households receiving social benefits; source: Slovakia/Ústredie práce, sociálnych vecí a rodiny (2009) *Štatistiky: Nezamestnanost' a sociálne dávky Február 2009*, available at: http://www.upsvar.sk/rsi/rsi.nsf/0/E95AC40BA6F6159EC125 75660031E9E7?OpenDocumen t (25.03.2009).

17. Slovakia/Zákon č. 599/2003 Z. Z. o pomoci v hmotnej núdzi (11.11.2003).

18. M. Hojsík et al. (2007) *Forced Evictions in Slovakia—2006 (Executive Summary)*, Bratislava: Nadácia Milana Šimečku, p. 5, available at: http://www.nadaciamilanasimecku.sk/fileadmin/user_upload/dokumenty/Evictions_ENG_-_Web_version_22_Jan.pdf (22.03.2009).

19. Slovakia/Zákon č. 599/2003 Z. z. o pomoci v hmotnej núdzi a o zmene a doplnení niektorých predpisov (11.11.2003).

20. The mapping covered 1,087 municipalities in Slovakia and identified 1,575 settlements described by their social environment as Roma. Roma communities have been identified through self-identification of their inhabitants or through identification by their social environment.

21. M. Jurásková, E. Kriglerová, J. Rybová (2004) *Atlas rómskych komunít na Slovensku 2004*, Bratislava: Úrad vlády SR. Some data are available at the webpage of the OPGRC: http://romovia.vlada.gov.sk/3554/list-faktov.php.

22. See Annex 1, Table 1.

23. Slovakia/Uznesenie vlády SR č. 335/2001 o k návrhu programu podpory výstavby obecných nájomných bytov odlišného štandardu, určených pre bývanie občanov v hmotnej núdzi ako i technickej vybavenosti v rómskych osadách (11.04.2001).

24. lovakia/Správa o činnosti Úradu splnomocnenca vlády SR pre rómske komunity za rok 2007 (Informatívny mteriál z rokovania vlády SR), Úrad vlády SR (21.05.2008).

25. Slovakia/Výnos Ministerstva výstavby a regionálneho rozvoja Slovenskej republiky č. V-2/2008 (21.11.2008).

26. See Annex 1, Table 2.

27. Slovakia/Výnos Ministerstva výstavby a regionálneho rozvoja Slovenskej republiky č V-2/2008 (21.11.2008).

28. Slovakia/Nariadenie vlády SR č. 406/2006 o podrobnostiach o požiadavkách na vnútorné prostredie budov a o minimálnych požia davách na byty nižšieho štandardu a na ubytovacie zariadenia (vyhodnotenie medzirezortného pripomienkového konanie) (10.05.2006).

29. See: M. Hojsík (2008) *Evaluácia obecných nájomných bytov v rómskych osídleniach*, Bratislava: Nadácia Milana Simečku, available at: http://www.nadaciamilanasimecku.sk/fileadmin/user_upload/dokumenty/Ine/Evalu__cia_FINAL.pdf (27.03.2009).

30. Slovakia/Uznesenie vlády SR č. 63/2005 (19.01.2005), available at: http://www.rokovania.sk/appl/material.nsf/0/6B89FF316E70A13EC1256F7B002F2A35?OpenDocument (27.03.2009).

31. M. Hojsík (2008) *Evaluácia obecných nájomných bytov v rómskych osídleniach*, Bratislava: Nadácia Milana Simečku, available at: http://www.nadaciamilanasimecku.sk/fileadmin/user_upload/dokumenty/Ine/Evalu__cia_FINAL.pdf (27.03.2009).

32. *Úrad splnomocnenkyne vlády Slovenskej republiky pre rómske komunity (ÚSVRK)* [Office of the Plenipotentiary of the Slovak Republic Government for Roma Communities (OPGRC)].

33. References to the 'former mayor' quoted from interview with Ms Mária Bobáková, former mayor of Val'kovňa, 10.03.2009.

34. Schools for children with mental disabilities

35. Interview with a local authority representative, Val'kovňa, 10.03.2009.

36. Interview with a non-Roma respondent, 10.03.2009.

37. Interview with a local authority representative, Val'kovňa, 10.03.2009.

38. Interview with a local authority representative, Val'kovňa, 10.03.2009.

39. A similar situation occurred in the Svinia municipality in Slovakia. The municipality of Svinia was included in a PHARE project SR 0103.02 'Infrastructure Support for Roma Settlements'. The municipality was due to receive a grant of 1.5 million EUR for construction of infrastructure for the Roma settlement, which would be beneficial for the whole population as no infrastructure was accessible in the village, where Habitat for Humanity would organise the construction of housing for Roma. However, in 2002 the majority population withdrew support to a reform-minded mayor who supported pro-Roma projects in order to stop the initiatives. See for example: Chee-Hong Brian Chung *Habitat for Humanity in Slovakia: The Roma of Svinia A Case Study* (2005), available at: http://elearning.hfhu.org/hfhu/documents/case/HFHU_Slovakia.pdf (29.04.2009).

40. Interview with a local authority representative, Val'kovňa, 10.03.2009.

41. Interview with Ms Mária Bobáková, former mayor of Val'kovňa, 10.03.2009.

42. In 2002, the Val'kovňa housing project was awarded with the first prize of MCRD SR sponsored competition *Progresívne a cenovo dotupné bývanie 2002, V. ročník* [Progressive and Cost-Accessible Housing 2002, 5th Volume] in the category 'Different standard housing'.

43. Interview with a local authority representative, Val'kovňa, 10.03.2009.

44. Interview with several Roma and non-Roma respondents, 10-11.03.2009.

45. Interview with a Roma respondent, 11.03.2009.

46. www.nalepkovo.sk.

47. Interview with a local authority representative, Nálepkovo, 17.03.2009.

48. *Štátny fond rozvoja bývania (ŠFRB) [State Housing Development Fund (SHDF)]*.

49. For more information on ETP Slovakia ('Centre for Sustainable Development') see: http://www.etp.sk/en/index.php.

50. Interview with a local authority representative, Nálepkovo, 17.03.2009.

51. Interview with a Roma respondent, 17.03.2009.

52. *Fakulta architektúry Slovenskej technickej univerzity (FA STU)* [Faculty of Architecture of the Slovak University of Technology (FA SUT)].

53. Interview with a local authority representative, Nálepkovo, 17.03.2009.

54. Interview with a Roma respondent, 17.03.2009.

55. Interview with a local authority representative, Nálepkovo, 17.03.2009.

56. Interview with a local authority representative, Nálepkovo, 16.03.2009.

57. Interview with a Roma respondent, 17.03.2009.

58. Interview with a local authority representative, Nálepkovo, 16.03.2009.

59. Interview with a Roma respondent, 17.03.2009.

60. Interview with a local authority representative, Nálepkovo, 16.03.2009.

61. Interview with a local authority representative, Nálepkovo, 16.03.2009.

62. Interview with a local authority representative, Nálepkovo, 16.03.2009.

63. Interview with a Roma respondent, 16.03.2009.

64. Interview with a Roma respondent, 17.03.2009.

65. Interview with a local authority representative, Nálepkovo, 16.03.2009.

66. Interview with a local authority representative, Nálepkovo, 16.03.2009.

67. Interview with a Roma respondent, 17.03.2009.

68. Interview with a local authority representative, Nálepkovo, 16.03.2009.

69. Interview with a local authority representative, Nálepkovo, 17.03.2009.

70. See: www.etp.sk; *Projekt ETP: Rómovia z východného Slovenska si budú sporiť na zlepšenie budúcnosti*, Romano Nevo Ľil (02.07.2007), available at: http://www.rnl.sk/modules.php?name=News&file=article&sid=6885 (24.05.2009).

71. Interview with a local authority representative, 16.03.2009.

Annexes

Table 1: Figures on Roma Housing and Its Occupiers

Region	Integrated dispersed	Number of persons	Integrated dispersed	Number of persons	Settlements on edge of municipality	Number of persons	Settlements out of municipality	Number of persons	Settlements in total	Number of persons
Košice	171	23 053	43	9 835	105	27 683	111	23 705	430	84 276
Prešov	122	25 952	27	5 202	131	33 503	85	20 639	365	85 296
Banská Bystrica	233	36 798	41	8 185	55	6 053	63	4 780	392	55 816
Žilina	18	2 212	12	1 861	5	396	5	886	40	5 355
Nitra	117	19 317	17	3 115	14	1 327	4	250	152	24 009
Trenčín	46	3 005	4	880	7	440	0	0	57	4 325
Trnava	55	8 938	27	3 468	16	1 544	10	397	108	14 347
Bratislava	14	1 607	6	1 025	5	773	6	123	31	3 528
Total	776	120 882	177	33 571	338	71 719	284	50 780	1 575	276 952

Source: M. Jurásková, E. Kriglerová, J. Rybová (2004) Atlas rómskych komunít na Slovensku 2004, Bratislava: Úrad Vlády SR.

Table 2: Cost of Construction of Municipal Housing

Dwelling	Minimum cost per sq. m.	Maximum costs (total)	Grant (per cent)	Grant	Municipal co-funding
Standard 50 sq.m.	860 EUR	43 000 EUR	30	12 900 EUR	30 100 EUR
Standard 65 sq. m.	836 EUR	54 340 EUR	25	13 585 EUR	40 755 EUR
Standard 80 sq. m.	801 EUR	64 080 EUR	20	12 816 EUR	51 264 EUR
Lower–standard 40 sq. m	496 EUR	19 840 EUR	80	15 872 EUR	3 968 EUR
Lower–standard 60 sq. m	473 EUR	28 380 EUR	75	21 285 EUR	7 095 EUR

Source: Slovakia/Výnos Ministerstva výstavby a regionálneho rozvoja Slovenskej republiky č. V-2/2008 (21.11.2008).

[. . .]

ANNEX 3—BIBLIOGRAPHY

Centre on Housing Rights and Evictions (2007) *Housing Rights Awards Media Kit* Geneva: Centre on Housing Rights and Evictions.

Centre on Housing Rights and Evictions, Nadácia Milana Šimečku (2008) *Submission to the Office of the High Commissioner for Human Rights—Slovakia* Geneva/Bratislava: Centre on Housing Rights and Evictions, Nadácia Milana Šimečku.

Chee-Hong Brian Chung (2005) *Habitat for Humanity in Slovakia: The Roma of Svinia A Case Study* Habitat for Humanity International.

Council of Europe: European Commission Against Racism and Intolerance (ECRI)/*Third Report on Slovakia, Adopted on 27 June 2003*, (CRI(2004)4).

E. Havelková, B. Valentová (1998) 'Komparatívna analýza bytovej politiky v Slovenskej a Českej republike v rokoch 1990–1996', in: M. Potůček, I. Radičová (eds.) *Sociální politika v Čechách a na Slovensku po roce 1989*, Praha: Karolinum.

M. Hojsík (2008) *Evaluácia obecných nájomných bytov v rómskych osídleniach*, Bratislava: Nadácia Milana Simečku.

M. Hojsík (2009) 'Rómovia', in: M. Kollár, G. Mesežnikov, M. Bútora (eds.) *Slovensko 2008: Súhrnná správa o stave spoločnosti*, Bratislava: Inštitút pre verejné otázky.

M. Hojsík et al. (2007) *Forced Evictions in Slovakia – 2006 (Executive Summary)*, Bratislava: Nadácia Milana Šimečku.

M. Jurásková, E. Kriglerová, J. Rybová (2004) *Atlas rómskych komunít na Slovensku 2004*, Bratislava: Úrad vlády SR.

T. Loran (2009) 'Marginalizovaní Rómovia ako špecifický potenciál ľudského kapitálu', in: Romano Nevo Ľil (16.02.2009).

Ministerstvo práce, sociálnych vecí a rodiny SR (2001) *Bytová politika na miestnej úrovni. Metodická príručka pre miestne samosprávy*. Bratislava: Ministerstvo práce, sociálnych vecí a rodiny SR.

A. Mušinka (2003) 'Roma Housing', in: M. Vašečka, M. Jurásková, T. Nicholson (eds.) *Čačipen pal o Roma: A Global report on Roma in Slovakia*, Bratislava: Inštitút pre verejné otázky.

Projekt ETP: Rómovia z východného Slovenska si budú sporiť' na zlepšenie budúcnosti, Romano Nevo Ľil (02.07.2007).

I. Radičová (2001) *Hic sunt Romales*, Bratislava: S.P.A.C.E.

Slovakia/Nariadenie vlády SR č. 406/2006 *o podrobnostiach o požiadavkách na vnútorné prostredie budov a o minimálnych požiadavkách na byty nižšieho štandardu a na ubytovacie zariadenia (vyhodnotenie medzirezortného pripomienkového konania)* (10.05.2006).

Slovakia/Správa o činnosti Úradu splnomocnenca vlády SR pre rómske komunity za rok 2007 (*Informatívny mteriál z rokovania vlády SR)*, Úrad vlády SR (21.05.2008).

Slovakia/Štatistický úrad Slovenskej republiky (2008) *Informácia o demografickom vývoji v roku 2007.*

Slovakia/Ústredie práce, sociálnych vecí a rodiny (2009) *Štatistiky: Nezamestnanosť a sociálne dávky Február 2009.*

Slovakia/*Uznesenie vlády SR č. 547/2008* (20.08.2008).

Slovakia/*Uznesenie vlády SR č. 63/2005* (19.01.2005).

Slovakia/*Výnos Ministerstva výstavby a regionálneho rozvoja Slovenskej republiky č. V-2/2008* (21.11.2008).

Slovakia/*Zákon č. 453/2001 Z. z. ktorým sa mení a dopĺňa zákon č. 369/1990 Zb. o obecnom zriadení v znení neskorších predpisov a menia a dopĺňajú sa niektoré ďalšie zákony* (02.10.2001).

Slovakia/*Zákon č. 599/2003 Z. Z. o pomoci v hmotnej núdzi* (11.11.2003).

Slovakia/*Zákon č. 599/2003 Z. z. o pomoci v hmotnej núdzi a o zmene a doplnení niektorých predpisov* (11.11.2003).

Slovakia/*Zákon č. 74/1958 Zb. o trvalom usídlení kočujúcich osôb* (17.10.1958).

J. Zapletalova, M. Antalikova, E. Smatanova (2003) 'The Role of Self-government in Housing Development in Slovakia: Local Government and Housing in Slovakia', in: M. Lux (ed.) *Housing Policy: An End or a New Beginning?*, Budapest: LGI Books.

*The European Union Agency for Fundamental Rights is an advisory body of the European Union; it collects evidence about the condition of fundamental rights across the European Union and provides advice, based on evidence, about how to improve the situation.

European Union Agency for Fundamental Rights, "Roma Housing Projects in Small Communities, Slovakia," October 2009. Available at: http://fra.europa.eu/fraWebsite/attachments/ROMA_Housing_Case-final-ENSK.pdf.

Used by Permission.

Appendix 1: An EU Framework for National Roma Integration Strategies up to 2020

by European Commission

---

1. Improving the Situation of Roma: A Social and Economic Imperative for the Union and Its Member States

Many of the estimated 10–12 million[1] Roma in Europe face prejudice, intolerance, discrimination and social exclusion in their daily lives. They are marginalised and live in very poor socio-economic conditions. This is not acceptable in the European Union (EU) at the beginning of the 21st century.

The EU's Europe 2020 strategy for a new growth path—smart, sustainable and inclusive growth—leaves no room for the persistent economic and social marginalisation of what constitutes Europe's largest minority. Determined action, in active dialogue with the Roma, is needed both at national and EU level. While primary responsibility for that action rests with public authorities, it remains a challenge given that the social and economic integration of Roma is a two-way process which requires a change of mindsets of the majority of the people as well as of members of the Roma communities[2].

First of all, Member States need to ensure that Roma are not discriminated against but treated like any other EU citizens with equal access to all fundamental rights as enshrined in the EU Charter of Fundamental Rights. In addition, action is needed to break the vicious cycle of poverty moving from one generation to the next. In many Member States, Roma represent a significant and growing proportion of the school age population and therefore the future workforce. The Roma population is young: 35.7% are under 15 compared to 15.7% of the EU population overall. The average age is 25 among Roma, compared with 40 across the EU[3]. The vast majority of working-age Roma lack the education needed to find good jobs. It is therefore of crucial importance to invest in the education of Roma children to allow them later on to successfully enter the labour market. In Member States with significant Roma populations, this already has an economic impact. According to estimates, in Bulgaria, about 23% of new labour entrants are Roma, in Romania, about 21%[4].

A significant number of Roma living in the EU are legally residing third-country nationals. They share the same severe living conditions as many Roma holding EU citizenship, whilst facing also challenges of migrants coming from outside the EU. These challenges are addressed in the context of EU policies to stimulate integration of third-country nationals, while taking into account the needs of especially vulnerable groups[5].

Integrating the Roma people will not only bring social benefits, but will also economically benefit both Roma people as well as the communities they are part of. According to a recent research by the World Bank[6], for instance, full Roma integration in the labour market could bring economic benefits estimated to be around €0.5 billion annually for some countries. Greater participation of Roma in the labour market would improve economic productivity, reduce government payments for social assistance and increase revenue from income taxes. According to the same World Bank study, the tax benefits of Roma integration in the labour market are estimated to be around €175 million annually per country. All of these important economic and financial consequences of Roma integration could in turn foster a climate of greater openness to the Roma people with the general public and thereby contribute to their smooth integration in the communities of which they are part of.

Economic integration of the Roma will also contribute to social cohesion and improve respect for fundamental rights, including the rights of persons belonging to minorities, and help eliminating discrimination based on someone's race, colour, ethnic, social origin or membership of a minority[7].

The EU has made several proposals for Member States to promote the social and economic integration of Roma, most recently in its Communication of April 2010[8]. Member States are already under an obligation to give Roma (like other EU citizens) non-discriminatory access to education, employment, vocational training, healthcare, social protection and housing through Directive 2000/43/EC. The rigorous monitoring of the implementation of this Directive can be a useful instrument for measuring the integration of Roma[9].

In spite of some progress achieved both in the Member States and at EU level[10] over the past years, little has changed in the day-to-day situation of most of the Roma. According to the Commission's Roma Task Force findings[11], strong and proportionate measures are still not yet in place to tackle the social and economic problems of a large part of the EU's Roma population.

To address this challenge, and since non-discrimination alone is not sufficient to combat the social exclusion of Roma, the Commission asks the EU institutions to endorse this EU Framework for National Roma Integration Strategies. It is a means to complement and reinforce the EU's equality legislation and policies by addressing, at national, regional and local level, but also through dialogue with and participation of the Roma, the specific needs of Roma regarding equal access to employment, education, housing and healthcare.

This EU Framework seeks to make a tangible difference to Roma people's lives. It is the EU's response to the current situation and does not replace Member States' primary responsibility in this regard. With this EU Framework, the European Commission encourages Member States, in proportion to the size of the Roma population living in their territories[12] and taking into account their different starting points, to adopt or to develop further a comprehensive approach to Roma integration and endorse the following goals.

2. A Need for a Targeted Approach: An EU Framework for National Roma Integration Strategies

To achieve significant progress towards Roma integration, it is now crucial to step up a gear and ensure that national, regional and local integration policies **focus on Roma** in a **clear and specific** way, and address the needs of Roma with **explicit measures** to prevent and compensate for disadvantages they face. A targeted approach, within the broader strategy to fight against poverty and exclusion—which does not exclude other vulnerable and deprived group from support—is compatible with the principle of non-discrimination both at EU and national level. The principle of equal treatment does not prevent Member States from maintaining or adopting specific measures to prevent or compensate for disadvantages linked to racial or ethnic origin[13]. Some Member States have already successfully used positive action in favour of Roma, considering that classical social inclusion measures were not sufficient to meet Roma specific needs[14].

To ensure that effective policies are in place in the Member States, the Commission proposes that **national Roma integration strategies** are designed or, where they already exist, are adapted to meet **EU Roma integration goals**, with targeted actions and sufficient funding (national, EU and other) to deliver them. It proposes solutions to address the current barriers to a more effective use of EU funds and lays the foundations of a **robust monitoring mechanism** to ensure concrete results for Roma.

3. Expressing the EU Ambition: Setting Roma Integration Goals

The European Commission's Annual Growth Survey[15] showed that much needs to be done by Member States and the EU to implement the Europe 2020 strategy and to achieve its headline targets, supported by flagship initiatives[16].

For a number of Member States, addressing the situation of Roma in terms of employment, poverty and education will contribute to progress towards Europe 2020 employment, social inclusion and education targets.

EU Roma integration goals should cover, in proportion to the size of the Roma population, **four crucial areas: access to education, employment, healthcare and housing.** These minimum standards should be based on common, comparable and reliable indicators. The achievement of these goals is important to help Member States reaching the overall targets of the Europe 2020 strategy.

- Access to education: *Ensure that all Roma children complete at least primary school*

Educational achievement within the Roma population is much lower than the rest of the population, although the situation differs among Member States[17].

While primary school attendance is compulsory in all Member States, Member States have a duty to ensure that primary education is available to all children at the compulsory ages. According to the best available evidence from the Labour Force Survey 2009[18], an average of 97.5% of children completes primary education across the EU.

Surveys suggest that in some Member States, only a limited number of Roma children complete primary school[19]. Roma children tend to be over-represented in special education and segregated schools. There is a need to strengthen links with communities through cultural/school mediators, churches, religious associations or communities and through active participation of the parents of Roma, to improve the intercultural competences of teachers, to reduce segregation and to ensure compliance with the duty to primary school attendance. The Commission plans a joint action with the Council of Europe to train about 1000 mediators over two years. Mediators can inform and advise parents on the workings of the local education system, and help to ensure that children make the transition between each stage of their school career.

It is well known that children who miss out on, enter late into the school system, or leave too early will subsequently experience significant difficulties, ranging from illiteracy and language problems to feelings of exclusion and inadequacy. As a result, they will have a harder time getting into further education, university or a good job. Therefore, initiatives of second chance programmes for drop-out young adults are encouraged, including programmes with an explicit focus on Roma children. Support should also be given to reform teachers' training curricula and to elaborate innovative teaching methods. Attendance of multiply disadvantaged children requires a cross-sectoral cooperation and appropriate support programmes. The High Level Group on Literacy and the Literacy Campaign the Commission is launching as a contribution to the Europe 2020 flagship "New Skills and Jobs" will stress the importance of combating illiteracy among Roma children and adults.

The Commission adopted a Communication on Early Childhood Education and Care[20] which highlighted that participation rates of Roma children are significantly lower, although their needs for support are greater. Increased access to high quality non-segregated early childhood education can play a key role in overcoming the educational disadvantage faced by Roma children, as highlighted by pilot actions on Roma integration currently underway in some Member States with contributions from the EU budget[21].

This is why Member States should ensure that all Roma children have access to quality education and are not subject to discrimination or segregation, regardless of whether they are sedentary or not. Member States should, as a minimum, ensure primary school completion. They should also widen access to quality early childhood education and care and reduce the number of early school leavers from secondary education pursuant to the Europe 2020 strategy. Roma youngsters should be strongly encouraged to participate also in secondary and tertiary education[22].

- Access to employment: *Cut the employment gap between Roma and the rest of the population*

The Europe 2020 strategy sets a headline target of 75% of the population aged 20-64 to be employed (on average, the employment rate in the EU amounts to 68.8%[23]). The 2011 Annual Growth Survey outlined how Member States are setting national employment targets in national reform programmes against which progress can be measured. Empirical evidence and research on the socio-economic situation of Roma show that there is a significant gap between the employment rate for Roma and the rest of the population.

The World Bank found that Roma employment rates (especially for women) fall well behind those of the non-Roma majority[24]. A survey by the European Agency for Fundamental Rights in seven Member States also highlights important gaps and indicates that Roma consider themselves to be highly discriminated against in the field of employment[25].

This is why Member States should grant Roma people full access in a

non-discriminatory way to vocational training, to the job market and to self-employment tools and initiatives. Access to micro-credit should be encouraged. In the public sector, due attention should be given to employment of qualified Roma civil servants. Public Employment Services can reach out to the Roma by providing personalised services and mediation. This can help attract Roma to the labour market and thus increase the employment rate.

- Access to healthcare: *Reduce the gap in health status between the Roma and the rest of the population*

Life expectancy at birth in the EU is 76 for men and 82 for women[26]. For Roma, it is estimated to be 10 years less[27]. In addition, while the infant mortality rate in the EU is 4.3 per thousand live births[28], there is evidence that the rate is much higher among Roma communities. A United Nations Development Programme report on five countries noted that Roma child mortality rates are 2 to 6 times higher than those for the general population, depending on the country. High levels of infant mortality among the Roma community are reported in other countries[29].

This disparity reflects the overall gap in health between Roma and non-Roma. This difference is linked to their poor living situations, lack of targeted information campaign, limited access to quality healthcare and exposure to higher health risks. In the Fundamental Rights Agency survey, discrimination by healthcare personnel also emerged as a particular problem for the Roma[30]: 17% indicated they had experienced discrimination in this area in the previous 12 months. Use of prevention services among the Roma population is low and, according to some studies, over 25% of Roma children are not fully vaccinated[31].

This is why Member States should provide access to quality healthcare especially for children and women as well as preventive care and social services at a similar level and under the same conditions to the Roma as to the rest of the population. Where possible, qualified Roma should be involved in healthcare programmes targeting their communities.

- Access to housing and essential services: *Close the gap between the share of Roma with access to housing and to public utilities (such as water, electricity and gas) and that of the rest of the population*

Between 72% and 100% of households across the EU are connected to a public water supply[32]. Yet the situation for Roma is much worse. Their often poor housing conditions include an inadequate access to public utilities such as water, electricity or gas and non-sedentary Roma often have difficulty finding sites with access to water[33]. This has a negative impact on their health and overall integration in society.

This is why Member States should promote non-discriminatory access to housing, including social housing. Action on housing needs to be part of an integrated approach including, in particular, education, health, social affairs, employment and security, and desegregation measures. Member States should also address the particular needs of non-sedentary Roma (e.g. provide access to suitable halting sites for non-sedentary Roma). They should actively intervene with targeted programmes involving regional and local authorities.

4. National Roma Integration Strategies: A Clear Policy Commitment from Member States

Building on the experience of the Member States including these participating in the Roma Decade[34], the Commission calls on Member States to align their national Roma integration strategies to the targeted approach set out above and extend their planning period up to 2020. Member States that do not have national Roma strategies in place yet are called upon to set similar goals, in proportion to the size of the Roma population living in their territories[35] and taking into account their different starting points as well as the specificities of such populations.

Member States' national strategies should pursue a targeted approach which will, in line with the **Common Basic Principles on Roma Inclusion**[36], actively contribute to the social integration of Roma in mainstream society and to eliminating segregation where it exists. They should fit into and contribute to the broader framework of the Europe 2020 strategy and should therefore be **consistent with national reform programmes.**

When developing national Roma integration strategies, Member States should bear in mind the following approaches:

* Set achievable **national goals for Roma integration** to bridge the gap with the general population. These targets should address, as a minimum, the four EU Roma integration goals relating to access to education, employment, healthcare and housing.
* Identify where relevant those **disadvantaged micro-regions or segregated neighbourhoods,** where communities are most deprived, using already available socio-economic and territorial indicators (i.e. very low educational level, long-term unemployment, etc…).

- Allocate a **sufficient funding from national budgets,** which will be complemented, where appropriate, by international and EU funding.
- Include **strong monitoring methods** to evaluate the impact of Roma integration actions and a review mechanism for the adaptation of the strategy.
- Be designed, implemented and monitored in **close cooperation and continuous dialogue with Roma civil society, regional and local authorities.**
- Appoint a **national contact point for the national Roma integration strategy** with the authority to coordinate the development and implementation of the strategy or, where relevant, rely on suitable existing administrative structures.

Member States are requested to prepare or revise their national Roma integration strategies and present them to the Commission by the end of December 2011. In spring 2012, ahead of the annual Roma Platform meeting, the Commission will assess these national strategies and report to the European Parliament and to the Council about progress.

5. ACHIEVING CONCRETE RESULTS FOR ROMA PEOPLE

The implementation and success of national Roma integration strategies will very much depend on an effective and sufficient allocation of national resources. EU funding alone can certainly not solve the situation of Roma, but the Commission recalls that up to **€26.5 billion of EU funding** is currently programmed to support Member States' efforts in the field of social inclusion, including to support efforts to help the Roma[37].

In April 2010, the Commission[38] called on the Member States to ensure that existing EU financial instruments, and especially the Structural Funds and the European Agricultural Fund for Rural Development, were accessible to Roma. This approach was endorsed by the Council in June 2010[39]. However, most Member States currently do not make yet sufficient use of available EU funds to address the needs of the Roma.

Making progress under the present programming period (2007–2013)...
- In order to overcome the weaknesses in the development of appropriate strategies and effective measures to implement them where they exist, Members States are invited to amend their operational programmes co-financed by Structural Funds and the European Agricultural Fund for Rural Development in order to better support Roma targeted projects, and to align them with their national Roma integration strategies.
- The Commission will examine with Member States changes to their

operational programmes in order to address new needs, simplify delivery and speed up the implementation of priorities, including the use of the housing-related integrated approach foreseen in the European Regional Development Fund modified Regulation[40]. The Commission will swiftly examine requests for programme modifications that are in relation to the national Roma integration strategies.

• There are significant amounts of EU technical assistance at Member States' disposal (4% of all Structural Funds), out of which Member States on average had only used 31% of their planned allocations until late 2009. These amounts would be lost if not used. When designing their national Roma integration strategies, Member States should therefore make a greater use of EU technical assistance[41] to improve their management, monitoring and evaluation capacities also with regard to Roma-targeted projects. This instrument could also potentially be used by Member States to obtain the expertise of regional, national and international organisations in preparing, implementing and monitoring interventions.

• To surmount capacity issues, such as lack of know-how and administrative capacity of managing authorities and the difficulties of combining funds to support integrated projects, the Commission invites Member States to consider entrusting the management and implementation of some parts of their programmes to intermediary bodies such as international organisations, regional development bodies, churches and religious organisations or communities as well as non-governmental organisations with proven experience in Roma integration and knowledge of actors on the ground[42]. In this respect, the network of the European Economic and Social Committee could be a useful tool[43].

• Member States should also consider using the European Progress Microfinance Facility,[44] for which a total of €100 million of EU funding is available for the period 2010–2013. The Commission estimates that this amount can be leveraged to more than €500 million in microcredit over the coming eight years. Roma communities are one of the target groups of the instrument[45]. Giving Roma communities the opportunity to start autonomous productive activities could motivate people to actively participate in regular work, reduce benefit dependency and inspire future generations.

• When designing and implementing their national Roma integration strategies, Member States are encouraged to use the European Initiative on Social Innovation, which the Commission intends to launch in 2011 as set out in the Flagship Initiative "European Platform against Poverty and Social Exclusion". This innovation-based approach can contribute to improving the effectiveness of social inclusion policies.

...and beyond 2013

As the national Roma integration strategies should cover the period 2011–2020, making best use of the funding that will be made available under the new Multi-annual Financial Framework (MFF) is important. The MFF will set out the way in which the future EU budget will support the objectives of Europe 2020.

From its inception, Europe 2020 strategy takes into account the situation of the Roma population[46]. Actions to support the integration of the Roma will be part of the relevant EU financial instruments, in particular cohesion policy funds. When preparing its proposals for the future cohesion policy regulatory framework, based on the orientations put forward in the Budget Review[47] and in the conclusions of the fifth Cohesion Report, the Commission will strive to address the current potential barriers to an effective use of cohesion policy funds to support Roma integration.

It will be important to ensure that the investment priorities of the various funds that can be used in the area of social inclusion and fight against poverty underpin the implementation of the national reform programmes and the national Roma integration strategies. They should also set out the necessary pre-conditions for an effective and result-oriented support, including through better evaluation. In addition, the possibility to use positive incentives to redress inequalities will be explored. At the same time, simplifying procedures for the benefit of the programme users will be one of the main elements the Commission will take into account when preparing the future proposals. This is of particular importance for projects addressing Roma needs.

6. Promoting Roma Integration Beyond the EU: The Particular Situation of Enlargement Countries

The Commission's Enlargement Strategy[48] highlighted the precarious situation of many Roma in the Western Balkans and in Turkey. Their number is estimated at 3.8 million by the Council of Europe.

Roma in enlargement countries face similar or even more serious problems than in many EU Member States: social exclusion, segregation and marginalisation leading to lack of education, chronic unemployment, limited access to healthcare, housing and essential services as well as widespread poverty. In addition, due to the wars in the Balkan region, many Roma families had to move as displaced persons to other countries in the region or to Western Europe. In Turkey, Roma groups are diverse, but a large proportion suffers from multi-dimensional social exclusion.

Lessons learned from past accessions suggest that promoting Roma integration requires an enhanced political commitment to Roma inclusion, the allocation of appropriate resources under the national budgets, better coordination with all relevant donors and a systematic evaluation and reinforced monitoring. The EU Roma integration goals are equally relevant to these countries. Their national Roma integration strategies and Action Plans (developed in most cases in the framework of the 2005–2015 Decade of Roma Inclusion) should be reviewed in line with these goals. Turkey has yet to adopt a national framework to address Roma inclusion.

The Commission is committed to help, at regional and national level, the efforts of these countries to improve the social and economic inclusion of Roma through:

- improving the delivery of support under the Instrument on Pre-Accession Assistance towards a strategic and results oriented national and multi-beneficiary programming with a focus on a sector-wide approach for social development. The Commission is currently implementing or planning projects with a total value of more than €50 million which could also exclusively or partly benefit the Roma communities.
- strengthening the involvement of civil society by encouraging institutionalised dialogues with Roma representatives to become involved and take responsibility for policy formulation, implementation and monitoring on regional, national and local level.
- close monitoring of the progress made by each country regarding the economic and social situation of Roma and annual presentation of its conclusions in the enlargement Progress Reports.

7. Empowering Civil Society: A Stronger Role for the European Platform for Roma Inclusion

The European Platform for Roma Inclusion[49] is a useful forum for debate and concerted actions of all relevant stakeholders: EU institutions, national governments, international organisations, academia and Roma civil society representatives. The Platform has significantly contributed to making both European and national policies more sensitive to Roma needs.

The Commission is committed to playing a stronger role in the Platform and to reinforcing the Platform's role, building on past experience and by linking its work with the four priority areas of national Roma integration strategies.

Through the Platform, concerned stakeholders, especially representatives of the Roma communities, should have the possibility to play a role in the European Framework for National Roma Integration Strategies. The strengthened Platform can support Member States to find the relevant policy responses through the exchange of good practices and the discussion of approaches from international organisations with experience in promoting Roma inclusion. It will also provide the Commission with feedback on the results of national efforts on the ground through the voice of Roma civil society.

8. MEASURING PROGRESS: PUTTING IN PLACE A ROBUST MONITORING SYSTEM

At present, it is difficult to obtain accurate, detailed and complete data on the situation of Roma in the Member States and to identify concrete measures put in place to tackle Roma exclusion and discrimination. It is not possible to assess whether such measures have given the expected results. It is therefore important to collect reliable data.

This is why it is necessary to put in place a **robust monitoring mechanism** with clear benchmarks which will ensure that tangible results are measured, that money directed to Roma integration has reached its final beneficiaries, that there is progress towards the achievement of the EU Roma integration goals and that national Roma integration strategies have been implemented.

The Commission will **report annually to the European Parliament and to the Council** on progress on the integration of the Roma population in Member States and on the achievement of the goals.

The Commission will do so by building on the Roma household survey pilot project carried out by the United Nations Development Programme in cooperation particularly with the World Bank and the Fundamental Rights Agency[50]. The Commission requests the Fundamental Rights Agency to expand this survey on Roma to all Member States and to run it regularly to measure progress on the ground. The Fundamental Rights Agency, working together with other relevant bodies, such as the European Foundation for the Improvement of Living and Working Conditions, will collect data on the situation of Roma with respect to access to employment, education, healthcare and housing. Data collection will also be drawn from specific research funded by Socio-economic Sciences and Humanities Programme of the 7th Framework Programme. Throughout this process, the Commission, the Fundamental Rights Agency and other Union bodies will, in line with Article 4(2)TEU, respect the national identities of the Member States, inherent to their fundamental structures, political and constitutional, inclusive to their regional and self-government.

The Commission will also take into account ongoing work within the Open Method of Coordination in the field of social policies and other Member States contributions based on their own monitoring systems of Roma integration. The in-depth monitoring by Member States and stakeholders of the implementation of national Roma integration strategies is a sound method for enhancing transparency and accountability in order to ensure the most effective impacts of Roma integration.

National reform programmes together with the monitoring and peer review process of the Europe 2020 strategy should be an additional source of information for assessing progress and giving guidance to Member States.

In order to get useful data in the long term, the Commission will also foster cooperation between national statistical offices and Eurostat so as to be able to identify methods to map the EU's least developed micro-regions, where the most marginalised groups live, and in particular Roma, as a first step. This territorial approach to data collection has a direct relevance to tackling Roma poverty and exclusion. In addition, the Fundamental Rights Agency should work with Member States to develop monitoring methods which can provide a comparative analysis of the situation of Roma across Europe.

9. CONCLUSION: 10 YEARS TO MAKE A DIFFERENCE

This EU Framework for National Roma Integration Strategies provides the opportunity for joining forces at all levels (EU, national, regional) and with all stakeholders, including the Roma, to address one of the most serious social challenges in Europe: putting an end to the exclusion of Roma. It is complementary to the existing EU legislation and policies in the areas of non-discrimination, fundamental rights, the free movement of persons, and the rights of the child[51]. The framework spells out EU level goals for Roma integration to be achieved at national, regional and local level. Those ambitious goals will only be reached if there is a clear commitment from Member States and national, regional and local authorities coupled with involvement of Roma civil society organisations.

The Commission invites the European Parliament, the European Council, the Council, the Committee of the Regions and the European Social an Economic Committee to endorse the EU Framework for National Roma Integration Strategies. For over a decade, the EU institutions have been regularly calling on Member States and candidate countries to improve the social and economic integration of Roma. Now is the time to change good intentions into more concrete actions.

Annex—Table Elaborated on the Basis of Council of Europe's Data (http://www.coe.int/t/dg3/romatravellers/default_en.asp)

European countries (EU Member States)	Total country population (July 2009)	Official number (last census)	Minimum estimate	Maximum estimate	Average estimate	% of total population (from averages)	Updated
\multicolumn{8}{l}{Figures taken from a document prepared by the Council of Europe Roma and Travellers Division}
Austria	8.205.533	No data available	20.000	30.000	25.000	0,30%	14/09/2010
Belgium	10.414.336	No data available	20.000	40.000	30.000	0,29%	14/09/2010
Bulgaria	7.262.675	370 908 (2001)	700.000	800.000	750.000	10,33%	14/09/2010
Cyprus	792.604	560 (1960)	1.000	1.500	1.250	0,16%	3/08/2009
Czech Republic	10.220.911	11 718 (2001)	150.000	250.000	200.000	1,96%	14/09/2010
Denmark	5.484.723	No data available	1.000	10.000	5.500	0,10%	3/08/2009
Estonia	1.307.605	584 (2009)	1.000	1.500	1.250	0,10%	3/08/2009
Finland	5.244.749	No data available	10.000	12.000	11.000	0,21%	3/08/2009
France	64.057.790	No data available	300.000	500.000	400.000	0,62%	14/09/2010
Germany	82.400.996	No data available	70.000	140.000	105.000	0,13%	14/09/2010
Greece	10.722.816	No data available	180.000	350.000	265.000	2,47%	14/09/2010
Hungary	9.930.915	190 046 (2001)	400.000	1.000.000	700.000	7,05%	14/09/2010
Ireland	4.156.119	22 435 (2006)	32.000	43.000	37.500	0,90%	14/09/2010
Italy	59.619.290	No data available	110.000	170.000	140.000	0,23%	14/09/2010
Latvia	2.245.423	8 205 (2000)	13.000	16.000	14.500	0,65%	3/08/2009
Lithuania	3.565.205	2 571 (2001)	2.000	4.000	3.000	0,08%	3/08/2009
Luxembourg	486.006	No data available	100	500	300	0,06%	3/08/2009
Malta	403.532	No data available	0	0	0	0,00%	3/08/2009
The Netherlands	16.645.313	No data available	32.000	48.000	40.000	0,24%	14/09/2010
Poland	38.500.696	12 731 (2002)	15.000	60.000	37.500	0,10%	14/09/2010
Portugal	10.676.910	No data available	40.000	70.000	55.000	0,52%	14/09/2010
Romania	22.246.862	535 140 (2002)	1.200.000	2.500.000	1.850.000	8,32%	14/09/2010
Slovak Republic	5.455.407	89 920 (2001)	400.000	600.000	500.000	9,17%	14/09/2010
Slovenia	2.007.711	3 246 (2002)	7.000	10.000	8.500	0,42%	3/08/2009
Spain	46.157.822	No data available	650.000	800.000	725.000	1,57%	14/09/2010
Sweden	9.276.509	No data available	35.000	50.000	42.500	0,46%	14/09/2010
United Kingdom	60.943.912	No data available	150.000	300.000	225.000	0,37%	14/09/2010
Total in the EU					6.172.800	1,73%	

European countries (Non-EU Member States)	Total country population (July 2009)	Official number (last census)	Minimum estimate	Maximum estimate	Average estimate	% of total population (from averages)	Updated
Albania	3.619.778	1261 (2001)	80.000	150.000	115.000	3,18%	14/09/2010
Andorra	72.413	No data available	0	0	0	0,00%	3/08/2009
Armenia	2.968.586	No data available	2.000	2.000	2.000	0,07%	3/08/2009
Azerbaijan	8.177.717	No data available	2.000	2.000	2.000	0,02%	3/08/2009
Belarus	9.685.768	No data available	10.000	70.000	40.000	0,41%	14/09/2010
Bosnia and Herzegovina	4.590.310	8 864 (1991)	40.000	60.000	50.000	1,09%	14/09/2010
Croatia	4.491.543	9 463 (2001)	30.000	40.000	35.000	0,78%	14/09/2010
Georgia	4.630.841	1 744 (1989)	2.000	2.500	2.250	0,05%	3/08/2009
Iceland	304.367	No data available	0	0	0	0,00%	3/08/2009
Kosovo*	2.542.711	45 745 (1991)	25.000	50.000	37.500	1,47%	14/09/2010
Liechtenstein	34.498	No data available	0	0	0	0,00%	3/08/2009
"The former Yugoslav Republic of Macedonia"	2.061.315	53 879 (2002)	135.500	260.000	197.750	9,59%	14/09/2010
Moldova	4.324.450	12 280 (2004)	15.000	200.000	107.500	2,49%	14/09/2010
Monaco	32.796	No data available	0	0	0	0,00%	3/08/2009
Montenegro	678.177	2 826 (2003)	15.000	25.000	20.000	2,95%	14/09/2010
Norway	4.644.457	No data available	4.500	15.700	10.100	0,22%	3/08/2009
Russian Federation	140.702.094	182 617 (2002)	450.000	1.200.000	825.000	0,59%	14/09/2010
SanMarino	29.973	No data available	0	0	0	0,00%	3/08/2009
Serbia (excl. Kosovo)	7.334.935	108 193 (2002)	400.000	800.000	600.000	8,18%	14/09/2010
Switzerland	7.581.520	No data available	25.000	35.000	30.000	0,40%	14/09/2010
Turkey	71.892.807	4 656 (1945)	500.000	5.000.000	2.750.000	3,83%	14/09/2010
Ukraine	45.994.287	47 917 (2001)	120.000	400.000	260.000	0,57%	14/09/2010
Total Non-EU					5.084.100	1,63%	
Total in Europe					11.256.900		

*under UNSCR 1244/99

Notes

1. The term "Roma" is used—similarly to other political documents of the European Parliament and the European Council—as an umbrella which includes groups of people who have more or less similar cultural characteristics, such as Sinti, Travellers, Kalé, Gens du voyage, etc. whether sedentary or not; around 80% of Roma are estimated to be sedentary (SEC(2010)400).

2. COM(2010) 133, p. 5.

3. Fundación Secretariado Gitano, *Health and the Roma community, analysis of the situation in Europe*, 2009. The study looks at Bulgaria, the Czech Republic, Greece, Portugal, Romania, Slovakia and Spain.

4. World Bank, Roma Inclusion: An Economic Opportunity for Bulgaria, the Czech Republic, Romania and Serbia, September 2010.

5. A Communication on a European Agenda for the Integration of Third-Country Nationals is foreseen in 2011.

6. World Bank, Roma Inclusion: An Economic Opportunity for Bulgaria, the Czech Republic, Romania and Serbia, September 2010.

7. Treaty on the European Union, Article 2 and Charter of Fundamental Rights of the European Union, Article 21.

8. COM(2010) 133, *The social and economic integration of the Roma in Europe*.

9. Council Directive 2000/43/EC of 29 June 2000 implementing the principle of equal treatment between persons irrespective of racial or ethnic origin (OJ L 180, 19.7.2009).

10. COM(2010) 133, section 2.

11. The Commission Roma Task Force was created on 7 September 2010 to streamline, assess and benchmark the use (including the effectiveness) of EU funds by all Member States for Roma integration and identify underpinning deficiencies in the use of funds.

12. See the estimates of the Council of Europe at http://www.coe.int/t/dg3/romatravellers/default_EN.asp, which are included in the Annex to this Communication.

13. Council Directive 2000/43/EC (OJ L 180 19.7.2000).

14. For example, the United Kingdom's local Traveller Education Support Services (TESS) is a tailored service to achieve equal access to education and equal educational outcomes for Traveller and Roma children. Another example is the JOBS for Roma project in Bulgaria which offers assistance for unemployed Roma and support for entrepreneurs. Other examples can be found in the Commission's report "Improving the tools for the social inclusion and non-discrimination of Roma in the EU", 2010. See also European Commission, "International perspectives on positive action measures", 2009.

15. COM(2011) 11, Annual Growth Survey: advancing the EU's comprehensive response to the crisis.

16. Out of seven flagship initiatives, the most relevant in this context are the *European Platform against Poverty and Social Exclusion*, *An Agenda for New Skills and Jobs* and the *Innovation Union*.

17. As regards secondary education, the Roma attendance is about 10% as estimated on the basis of the Open Society Institute (OSI) Survey 2008 (data available for seven Member States).

18. Labour Force Survey, 2009—http://epp.eurostat.ec.europa.eu/portal/page/portal/microdata/lfs

19. Open Society Institute, *International Comparative Data Set on Roma Education*, 2008. Data on primary education is available for 6 Member States: Bulgaria, Hungary, Latvia, Lithuania, Romania, and Slovakia. 42% is the weighted average for these Member States.

20. COM(2011) 66.

21. Pilot project: "A Good Start: scaling-up access to quality services for young Roma children".

22. In this context, the potential use of innovative approaches such as ICT-based access to learning and skill acquisition should be actively explored.

23. COM(2011) 11, Annex 3, *Draft Joint Employment Report*. See also Labour Force Survey, 2009: for 2009 the employment rate was 62.5% for women, 75.8% for men—http://epp.eurostat.ec.europa.eu/tgm/table.do?tab=table&init=1&plugin=1&language=en&pcode=t2020_10

24. World Bank, op.cit.

25. Fundamental Rights Agency, European Union Minorities and Discrimination Survey, Main Results Report, 2009.

26. http://epp.eurostat.ec.europa.eu/portal/page/portal/product_details/dataset?p_product_code=TSDPH100

27. COM(2009) 567, *Solidarity in Health: Reducing Health Inequalities in the EU*. See also Fundación Secretariado Gitano, op cit. and Sepkowitz K, "Health of the World's Roma population", 2006, based on the situation in the Czech Republic, Ireland, Slovakia and Bulgaria.

28. Ratio of the number of deaths of children under one year of age during the year, to the number of live births in that year. Eurostat Data, 2009 - http://appsso.eurostat.ec.europa.eu/nui/show.do?dataset=demo_minfind&lang=en

29. UNDP, The Roma in Central and Eastern Europe, Avoiding the Dependency Trap, 2003. Bulgaria, Romania, Slovakia, Hungary and the Czech Republic. Equality and Human Rights Commission, Inequalities Experienced by Gypsy and Traveller Communities: A review, 2009.

30. Fundamental Rights Agency, European Union Minorities and Discrimination Survey, Main Results Report, 2009.

31. Fundación Secretariado Gitano, op.cit. See also University of Sheffield, *The Health Status of Gypsies and Travellers in England*, 2004.

32. Eurostat data, 2002 — http://epp.eurostat.ec.europa.eu/cache/ITY_PUBLIC/8-21032006-AP/EN/8- 21032006-AP-EN.PDF

33. Fundamental Rights Agency, Housing conditions of Roma and Travellers in the European Union, Comparative Report, 2009.

34. The Decade of Roma Inclusion 2005–2015 is an international initiative that brings together governments, international partner organisations and civil society, to accelerate progress towards Roma inclusion and review such progress in a transparent and quantifiable way. The twelve countries currently taking part in the Decade are Bulgaria, the Czech Republic, Hungary, Romania, Slovakia, Spain as well as Albania, Bosnia and Herzegovina, Croatia, FYROM, Montenegro and Serbia. Slovenia has observer status. The international partner organisations of the Decade are the World Bank, OSI, UNDP, Council of Europe, Council of Europe Development Bank, OSCE, ERIO, ERTF, ERRC, UN-HABITAT, UNHCR, and UNICEF.

35. See the estimates of the Council of Europe at http://www.coe.int/t/dg3/romatravellers/default_EN.asp, which are included in the Annex to this Communication.

36. The 10 Common Basic Principles on Roma Inclusion were presented at the first Platform meeting on 24 April 2009. They were annexed to the Council conclusions of 8 June 2009. They comprise: 1) constructive, pragmatic and non-discriminatory policies 2) explicit but not exclusive targeting 3) inter-cultural approach 4) aiming for the mainstream 5) awareness of the gender dimension 6) transfer of evidence-based policies 7) use of EU instruments 8) involvement of regional and local authorities 9) involvement of civil society 10) active participation of Roma.

37. For the European Social Fund, €9.6 billion have been allocated in the period 2007–2013 for measures targeting socio-economic inclusion of disadvantaged people—among them marginalised Roma—and €172 million have been explicitly allocated for actions aiming at integrating the Roma. In the case of the European Regional Development Fund (ERDF), more than €16.8 billion are planned for social infrastructure.

38. COM(2010) 133.

39. Council Conclusions of 7 June 2010, 10058/10+COR 1.

40. European Parliament and Council Regulation No 437/2010 (OJ L 132, 29.5.2010). On 9 February 2011, the Commission issued a guidance note on the implementation of integrated housing interventions in favour of marginalised communities under the ERDF, approved by the Committee of Coordination of the Funds.

41. COM(2010) 110, *Cohesion policy: Strategic Report 2010 on the implementation of the programme 2007–2013* and SEC(2010) 360, reported that Member States used on average only 31% of their allocations in support of preparation, implementation and monitoring of cohesion policy.

42. In accordance with Council Regulation No 1083/2006, Articles 42 and 43 relating to global grants (OJ L 210, 31.7.2006).

43. The European Economic and Social Committee has a network of national contact points in the organised civil society through national Economic and Social committees and similar organisations.

44. European Parliament and Council Decision No 283/2010/EU of 25 March 2010.

45. The Commission already supports, for example, the Kiútprogram, a small scale pilot project targeting the Roma community in Hungary, which provides relatively small microloans.

46. The Integrated Guidelines for economic and employment policies (no 10) contain an explicit reference to Roma. Furthermore, the "Platform against Poverty and Social Exclusion" flagship initiative outlines how to address the integration of Roma within the overall policy to fight poverty and social exclusion. Other Guidelines for the employment policies promote employability in a way which helps the socio-economic integration of Roma people.

47. COM(2010) 700, *The EU Budget Review*.

48. COM(2010) 660, *Enlargement Strategy and Main Challenges 2010–2011*.

49. The first meeting of the Platform took place in 2009, following the General Affairs Council conclusions of 8 December 2008, which called upon the Commission to organise an exchange of good practices and experiences between Member States in the sphere of inclusion of the Roma, provide analytical support and stimulate cooperation between all parties concerned by Roma issues, including the organisations representing Roma, in the context of an integrated European platform. General Affairs Council Conclusions 15976/1/08 REV 1.

50. UNDP Survey, co-financed by DG REGIO and developed in cooperation with DG REGIO, the FRA, the World Bank and OSI (Spring 2011-Results in the Autumn): 11 Member States

covered (Bulgaria, the Czech Republic, Greece, Hungary, Poland, Romania, Slovakia, France, Italy, Spain and Portugal).

51. COM(2011) 60, *An EU Agenda for the Rights of the Child.*

European Commission, "An EU Framework for National Roma Integration Strategies up to 2020," COM(2011) 173, Brussels. Available at: http://ec.europa.eu/justice/policies/discrimination/docs/com_2011_173_en.pdf.

Used by Permission.

Appendix 2: Common Basic Principles for Roma Inclusion

by European Commission

[. . .]

Principle no 1: Constructive, pragmatic and non-discriminatory policies

Policies aiming at the inclusion of Roma people respect and realise the core values of the European Union, which include human rights and dignity, non-discrimination and equality of opportunity as well as economic development. Roma inclusion policies are integrated with mainstream policies, particularly in the fields of education, employment, social affairs, housing, health and security. The aim of these policies is to provide the Roma with effective access to equal opportunities in Member State societies.

Principle no 2: Explicit but not exclusive targeting

Explicit but not exclusive targeting of the Roma is essential for inclusion policy initiatives. It implies focusing on Roma people as a target group but not to the exclusion of other people who share similar socio-economic circumstances. This approach does not separate Roma- focused interventions from broader policy initiatives. In addition, where relevant, consideration must be given to the likely impact of broader policies and decisions on the social inclusion of Roma people.

Principle no 3: Inter-cultural approach

There is a need for an inter-cultural approach which involves Roma people together with people from different ethnic backgrounds. Essential for effective communication and policy, inter-cultural learning and skills deserve to be promoted alongside combating prejudices and stereotypes.

Principle no 4: Aiming for the mainstream

All inclusion policies aim to insert the Roma in the mainstream of society (mainstream educational institutions, mainstream jobs, and mainstream housing). Where partially or entirely segregated education or housing still exist,

Roma inclusion policies must aim to overcome this legacy. The development of artificial and separate "Roma" labour markets is to be avoided.

Principle no 5: Awareness of the gender dimension

Roma inclusion policy initiatives need to take account of the needs and circumstances of Roma women. They address issues such as multiple discrimination and problems of access to health care and child support, but also domestic violence and exploitation.

Principle no 6: Transfer of evidence-based policies

It is essential that Member States learn from their own experiences of developing Roma inclusion initiatives and share their experiences with other Member States. It is recognised that the development, implementation and monitoring of Roma inclusion policies requires a good base of regularly collected socio-economic data. Where relevant, the examples and experiences of social inclusion policies concerning other vulnerable groups, both from inside and from outside the EU, are also taken into account.

Principle no 7: Use of Community instruments

In the development and implementation of their policies aiming at Roma inclusion, it is crucial that the Member States make full use of Community instruments, including legal instruments (Race Equality Directive, Framework Decision on Racism and Xenophobia), financial instruments (European Social Fund, European Regional Development Fund, European Agricultural Fund for Rural Development, Instrument for Pre-Accession Assistance) and coordination instruments (Open Methods of Coordination). Member States must ensure that use of financial instruments accords with these Common Basic Principles, and make use of the expertise within the European Commission, in respect of the evaluation of policies and projects. Peer review and the transfer of good practices are also facilitated on the expert level by EURoma (European Network on Social Inclusion and Roma under the Structural Funds).

Principle no 8: Involvement of regional and local authorities

Member States need to design, develop, implement and evaluate Roma inclusion policy initiatives in close cooperation with regional and local authorities. These authorities play a key role in the practical implementation of policies.

Principle no 9: Involvement of civil society

Member States also need to design, develop, implement and evaluate Roma inclusion policy initiatives in close cooperation with civil society actors such as non-governmental organisations, social partners and academics/researchers. The involvement of civil society is recognised as vital both for the mobilisation of expertise and the dissemination of knowledge required to develop public debate and accountability throughout the policy process.

Principle no 10: Active participation of the Roma

The effectiveness of policies is enhanced with the involvement of Roma people at every stage of the process. Roma involvement must take place at both national and European levels through the input of expertise from Roma experts and civil servants, as well as by consultation with a range of Roma stakeholders in the design, implementation and evaluation of policy initiatives. It is of vital importance that inclusion policies are based on openness and transparency and tackle difficult or taboo subjects in an appropriate and effective manner. Support for the full participation of Roma people in public life, stimulation of their active citizenship and development of their human resources are also essential.

European Commission, excerpt from "Roma in Europe: The Implementation of European Union Instruments and Politics for Roma Inclusion—Progress Report 2008–2010," SEC 400, (Brussels, 2010) : 35–37. Available at: ec.europa.eu/social/BlobServlet?docId=4823&langId=en.

Appendix 3: Roma People Living in the EU: Frequently Asked Questions

Europa Press Release

There are between 10 million and 12 million Roma in the EU, in candidate countries and potential candidate countries in the Western Balkans. Roma people living in the European Union are EU citizens and have the same rights as any other EU citizen. A significant number of Roma live in extreme marginalisation in both rural and urban areas and in very poor social-economic conditions. They are disproportionally affected by discrimination, violence, unemployment, poverty, bad housing and poor health standards.

What is the European Commission doing to help the integration of Roma people?

The social and economic inclusion of Roma is a priority for the EU and needs the commitment and joint efforts of national and local authorities, civil society and EU institutions. The European Commission is committed to taking the necessary steps to improve the situation of Roma people and their social and economic integration in society. On 7 April 2010 the Commission adopted a Communication on the social and economic integration of Roma in Europe (IP/10/407; MEMO/10/121)—the first ever policy document dedicated specifically to Roma. It outlines an ambitious programme to help making policies for Roma inclusion more effective and defines the main challenges ahead.

The Communication also outlines the complexity and interdependence of the problems faced by Roma in terms of discrimination, poverty, low educational achievement, labour market barriers, housing segregation and poor health.

Although the situation of many of Europe's Roma people remains difficult, important progress has been made at EU and national levels. In the last two years, the EU and Member States have focused on adopting non-discrimination laws and making EU funding more effective in promoting Roma inclusion. This includes fighting discrimination, segregation and racist violence as well as supporting programmes to address the vicious circle of poverty, social marginalisation, low school achievement and poor housing and health.

What funding is available at EU level for Roma?

The EU and Member States have a joint responsibility for Roma inclusion and use a broad range of funds in their areas of responsibility, namely the European Social Fund (ESF), European Regional Development Fund (ERDF) and the European Agricultural Fund for Rural Development (EAFRD) to support the implementation of national policies in these fields. The EU already co-finances projects for the Roma in sectors like education, employment, microfinance and equal opportunities (in particular equality between men and women).

Concrete amounts of EU funds specifically allocated to Roma are hard to quantify. However, according to an analysis of the European Social Fund (ESF) 2007-2013 Operational Programmes in 12 Member States (BG, CZ, ES, FI, GR, HU, IE, IT, PL, RO, SI, SK) target Roma (among other vulnerable groups). Overall, these countries have allocated a total budget of €17.5 billion (including €13.3 billion of ESF funds) to measures benefiting Roma and other vulnerable groups. This represents 27% of their total European Social Fund budget. In Hungary and Romania, Roma are potential beneficiaries in more than 50% of the planned ESF interventions, while in Ireland, travellers are a potential target of 99.5% of the planned ESF supported activities for 2007–2013.

Czech Republic, Poland, Romania, Slovakia, and Spain have dedicated €172 million for activities aimed solely at Roma.

Examples of projects for the 2000–2006 operational programmes and for what is planned under the 2007–2013 operational programmes are available here: http://ec.europa.eu/employment_social/esf/docs/esf_roma_en.pdf

Since May 2010 the rules to use money from the European Regional Development Fund (ERDF) have been changed, which makes it easier to ask for EU funding for projects to help minority groups, like Roma, to get a house (IP 10/589).

In the past, not all Member States could use ERDF money to fund housing projects for Roma or other minority groups. This is now possible for all Member States, with easier procedures. It's not possible to provide an exact amount of how much money will be available. In all Member States where housing is concerned, projects for Roma or other minority groups can be accepted. The figure depends on how many projects are developed in the Member States and how much money the Commission could invest in certain projects.

Another example of funding for Roma is the €1.11 million for a new urban regeneration project in the Hungarian town of Nyíregyháza, which has one of the highest Roma populations in the country. The segregated school will be torn down and the roads, playgrounds and childcare facilities renovated.

In addition, the European Agricultural Fund for Rural Development (EA-FRD) has been used by some Member States to further the integration of Roma.

Rural development can make a vital contribution to the socio-economic development of rural areas, the prevention of poverty and elimination of social exclusion in rural areas. The EAFRD promotes the non-discrimination principle: Member States have to describe in their rural development programmes how discrimination based on ethnic origin is prevented during the various stages of programme implementation. The respect of this provision has been verified by the Commission during the assessment of the rural development programmes for the period 2007–2013. Several programmed actions or project selection rules ensure that Roma are benefiting from the EAFRD support.

In the implementation of the EAFRD programmes, several actions or project selection rules ensure that Roma are benefiting from the EAFRD support. For example, in the Czech Republic, under the programmes "Village renewal and development" and "Public basic services to the rural population", priority criteria for the approval of projects are targeting the disadvantaged areas with higher unemployment rates (both measures) or projects with disadvantaged groups of population (basic services). These criteria ensure that areas with a high share of Roma are benefiting from the available support.

The European Year 2010 is specifically dedicated to the fight against poverty and social exclusion and the Roma have been identified as a group at high risk of poverty. A special focus has been dedicated to this group and a number of countries have mentioned the Roma as a group at risk in their country and proposed them as a priority for the activities during the Year: Hungary, Greece, and Slovakia for instance._Several countries have funded projects involving Roma populations: Hungary, Italy, Spain, Slovakia and France. For example, in France, Secours Catholique—Caritas France is running a project for the inclusion of the Roma called "*Pour une inclusion réelle et effective des Roms en Europe*".

In addition to funding, the Commission has also convened **high-level events in several Member States to raise awareness of the opportunities offered by EU funds** to improve the social and economic situation of Roma and to promote a more efficient use of these funds. After a first series of events took place in Hungary in 2009 and are scheduled for September 2010, another series of high-level events will take place in Romania in October 2010 and more are planned for next year.

Who checks how EU funding is spent?

As is always the case with EU funds, it is up to Member States and managing authorities to come up with viable projects. It is not the role of the European Commission to propose projects.

Standard practice for all projects is that Member States have certifying and auditing authorities and on top of that the European Commission does sample controls to see if the money has been spent on projects which have been approved. If there are any irregularities, there will be so-called "financial corrections", meaning that the sum will be deducted from a next payment and no EU money will be spent on the projects for which irregularities have been found.

What EU policies are available to fight against possible discrimination of Roma?

The European Commission is fully committed to fighting against any form of discrimination, according to standards laid down in EU law. EU Justice Commissioner Viviane Reding has warned against Roma discrimination:

"The European Union is built on fundamental rights and values, and in the respect for cultural and linguistic diversity. Our European values include the protection of people belonging to minorities, the principle of free movement, and the prohibition of all forms of discrimination," Commissioner Reding said during a speech in Cordoba, Spain on 9 April (SPEECH/10/147). *"As Vice-President of the European Commission with responsibility for Justice, Fundamental Rights and Citizenship, I am committed to combating all forms of racism and xenophobia, discrimination and social exclusion on grounds of ethnic origin,"* she said.

EU Employment and Social Affairs Commissioner László Andor is fully committed to the social inclusion dimension of the Roma saying in his speech at the last summit on the Roma (SPEECH/10/148): *"Our support for Roma inclusion needs to be explicit, but not exclusive, and must aim at ensuring all Roma people to enjoy equality and opportunity."* He has continuously stressed the opportunities for Member States to draw on EU funds, saying: *"We need to use all available European and national funds available to respond the needs and circumstances of Roma people in a culturally sensitive and reasonable way in all our policies."*

There are clear EU rules in place regarding the free movement of EU citizens: Article 21 of the Treaty on the Functioning of the European Union (TFEU) provides that every citizen of the Union has the right to move and reside freely within the territory of the Member States, subject to certain limitations. These limitations are laid down in Directive 2004/38/EC.

When it comes to discrimination in employment situations, the main legislative instruments available to the Commission are the non-discrimination Directive 2000/43/EC and the Framework Decision on combating racism and xenophobia 2008/913/JHA.

The Commission also promotes the use of best practices and the exchange of information in the framework of the annual European Roma Summits. The most recent summit was held in Cordoba, Spain on 8–9 April. The European Platform for Roma Inclusion meets twice a year. The Platform's main principle is that all Roma policies should aim at integrating Roma into standard schools, labour market and society rather than creating a parallel society. Action should be explicitly targeted towards Roma without excluding people of other ethnicities who are in a similar socio-economic situation.

Can Roma people from Bulgaria and Romania work in the EU?

Starting in January 2014—seven years after accession—there will be complete freedom of movement for workers from Bulgaria and Romania. For EU citizens, the free movement of persons is one of the fundamental freedoms guaranteed by EU law and includes the right to work in another Member State without needing a work permit. It is an essential part of the Single Market and of European citizenship.

Roma people who are Bulgarian or Romanian nationals enjoy the same rights under EU law as other EU nationals. But as transitional arrangements still apply regarding the right to free movement of workers on the basis of Bulgaria's and Romania's Accession Treaty this means that all Bulgarian or Romanian nationals may face restrictions to this right until 31 December 2013 at the latest.

The situation for Bulgarian and Romanian nationals is as follows:

Workers from Bulgaria and Romania currently enjoy full rights to free movement pursuant to EU law in 14 (of 25) Member States (Denmark, Estonia, Cyprus, Latvia, Lithuania, Poland, Slovenia, Slovakia, Finland, Sweden, Hungary, Greece, Spain and Portugal) and also have free access to the labour market of the Czech Republic under national Czech law (+1).

The restrictions that the remaining 10 Member States (Belgium, Germany, Ireland France, Italy, Luxembourg, Netherlands, Austria. UK, Malta) apply vary from one Member State to another but typically require Bulgarian and Romanian citizens to have a work permit. Only the individual Member States can give detailed information on the restrictions they apply. Nevertheless, the Commission understands that several Member States have eased conditions or simplified procedures to access the labour market in comparison to the conditions and procedures that applied in these Member States to Bulgarian and Romanian citizens prior to EU accession.

First phase: 1 January 2007–31 December 2008: During the two first years following the accession of Bulgaria and Romania, access to the labour markets of the EU Member States depending on national measures and policies, as well as bilateral agreements they may have had with the new Member States.

Second phase: 1 January 2009–31 December 2011: At the end of 2008 the Commission drafted a report, which was the basis for a review by the Council of Ministers of the functioning of the transitional arrangements. In addition to the Council's review, Member States had the obligation to notify the Commission before 31 December 2008 as to their intention for the next three-year period—either to continue with national measures, or to allow free movement of workers.

Third phase: 1 January 2012–31 December 2013: Free movement should be applied as of 1 January 2012. However, if a current Member State notifies the Commission of a serious disturbance of its labour market, or threat thereof, restrictions continue to apply.

The transitional arrangements on the free movement of workers from Bulgaria and Romania are currently in the second phase that started on 1 January 2009.

Who is covered by the transitional arrangements?

The transitional arrangements apply to any national of Bulgaria or Romania who wants to work as an employed person in one of the current Member States. It does not apply to those wishing to reside in one of the current Member States for purposes such as study, or those who wish to establish themselves as self-employed persons. Only Austria and Germany may, under certain conditions, also apply restrictions to Bulgarian and Romanian companies who post workers for the purpose of providing services in certain sectors, notable the construction industry.

On what grounds can Member States seek to remove EU citizens, including Roma, from their territory?

Free movement of persons is one of the pillars of the EU and a fundamental right of EU citizens. It brings great benefits to EU citizens, Member States and the European economy as a whole. In 2008, EU citizens residing in a Member State other than the one of origin were estimated at 11.3 million.

The Roma population living in the EU are EU citizens and have the same rights as any other citizen.

Article 21 TFEU provides that every citizen of the Union has the right to move and reside freely within the territory of the Member States. This right is not unconditional. Limitations are laid down in Directive 2004/38/EC on the right of citizens of the EU and their family members to move and reside freely within the territory of the Member States.

For stays for up to three months, the only condition is to have a valid passport or identity card. No entry visas, employment or sufficient resources can be required.

EU citizens staying **for more than three months** must be economically active (i.e. they must work or be self-employed) or have sufficient resources not to become a burden on the social assistance system and have comprehensive sickness insurance cover (Article 7). EU citizens can be removed from the host country if after three months the EU citizen does not meet the above conditions on economic resources and health insurance.

After residing in the country **for a continuous period of five years**, EU citizens become permanent residents and are free from meeting any conditions.

Restrictions on the right of free movement and residence can be based on grounds of public policy, public security or public health (Article 27 of the Directive).

When deciding to remove an EU citizen, Member States must first ensure that the decision is proportionate to the threat to public policy or to the burden on public funds that the EU citizen concerned represents.

A decision to remove an EU citizen should not be taken lightly. EU law provides for **safeguards** ensuring that the final decision is fair. The safeguards protect both the interests of EU citizens and of the countries in which they live.

A decision on the grounds of public policy or public security must be based exclusively on the personal conduct of the individual concerned. This means that the personal conduct must represent a genuine, present and sufficiently serious threat affecting one of the fundamental interests of society (Article 27).

In the framework of this individual assessment, the host EU country must take account of considerations such as how long the EU citizens have resided on its territory, their age, state of health, family and economic situation, social and cultural integration into the host Member State and the extent of their links with the country of origin.

If Member States conclude that the threat represented by the EU citizens and their family members is sufficiently serious and the expulsion is warranted, they must notify the decision to the person concerned in writing and indicate, in full, all the grounds on which the decision was taken (Article 30).

Except in duly substantiated cases of urgency (to be defined by Member States, but for example where there is a risk of serious reoffending), persons concerned should have at least one month to leave (Article 30).

Such decisions can be appealed at a national court. People can also apply to suspend the removal until the court decision. In that case, they may not be actually removed from the country except where they already had access to judicial review or where the decision is based on grounds of public security (Article 31).

The Commission is committed to ensuring that EU citizens fully benefit from their free movement rights. Member States are responsible for the application of the Directive. The Commission issued Guidelines (IP/09/1077) in July 2009 to help Member States to correctly apply the Directive. The Guidelines are not binding. They are intended to provide information to both Member States and EU citizens and to make the application of the Directive more effective.

European Union, "Roma People Living in the EU: Frequently Asked Questions," (Europa press release, MEMO/10/383, Brussels). Available at: http://europa.eu/rapid/pressReleasesAction. do?reference=MEMO/10/383.

Appendix 4: Improving the Tools for the Social Inclusion and Non-discrimination of Roma in the EU

by European Commission

[...]

2.2. EU legislative instruments

At the EU level, several important legislative developments in the last ten years have established a framework for greater protection against racism and racial discrimination for all EU citizens. These are:

- **Directive 2000/43/EC implementing the principle of equal treatment between persons irrespective of racial or ethnic origin (Racial Equality Directive).**[17] By the end of 2009 all EU Member States had transposed the Racial Equality Directive into their national legislation.[18]
- **Framework Decision on combating certain forms and expressions of racism and xenophobia.** This ruled that such behaviour must constitute an offence in all Member States and should be punishable by the penalty of up to three years imprisonment. The Decision was adopted in November 2008 and is applicable from July 2010.[19]
- Charter of Fundamental Rights of the European Union of 7 December 2000. It incorporates fundamental rights into European Union law and reaffirms the EU commitment to non-discrimination and equality. It became legally binding,[20] after the entry into force of the Lisbon treaty on 1 December 2009[21].

2.3 EU policy and financial instruments

At a **policy level**, the **Lisbon Strategy of 2000** and the **Social Agenda 2005–2010** aim at achieving sustainable economic growth and the harmonious operation of the single market, while respecting fundamental rights and promoting the social dimension of economic growth. The realisation of these objectives relies on a combination of instruments. These include **EU legislation**, implementing the **Open Method of Coordination on Social Inclusion (OMC)** and financial instruments such as the **European Social Fund**. Subsequently, in 2006, the Community Programme for Employment and Social Solidarity—**PROGRESS**—was adopted by the European Parliament and Council.[22] Particular attention is to be paid to the most vulnerable groups, those suffering from multiple discrimination and those at high risk of exclusion. Among these are ethnic minorities and clearly identifiable as some of the most marginalised groups are many Romani communities.

The main **financial instruments**[23] providing support for Roma are **European funds**:

- The **European Social Fund (ESF)** including the Community Initiative **EQUAL**. The current programming period foresees **Operational Programmes**, which can be used to support targeted initiatives. Over the period 2007–2013 the European Social Fund expects to distribute some 75 billion EUR.[24]
- The **European Regional Development Fund (ERDF)**. This aims to strengthen economic and social cohesion by correcting imbalances between EU regions and is particularly relevant for infrastructure and environmental projects for Roma.
- The **European Agricultural Fund for Rural Development (EAFRD)**. Although not a structural fund, this resource can improve the employment prospects of Roma living in underdeveloped rural areas.

The EU's current overarching strategy for Roma is described as "Mainstreaming Roma Inclusion in All Policies of the European Union." This approach is defined as "explicit but not exclusive" since "it does not separate Roma-focused interventions from broader policy initiatives." Some coordinating initiatives have been launched that link EU Member States with other countries. These include the European Network on Social Inclusion and Roma under the Structural Funds.[25]

Meanwhile the growing significance of the social inclusion of Romani populations had been reflected in a **progress report** by the Commission,[26] followed by two high-level EU conferences on Roma issues, **the 2008 and 2010 Roma Summits**.[27] This brought together representatives of EU institutions, Member State governments, national parliaments and civil society, as well as other European states participating in the Decade of Roma Inclusion.

The first meeting of the integrated **European Platform for Roma Inclusion**,[28] was held in 2009. It is an open and flexible mechanism organised by the Commission and the EU Presidency at the request of the Council, in which key actors—EU institutions, national governments, international organisations, NGOs and experts—can interact with a view to exchange experience and good practice. It aims at making the existing policy processes more coherent and prepares the ground for synergies.

The **ten Common Basic Principles for Roma Inclusion** were discussed in the Platform and were annexed to the Council conclusions of June 2009.[29] These Principles are non-binding guidelines for policy makers working at the European, national, regional and local levels.

The ten Common Basic Principles for Roma Inclusion, annexed to the Council Conclusions in June 2009, non-binding guidelines for policy makers in Europe—set the context for this study, which confirmed their relevance.

The Principles are:

1. Constructive, pragmatic and non-discriminatory policies;

2. explicit but not exclusive targeting;

3. inter-cultural approach;

4. aiming for the mainstream;

5. awareness of the gender dimension;

6. transfer of evidence-based policies;

7. use of Community instruments;

8. involvement of regional and local authorities;

9. involvement of civil society; and

10. active participation of the Roma.

2.4. Related international structures and actions on Roma

In addition to the EU initiatives outlined above, some international bodies have taken action to promote Roma inclusion and combat discrimination.

- The **Committee of Experts on Roma and Travellers (MG-S-ROM)**, established in 1995, was the first Council of Europe (CoE) body responsible for reviewing the situation of Roma and Travellers in Europe.[30] This committee analyses and evaluates the implementation of policies and practices of CoE Member States concerning Roma and Travellers, is a forum for the exchange of information and experience[31] and draws up policy guidelines and Recommendations. The CoE **Commissioner for Human Rights** also devotes significant attention to the situation of Roma through Viewpoints, Recommendations and Country Reports based on country visits[32]. The **European Roma and Travellers Forum (ERTF)** was created in July 2004 to institutionalise the voice of Roma and Travellers at the CoE level.

- The **Action Plan on improving the situation of Roma within the OSCE Area** was adopted in 2003 by the OSCE and the 55 OSCE participating states.[33] The 2008 **status report** on its implementation found that although progress had been made, this was often slowed by lack of political will at the national level, failures to carry out policies at the local level and insufficient funding to support large-scale programmes.[34] The OSCE **High Commissioner on National Minorities** issued two reports in 1993 and 2000 on the **Situation of Roma and Sinti in the OSCE Area**[35] as well as more recent statements, such as on Roma migration and freedom of movement.[36]
- At the **United Nations** level, treaty-monitoring bodies have paid attention to the human rights situation of Roma, issuing Concluding Comments with recommendations for reducing human rights violations and issuing decisions on individual complaints filed by Roma. The **Committee on the Elimination of Racial Discrimination (CERD)** issued a General Comment on Discrimination against Roma[37] and several Special Procedures have also focused on Roma issues.[38]
- The **Decade of Roma Inclusion (2005–2015)**, an international political initiative, involves 12 European governments that have pledged to improve the situation of the Roma.[39] Their National Action Plans are "intended to complement and reinforce—and not duplicate—national strategies for Roma that are in place in nearly all of the [participating] countries"[40] in the priority areas: education, employment, health and housing. The implementation of these plans is to be guided by an overarching focus on poverty, discrimination and gender mainstreaming. In this task, states were joined by intergovernmental and nongovernmental organisations, as well as Romani civil society.[41] With the exception of the Roma Education Fund (REF) and some administrative support, no additional funding has been provided by the sponsors.[42] Instead, members were to draw on Structural Funds, pre-accession funds like PHARE, national and other resources to support Decade initiatives.

Notes

[...]

17. Council of the European Union 2000.

18. Transposition does not necessarily equate with adequate implementation. In 2007, the European Commission sent Formal Requests to 11 Members States for inadequate transposition of the Directive. See: http://ec.europa.eu/social/main.jsp?catId=613&langId=en

19. See: http://europa.eu/legislation_summaries/justice_freedom_security/combating_discrimination/l33178_en.htm

20. See: http://eur-lex.europa.eu/LexUriServ/site/en/oj/2007/c_303/c_30320071214en00010016.pdf

21. See: http://europa.eu/lisbon_treaty/index_en.htm

22. European Parliament and Council of the European Union 2006.

23. For the kinds of practices supported through these instruments, see: http://ec.europa.eu/social/main.jsp?catId=634&langId=en

24. European Commission 2006.

25. This initiative brings together Bulgaria, the Czech Republic, Finland, Greece, Hungary, Italy, Portugal, Romania, Slovakia, Slovenia, Spain and Sweden from this study, as well as Poland. See: http://www.euromanet.eu/about/index.html

26. European Commission 2008.

27. See: http://ec.europa.eu/social/main.jsp?catId=88&langId=en&eventsId=105

28. See: http://ec.europa.eu/social/main.jsp?catId=761&langId=en

29. Council of the European Union (2009: 4–6).

30. See: http://www.coe.int/T/DG3/RomaTravellers/mgsrom_en.asp

31. See: http://www.coe.int/T/DG3/RomaTravellers/Default_en.asp

32. See: http://www.coe.int/t/commissioner/Default_en.asp

33. OSCE 2003.

34. OSCE 2008.

35. OSCE (formerly CSCE) 1993 and OSCE 2000.

36. See: http://www.osce.org/documents/hcnm/2009/11/41409_en.pdf

37. UNHCHR 2000.

38. Notably, the Special Rapporteur on the right to adequate housing **as a component of the right to an adequate standard of living and on the right to non-discrimination in this context,** and the Independent Expert on minority issues.

39. The participants are the governments, intergovernmental and nongovernmental organisations, including Romani civil society, from twelve countries: Albania, Bosnia and Herzegovina, Bulgaria, Croatia, the Czech Republic, Hungary, FYROM, Montenegro, Romania, Serbia, Slovakia and Spain. Slovenia and the European Commission are observers.

40. Roma Education Fund (2004: 3).

41. The World Bank, the Open Society Institute, the United Nations Development Program, the Council of Europe, Council of Europe Development Bank, the Contact Point for Roma and Sinti Issues of the Office for Democratic Institutions and Human Rights of the Organisation for Security and Co-operation in Europe, the European Roma Information Office and the European Roma Rights Centre were the original international partner organisations of the Decade, joined subsequently by UN-HABITAT, UNHCR and UNICEF.

42. See: http:// romaeducationfund.hu

European Commission, excerpts from "Improving the Tools for the Social Inclusion and Non-discrimination of Roma in the EU," (June 2010): 12–15. Available at: ec.europa.eu/social/Blob Servlet?docId=6784&langId=en.

Used by Permission.

Appendix 5: Recent Migration of Roma in Europe

by Claude Cahn and Elspeth Guild*

[...]

II. Romani Migration, Stigma, Romani Expulsion: The Historical Context

It is now generally accepted by scholars that the Romani people of Europe are descended from groups which left India around 1,000 years ago and began arriving on the territory of today's European Union in or around the 14th century.[4] The history of Roma in Europe—and the Romani identity itself—is to a great extent bound up with ideas around migration, "nomadism", diaspora and exile. Nevertheless, the great majority of the Roma of Europe is sedentary, and the Romani language—notwithstanding its close links to modern Hindi, Urdu and Punjabi[5]—appears to have taken its present form in Byzantine Greece and the Ottoman Empire.[6]

Today, more than ten million Roma live in Europe,[7] a large proportion of them in the EU. The Roma of Europe are an immensely diverse group of individuals and communities. Some speak Romani and their national language. Some speak only their national language, possibly together with second languages. Some may speak as a home language other minority languages such as Beash, Jenisch, Shelta or Pogadi Chib, although there is a dispute as to whether some of these persons should be regarded as Roma.[8] Some may have no affinity with Romani communities; others on the other hand may have been raised and/or now live in traditional communities governed by extensive internal codes. Common unifying features—to the extent that such may exist—include common identification as members of the "communities of fate" regarded as "Gypsies" in Europe and, indeed, the occasional or frequent experience of being "outed" as "Gypsy", often for negative treatment, or at least suspicion. For the latter reason, many Roma and others identified as "Gypsies" choose to conceal their ethnic identity—particularly when asked by a public authority. In addition to the concerns for dignity this raises, it also has real implications with respect to statistical data about the situation of Roma (see below Part 1, section III.2).

Roma occupy a particular place in the European imagination as "nomads",[9] a fact many if not most regard as stigmatizing and erroneous. The reasons for the association of Roma with "nomadism" are complex and include the fact that some Romani and related "Gypsy" groups (albeit now a very small number of persons) have remained nomadic or partially nomadic, particularly in Western Europe, Romania and parts of the former Soviet Union. Supplementing this otherwise neutral fact, however, is the fact that "Gypsies" occupy a rich place in the European folk imagination, with a stereotypical idea about "Gypsies" enduring to the present day. Arriving Roma—particularly those Roma continuing to maintain traditions, including traditional dress—have frequently found that there is extensive speculation attached to their arrival; the past 200 years of European history has seen regular and frequent sensationalism of "the arrival of the wild Gypsies".[10]

After the 14th century, Romani migration in Europe is a historical fact of primarily the past century and a half. The abolition of slavery of Roma in Romania,[11] and the subsequent destitution of the freed slaves and their descendents made the end of the 19th century and the early part of the 20th century a time when many Roma fled South-Eastern Europe for points West and North, in search of a better life, and at times in search simply of food. The Cold War for the most part sealed closed countries with major Romani populations—Albania, Bulgaria, Czechoslovakia, Romania and the former Yugoslavia, among others—before borders began opening with the former Yugoslavia in the mid- 1980s.

The end of bipolarity in 1989 saw larger movements of persons across Europe than Western European governments had been accustomed to in the preceding years. The re- emergence and emergence of states in Europe, which followed 1989 was accompanied by new questions about identity and nationality. The lines of belonging and exclusion—the definitions of citizens, foreigners and entitlements based on ethnicity and language—were reformulated in ways that were not always benign for Roma and other groups, which have been the target of discrimination and exclusion in the 20th century. Some Roma were excluded from citizenship of new states as the three major Communist federations—Czechoslovakia, Yugoslavia and the Soviet Union—collapsed and new nation-states were formed. Following 1989, old ideas about "Gypsies" have been dramatically reawakened in Western Europe, in part as a result of the return of Romani migration from Central and South-Eastern Europe.

These facts have interacted with policy- and law-making and implementation in the post-1989 period. In the first place, the media has on a number of occasions provoked panic among the public about Roma immigration. Often the metaphors used ("wave", "deluge", etc.) have considerably distorted the scale of the issue, which frequently involves no more than a few score or several hundred persons. Secondly, the impact of this media attention, as well as other factors, seems to have resulted in the authorities frequently regarding arriving Roma as "fraudulent" when they approach the public authority for legitimate entitlements, including social welfare assistance, access to refugee determination proceedings, etc. Finally, authorities at national level have come under pressure from the media and inflamed public opinion to undertake draconian measures to stop Roma from arriving.

The enlargement of the Council of Europe in the early 1990s, followed by the enlargement and integration of the EU (including the preparatory processes for the enlargement to include first eight and then a further two countries of the former East Block), coinciding with an outbreak of anti-Romani hostility, violence and systemic discrimination—particularly in Central and South-Eastern Europe[12]—has brought the social inclusion of Roma more forcefully into European policy concerns.[13] The pressure created by Romani migration in Europe has generally created conditions for the development of Roma policies by the major regional organizations—the EU,[14] the Council of Europe[15] and the OSCE[16]—and has also brought Roma into focus as a primary concern of the UN human rights machinery.[17] Roma policy as developed for example by the European Commission has come about, among other things, as a result of pressure from the Member States. States have also exercised bilateral influence. For example, Poland's Roma policy came about as a result of pressure by the United Kingdom Government to stop Roma from migrating to the country. Romani migration has also sometimes threatened to derail EU expansion and/or integration. For example, when scores of Roma from Hungary were granted asylum in France in 2000 in a high-profile case, questions were raised as to Hungary's readiness for free movement.[18] Similar discussions took place periodically in a number of EU Member States with respect to Slovakia's then-candidacy for the EU.[19] Roma inclusion issues featured prominently in the European Commission's regular reports in the accession process of the Central European 2004 accession countries, and European funding instruments have focused extensively on projects aiming to secure Roma inclusion.[20]

The transformation of Europe, accompanied by the extension of the role of the OSCE,[21] the doubling of the Council of Europe's membership and the enlargement of the EU has also led to new perspectives on rights. Human rights as entitlements beyond citizenship are at the heart of the OSCE and Council of Europe systems. The OSCE's 1990 Copenhagen Meeting of the Conference on the Human Dimension of the [CSCE] has provided the political framework for this: "the rights of persons belonging to national minorities as part of universally recognized human rights is an essential factor for peace, justice, stability and democracy in the participating States". The duty of states to ensure the protection of human rights for all persons within their jurisdiction is the core of the major Council of Europe human rights treaty, the European Convention on Human Rights (ECHR). The EU establishes a right for individuals to move and reside across state borders and to enjoy non-discrimination on the basis of nationality. In recent decades, the Union has expanded protection against discrimination, first in the field of gender, and then progressively to perceived race or ethnicity, and other grounds. The interchange of the law of free movement and establishment on the one hand, and the ban on discrimination on grounds including nationality, ethnicity and perceived race on the other, forms one key aspect of the legal assessments in this study.

The decade and a half between 1989 and the EU expansions of 2004 and 2007 was a period in which laws governing immigration to Western Europe became considerably more restrictive, particularly concerning non-privileged migrants (in particular persons seeking work, rather than arriving with previously contracted work). It was also a period of significant strain on refugee law and, particularly in Western Europe, the considerable erosion, in practice, of asylum rights. Nevertheless, many Roma fled persecution—particularly from Bosnia, Serbia and Kosovo, but also from now EU Member States including the Czech Republic, Slovakia, Romania, Bulgaria, Poland and the Baltics—and secured refugee status or temporary surrogate protection in Western European and other countries during the period. Among the public, and even among relevant policymakers, the distinction between migrants and refugees was often not as clear as was often asserted. In practice, it often splits families down the middle.

Following the expansion of the EU in 2004 and 2007, some of the previous urgency and intensity of debate around Romani migrants in Europe has, in some countries, subsided. However, in a number of European states public insecurity and intolerance vis-à-vis Romani migrants has, if anything worsened.[22] A number of Council of Europe and/or EU Member States have had national policy debates concerning the expulsion of Roma, often carried out in a crude or inflammatory manner.

To make matters even more complex, a number of European states—including EU Member States such as the Czech Republic, Hungary, Slovenia and Poland—have become both countries of migrant origin and countries of emigration for Roma. Roma from the Czech Republic, for example, continue to migrate particularly to the United Kingdom, while Roma from Romania and Slovakia— also EU Member States—migrate to, among other places, the Czech Republic.

Romani migration—and concerns related to the fundamental rights of Romani migrants—has also arisen in the OSCE area outside the EU, on occasion with impact in the EU. Thus, for example:

- Russia is a target country of migration for Roma from Moldova, Ukraine and the countries of Central Asia, as well as possibly from other countries; Ukraine is both a target country of Romani migrants (particularly from Moldova) and a country of Romani migrant origin.
- Canada has provided refugee status to large numbers of Roma from Central and Eastern Europe, particularly from the Czech Republic and Hungary. Canada also re-imposed visa requirements for Hungarian citizens, in order to stop Roma from migrating from Hungary to Canada, and discussions about lifting the visa requirement centred primarily around "seeking guarantees that Roma will not migrate to Canada". Following the abolition of the visa regime for Czech citizens in Canada in 2007, several hundred Roma from the Czech Republic have again sought asylum in Canada.
- Prior to the events of 11 September 2001 in particular, the United States resettled several thousand Roma from Bosnia, including Roma from Bosnia threatened with forced return to Bosnia by, in particular, the German Government. The United States also resettled several hundred Roma from Kosovo[23] who had secured temporary protection in the former Yugoslav Republic of Macedonia (FYROM).

The accession to the EU of the Czech Republic, Slovakia, Hungary, Poland, the Baltic States and Slovenia in 2004, followed by Bulgaria and Romania in 2007, has altered to a certain extent the nature of legal entitlements due to Roma from these countries. It has also created a situation in which, in countries of immigration, superficially unitary Romani communities may include persons with differing status and potentially differing legal entitlements, particularly as concerns EU rights, as well as rights under the Council of Europe's European Social Charter and Revised Charter. This study attempts to resolve a number of the factual, policy-related and legal questions at issue in this complex matter.

PART 1: THE LAW OF THE BORDER: ACCESS TO THE TERRITORY, EXPULSION, ESTABLISHMENT, STATUS AND POLICING OF ROMA IN AN INTERNATIONAL MIGRATION CONTEXT

III. The Right to Cross Borders

III.1.A The European Law and Policy Framework

Although the Universal Declaration of Human Rights (1948) provides for "everyone's right to leave any country, including his own", an absolute right to cross borders and to remain on the territory of a state only exists for the individual who is a national and is seeking to enter his or her home state. International treaties have recognized this as the fundamental right of citizenship—the right to enter the territory of the state of which one is a citizen.[24] Those claiming international protection, i.e. refugees, also have a right to arrive at borders, but international law in Europe only provides a right not to be sent back to a state where the individual fears persecution, torture, inhuman or degrading treatment, while their claim is under determination by the state from which they have sought protection.[25] Once the authorities have assessed the claim for protection, only those recognized as having a well-founded fear of persecution or where there is a substantial risk of torture, inhuman or degrading treatment in the country of origin are entitled to residence.[26] Minority rights as contained in international instruments provide little assistance regarding movement across international borders.[27] Instead, the emphasis is on the right to non-discrimination and the exercise of culture, religion and language.

Beyond the limited international exceptions to the sovereignty of a state over which foreigners it admits to its territory, states govern the crossing of international borders as a matter of national law. This prerogative has been strongly defended by states in the European region. It is a principle which is upheld by the OSCE, which reaffirms the rights of sovereign states.[28] The Council of Europe, too, has recently reaffirmed the principle of state sovereignty in its report on the Caucasus and Georgia.[29] Nonetheless, some instruments do move in the direction of modifying the sovereign right to control borders, not only as regards refugees and persons fleeing torture but also in the context of family reunification. The European Social Charter 1961 (revised 1996) is an important source of commitments as regards migrant workers. The EU, however, stands out as an exception, having been based on the right of individuals to cross borders for economic purposes. Discussion of each venue in turn follows below, with specific emphasis on the EU.

OSCE

The engagement of the OSCE in the field of migration begins with the principle in the Helsinki Final Act that borders are inviolable: "[T]he participating States regard as inviolable all one another's frontiers as well as the frontiers of all States in Europe and therefore they will refrain now and in the future from assaulting these frontiers." Further, in order to promote contact on the basis of family ties, the Helsinki Final Act calls for a favourable consideration of applications to travel for the purpose of allowing persons to enter or leave their territory temporarily or on a regular basis, in order to visit family members. The Act calls for the procedures of visas and travel documents to be facilitated and for the facilitation of travel for personal or professional reasons; though this is directed at the home state rather than the receiving state. Reference is also made in the Act to the importance of tourism, meetings between young people, sport and expansion of contacts.

> *Carmen S. is a 26-year-old Romani woman from a small village in Western Transylvania, Romania. She tried several times to take up employment in the regional capital Timisoara, but was unsuccessful because the wages provided did not cover the cost of rental accommodation. She then emigrated to Tuscany, Italy, where a local priest assisted her in finding work as a live-in minder for an elderly woman, as well as securing her access to health insurance and a local identity card. She never revealed her Romani ethnicity to anyone in Italy. Everyone in the village knew her as a "Romanian". After six months of this work, however, the elderly woman whom she was taking care of refused to pay her and seized her documents. With the assistance of a local labour union she recovered the documents and the unpaid wages, but returned to Romania.*
>
> (*The names of persons in the accounts in text boxes throughout this study have been fictionalized, although the accounts provided are of real persons.*)

Two further concerns of the OSCE deal with the question of border crossing: action against terrorism where the transborder element is present as a reason for common action in respect of the movement of persons across borders and secondly combating trafficking in human beings, where again there is a focus on the crossing of international borders by persons as a measure which requires states to coordinate their activities. While there are substantial undertakings in respect of the Roma, these are generally not framed in the context of border crossing. The OSCE's Office for Democratic Institutions and Human Rights (ODIHR) highlights the problem of trafficking in children as an issue of importance to some Romani communities. Similarly, it highlights the problem of Roma who are forced by fear of torture, inhuman or degrading treatment, to flee their country and seek asylum elsewhere. The focus is on the treatment of refugees in the states where they are currently living, rather than the legal regime which applies to movement of persons to seek asylum.

The Council of Europe

The Framework Convention on the Protection of National Minorities (1995), a Council of Europe treaty, is particularly important for Roma as regards the rights which groups are entitled to claim. However, as regards the crossing of borders the Convention only includes one relevant provision: Article 17(1)[30] which creates a duty on States Parties not to interfere with cross-border contacts between people who share a common, relevant background. This provision is sufficiently unclear as to represent no obvious obstacle to a state exercising sovereignty in the form of border controls.

The European Social Charter of 1961 (revised 1996) provides more assistance as regards the treatment of migrant workers. Article 19 provides rights on the basis of reciprocity—both the state of nationality and the host state must be party to the Charter for the individual to be entitled to rely on the provisions. The Parties commit themselves to providing information about migration, health services and medical attention as well as good hygienic conditions during the journey and to promoting cooperation among both public and private agencies involved in the migration process. In addition, the Appendix of the Revised Charter extends coverage to certain categories of third-party nationals: "Without prejudice to Article 12, paragraph 4, and Article 13, paragraph 4, the persons covered by Articles 1 to 17 and 20 to 31 include foreigners only in so far as they are nationals of other Parties lawfully resident or working regularly within the territory of the Party concerned, subject to the understanding that these articles are to be interpreted in the light of the provisions of Articles 18 and 19."

The ECHR—the core human rights treaty of the Council of Europe— provides somewhat more assistance on the question of movement across borders. Although the Convention itself does not deal with migration as such, as interpreted by the European Court of Human Rights (ECtHR) in individual cases, it has important consequences for movement of persons across borders. Further, the Protocols to the ECHR provide some protection for foreigners.

The ECHR sets out a number of rights to which individuals are entitled vis-à-vis any state which has jurisdiction over them. After exhausting domestic remedies the individual may bring a complaint before the ECtHR, which has the final word on whether the action of the state is consistent with the human rights contained in the ECHR or not. With respect to the crossing of state borders, the ECHR has no specific provision. The ECtHR has repeatedly stated, "[T]he Court recalls that the Convention does not guarantee the right of an alien to enter or to reside in a particular country. However, the removal of a person from a country where close members of his family are living may amount to an infringement of the right to respect for family life as guaranteed in Article 8 § 1 of the Convention".[31] However, the right to respect for private and family life provided by Article 8 has been interpreted by the ECtHR as including a right to enter a country in very specific circumstances. For the moment this right has been recognized to only apply to minor children of persons settled in a state where the family is seeking to effect family reunification.[32] However, it is to be expected that other categories may be added as the Court's case law develops. Under current case law, the fact that the child may never have been on the territory of the state where the rest of the family lives is not an insurmountable obstacle to the recognition of the right.

The European Union

Freedom of Movement of Persons in Primary EU Legislation

The right to free movement of persons under EU law means an inversion of the relationship of the state and the individual regarding the crossing of a border. The crossing is a right of the individual against which the state must justify any interference. When seeking to delineate the boundaries of the free movement of persons in the EU, one looks first to the provisions in the Treaty establishing the European Community (TEC), one of the two core EU treaties, which can have direct effect in the Member States. In such cases, the treaty provision does not need to be transposed into national law to be binding, but is rather directly accessible as a source of individual rights to be upheld both in national law and before national courts. All of the provisions on free movement of persons have been held to have such direct effect. To lend substance to the rights in the treaty, secondary legislation is adopted setting out administrative and other measures required for implementation at national level to secure effective exercise of the right. The EU treaties form the basis for strong legal framework with detailed rules on its exercise.

The organizing principle of EU law is nationality, not humanity. The individual acquires rights because he or she is a citizen of the Union or a family member of one. Rights flow from the fact that the individual belongs to one of the 27 Member States rather than other identities. However, through agreements with third countries the EU has extended rights almost identical to those of EU citizens to their nationals. Most important are the agreements with Iceland, Norway and Switzerland. The agreement with Turkey provides very important protection for Turkish workers already admitted to the Member States and a standstill provision (i.e., a ban on the introduction of new restrictions) for Turkish nationals seeking to go to the Member States as self-employed persons and service providers. The standstill dates from 1970 but applies to Member States only from the date they join the EU. Thus, the prohibition on new restrictions on self-employment provisions only applies to the 2004 Member States as regards their national legislation on 1 May 2004 when they joined the EU. There is a plethora of third country agreements with states in the neighbourhood of the EU, including provisions on workers and establishment, but these are mostly limited to providing protection against discrimination for workers lawfully admitted under national law and market access for companies based in those countries.

Esmerelda S. is a Romani woman from Romania who went to Tuscany and secured work as a minder of an elderly and incapacitated woman. She has not revealed her ethnicity to anyone, because she believes negative repercussions would surely follow if she did so. She has been in Italy for around a year and a half. She is currently saving money to be able to buy a house and, ultimately, open a small business. She sends home several hundred Euros per month in remittances.

The key source of the right of free movement is Article 18 TEC—citizenship of the Union. The concept of citizenship of the EU is somewhat different from the idea of citizenship derived from international human rights law. All nationals of the Members States are citizens of the Union. The key right is the right to move and reside anywhere in the EU (i.e. on the territory of the 27 Member States). Thus, while a citizen has the right to enter, move and reside in his or her state of nationality as a result of international human rights law, in the EU, he or she has—as a citizenship right—the right to leave his or her state of nationality and to cross an international border, enter another EU state and reside there. Thus, EU law provides rights to the migrant in the guise of a citizen.[33]

Article 39 TEC provides the right of free movement of workers. Anyone who is exercising an economic activity subordinate to another person and who receives remuneration for that activity over a period of time is a worker under EU law.[34] Anyone who is seeking work or taking up work has the right to cross EU borders for the purpose of doing so. The activity must not be marginal or ancillary to another purpose. For nationals of eight Central and Eastern European Member States, the right to free movement as workers was delayed for up to five years as of 1 May 2004 (with the exceptional option for an extension of a further two years). In fact, all Member States have lifted the restriction on free movement of workers, completely or almost so, except Austria, Germany, Belgium and Luxembourg. The same limitation applies for Bulgaria and Romania, as of

1 January 2007. While all the 2004 Member States did not apply any restriction on free movement of workers among the pre-2004 Member States, among the pre-2004 Member States themselves, only Sweden and Finland immediately allowed free movement of workers to citizens of the 2004 group.

Article 43 TEC sets out a right of establishment. Where an individual is crossing a border to set up as a self-employed person in another Member State, he or she has a right to do so under EU law. Establishment means self-employment, either individually or through a company. While the individual may have to fulfil criteria for regulated professions, he or she has a right to move and to exercise economic activities. For the activity to qualify as establishment, the individual must provide services for remuneration over a period of time but not be subordinate to another person. This is the main difference between the provisions of Article 43 TEC and those for workers as provided under Article 39 TEC, described above. So long as the activity is not prohibited by law, the individual is entitled to engage in it. This includes, for instance, prostitution, which the European Court of Justice has defined as an economic service.[35] There is no option for delay in the right of free movement for self-employment as regards the 2004 or 2007 Member States nationals.

TEC Article 49 concerns services. Persons have a right to move and reside in any Member State if the purpose is to provide or receive services there. The provision of services must be an economic activity, but can include minor activities such as occasional market trading so long as there is remuneration and the individual is not subordinate to any other person. The difference between the establishment provision and the service provision is in the amount of infrastructure the individual acquires and the duration of the service provision.[36] Receipt of services also gives rise to a right to cross borders in EU law. This includes going to another Member State to eat a restaurant meal, stay in a hotel, etc.[37]

Article 12 TEC provides a right to non-discrimination on the basis of nationality. The ground is unusual in international law, as border controls depend on the right of officials to discriminate on the basis of nationality. Article 13 TEC sets out a right to non-discrimination on more traditional grounds of sex, racial or ethnic origin, religion or belief, disability, age or sexual orientation.

Secondary EU Legislation

The EU elaborates the provisions of its two treaties, and makes the laws for the Union institutions and the EU Member States, by adopting secondary rules (Directives and Regulations) that give effect to the fundamental freedoms contained in the relevant EU/EC treaties.

Directive 2004/38 contains the measures on the right of citizens of the Union to move and reside. All nationals of the 27 Member States have the right to enter the territory of any other state on presentation of a valid ID card or passport. There is no obligation for an EU national to show that he or she has any money to support himself or herself and his or her family in order to exercise the right to cross the border. For residence up to three months, there is also no need to show any further documents, evidence of funds, accommodation, etc., though Member States are not obliged to confer social assistance on these persons for the first three months (Article 24(2)). There is a requirement that EU nationals must not become an unreasonable burden on the social assistance scheme of the particular state, but for this reason to be used to interfere with the right to cross the border and reside, the individuals must have actually sought social assistance (Article 14(4)).

Restrictions on entry are only permitted on the grounds of public policy, public security or public health. These grounds must not be invoked to serve economic ends (Article 27). Measures taken on these grounds must be proportionate and based exclusively on the personal conduct of the individual. Previous criminal convictions (let alone suspicion of involvement in criminal activities) shall not in themselves constitute grounds for taking such measures. Further, the personal conduct of the individual must represent a genuine, present and sufficiently serious threat affecting one of the fundamental interests of society. The state may only justify its actions on the particulars of the individual case and must not act on general preventative grounds.

Silvia L., 30 years-old, is a Romani woman from a village in southern Transylvania, Romania. She is currently living with relatives in rented accommodation in a medium-sized town in southern France. She is seeking work as a cleaner or minder of the elderly. She is Romani and has extensive management experience in Romani NGOs in Romania, but she has studiously deleted all of this experience from her curriculum vitae, because she is sure that if she is suspected of being Romani then she will not find work.

Julia P., from the same village in Transylvania, is a 32- year-old Romani woman. She and her husband are separated, and she is raising their two children alone. She has never emigrated, and indeed has never been outside Romania. She makes money primarily by picking through the Timisoara city dump for materials to recycle. In November 2007, while doing so, she was struck and run over by a bulldozer driven by municipal waste collection workers. Both of her legs were broken in the accident. Because she has no health insurance, she was given rudimentary emergency treatment and then sent home, incapacitated.

These rules not only apply to nationals of the Member States but also to their third-country national family members who accompany or join them. Family members are defined as:

- spouses;
- registered partners;
- children under 21 or who are dependent on the EU national or spouse;
- dependent relatives in the ascending line of the EU national or spouse (Article 2(2), Directive 2004/38).

In respect of these family members, the Member State must admit them and if they require visas must issue the visas free of charge. The state cannot apply national rules on family reunification for the issue of visas to these family members.[38]

There is also a duty on the Member States to facilitate the entry and residence of other family members, irrespective of their nationality, not coming within the above group but who, in the country from which they come, are dependents or members of the household of the EU citizen or on serious health grounds require the personal care of the EU national (Article 3(2), Directive 2004/38).

Dependency has been interpreted in EU law as meaning that there is a factual situation which has the following characteristics:

1. Material support (financial or in kind) is provided to the third-country national family member;

2. That material support must be provided by the EU national or his or her spouse;

3. The status of dependent does not presuppose a right to maintenance;

4. There is no need to determine why the family member is dependent;

5. There is no need to determine whether the dependent family member could work;

6. Member States must assess whether the family members are not in a position to support themselves having regard to their financial and social conditions;

7. The need for support must arise in the state where the family members have been living (not as a result of their move to the host Member State);

8. Dependency can be proven by any appropriate means;

9. Member States cannot require a document issued by the authorities of the state of residence attesting to the dependency of the family members (this is too onerous);

10. Member States do not need to accept as sufficient evidence a mere undertaking by family members from the European Economic Area that the third-country national is dependent (this is too easy);

11. There must be a situation of real dependence.[39]

Thus, extended family units where some family members may not be citizens of the Union are entitled to remain together when the EU national exercises the right to free movement to go to another Member State. For instance, a Romanian national who seeks to exercise his or her right to self employment (Article 43 TEC) in Italy is entitled to enter the territory accompanied by his or her family members according to EU law.

Third-Country Nationals in the EU

There is a right of movement across intra-EU borders[40] and residence for third-country nationals who have made the EU their home, provided they can fulfil the necessary conditions. Directive 2003/109 sets out the rights of third-country nationals who have lived for five years or more lawfully in the EU.[41] In order to qualify for the status of "long-term resident third-country nationals" under the Directive, the individual must fulfil three criteria: lawful residence (not including specific groups, such as diplomats, whose status is regulated outside the scope of the directive), stable and regular resources[42] and valid health insurance. Member States can apply an integration condition requirement and refuse the status on the basis of public policy or public security (Articles 5 and 6). Once the individual has such status he or she is entitled to move and reside, including for economic purposes, in any other Member State (Article 14). Only labour market access can be delayed for up to twelve months and made subject to national rules. The definition of public policy and public security is very close to that used for EU nationals.

The Directive requires a high level of integration into the administrative system of the EU state. Thus for instance, a Ukrainian national who has resided in the Netherlands for more than five years and has been economically active there, will have to prove his or her continuous residence on the territory, continuous economic activity to a level of support required by national law and health insurance cover for the full five-year period before he or she will be eligible for the status of long-term resident third-country national and the right to move and reside in another EU state. Further, he or she may, depending on the Member State at issue, have to pass an integration test. In the case of a number of EU Member States with stringent legislation on integration measures (such as in the current example, the Netherlands), an integration test will be required.

Directive 2003/86 provides for a right of family reunification for third-country nationals resident in the EU. The principle of the Directive is that as soon as a third-country national family member fulfils the conditions to join the spouse or parent in the EU, then he or she should be permitted to do so. However, family reunification for third-country nationals resident in the EU is more restrictive than for EU nationals. Third-country nationals must show they can support and accommodate their family members and that they have health insurance before they will qualify for admission. Further integration measures can be required of the family members.

Crossing the EU Border

Entering the territory of the EU is not automatic for third-country nationals. While some third-country nationals, such as United States nationals, rarely encounter difficulties, others are expected to meet various criteria every step of the way—starting with visa requirements. Short-stay visas in the EU are called "Schengen visas" and subject to harmonization.[43] There is a common list of countries whose nationals must have visas (or a document which is recognized as the equivalent such as a long-term resident card) before they can enter the EU. All of the EU's immediately neighbouring countries, except Croatia, are on the so-called "visa black list",[44] so their nationals must obtain visas before they can cross the EU border. The system is enforced by EU provisions on carriers. Carriers are fined if they bring third-country nationals to the EU who do not have the required documentation. In conjunction with the negotiation of readmission agreements, whereby the neighbouring states agree to take back their own nationals and third-country nationals who have entered the EU via their territory in certain circumstances, the EU has agreed visa facilitation agreements with Albania, Bosnia, the former Yugoslav Republic of Macedonia, Moldova, Montenegro, Russia, Serbia and Ukraine. The agreement with Russia entered into force in June 2007, the rest on 1 January 2008. The rules for the issue of Schengen visas are subject to substantially different interpretation at the consulates of the Member States.[45] At the time of the publication of this study, a proposal for a new EU regulation on the issue of visas is under consideration.

The Schengen Borders Code (Regulation 562/2006) came into force on 13 October 2006 and sets out the law applying to the crossing of the EU's external and internal borders.[46] It applies only to non-EU nationals, not to EU nationals and their third-country national family members. The grounds for refusing entry (other than the lack of documents or a visa) are that the individual is a threat to public policy or public health; or an alert on the individual has been entered in the Schengen Information System and is refused admission to the EU or is in a national no-entry database; or that the individual poses a threat to the international relations of any Member State. A person can be refused admission on the basis that he or she has insufficient funds. A foreigner needs to demonstrate that he or she has sufficient means for the given duration of stay on the territory; the amount is established by each Member State individually on the basis of a daily rate. A question arises once the individual has fulfilled the criteria, namely are there any other grounds on which a state can refuse admission; the answer seems to be no.

Article 6 of the Schengen Borders Code requires border guards to carry out their functions with respect for human dignity and in a proportionate manner. Further, officials are explicitly prohibited from discriminating on the grounds of sex, racial or ethnic origin, religion or belief, disability, age or sexual orientation. Where an individual is refused admission he or she is entitled to written notification, reasons, a right of appeal and information on how to exercise that right.

The Schengen Borders Code also provides for the abolition of intra-Member State border controls. Under this provision no controls are permitted at EU internal borders (Article 21). Police checks within the territory of a state are permitted but they must:
- not have border control as an objective;
- be based on general police information and experience regarding possible threats to public security; and
- aim to combat cross-border crime.

The checks must be devised and executed in a manner distinct from systematic checks on persons and only be carried out as spot checks. Residence permits and documents issued to non-EU nationals by the Member States are scheduled to indicate which are equivalent to a visa for the purpose of crossing the external border and for the purpose of movement across internal borders.

III.1.B. Non-Discrimination and Migration

With regard to Romani migration, preliminary discussion of the Law of the Border would be incomplete without summary examination of the ban on discrimination—including the particularly serious harm caused by racial discrimination—on the one hand, and border controls and migration, on the other.

The sources of political commitment and legal obligation on states regarding non-discrimination are numerous. The OSCE, both in the Helsinki Final Act and in many subsequent documents, has affirmed and reaffirmed states' political commitment to achieve equal rights and status for all citizens. The Universal Declaration of Human Rights, the International Covenant on Civil and Political Rights, the International Convention on the Elimination of All Forms of Racial Discrimination and many other instruments engage with the issue of discrimination. Several important aspects of discrimination as regards international human rights commitments are key in this context:

- Proscribed grounds: Human rights instruments prohibit discrimination mainly on grounds such as race, colour, sex, language, religion, political or other opinion, national or social origin, property, birth or other status.[47] The ECtHR has interpreted the prohibition on discrimination as also covering nationality as a prohibited ground in limited circumstances.[48] EU law prohibits discrimination on the basis of nationality (Articles 12 and 13 TEC).

- Non-discrimination and other rights: Some international and regional instruments limit the non-discrimination obligation to the enjoyment of rights contained in the instrument itself (for instance Article 14 of the ECHR). Protocol No 12 to the ECHR, however, provides a wider duty on states to ensure non-discrimination as regards any right set forth by law.

- Legitimate different treatment: some different treatment may not constitute discrimination (and therefore may not be illegal). As the ECtHR has held, "[a] difference of treatment is, however, discriminatory if it has no objective and reasonable justification; in other words, if it does not pursue a legitimate aim or if there is not a reasonable relationship of proportionality between the means employed and the aim sought to be realised. The Contracting State enjoys a margin of appreciation in assessing whether and to what extent differences in otherwise similar situations justify a different treatment."[49]

In light of the above, the limits of non-discrimination in a migration context are quickly apparent. States are entitled to operate immigration controls and to treat foreigners differently from their own nationals. This is not discrimination for two reasons. First of all, the different treatment is based on the fact that the circumstances are different—citizens have a right to enter the state while foreigners do not. Secondly, the differential treatment of foreigners from different countries—for instance between the treatment of a US national and a Nigerian national—will not normally constitute discrimination so long as it is based on nationality not disguised racial discrimination. Discrimination on the basis of nationality as concerns entry onto the territory is not normally prohibited (except in EU law, but primarily as regards nationals of the Member States). However, as noted below, discrimination based on nationality is banned in a range of sectoral fields outside areas directly concerning access to or expulsion from the territory.

Racial discrimination, i.e. discrimination based on perceived race or ethnicity, is regarded as a particularly serious form of harm under international law. This ban has been applied to decisions concerning border controls in Europe. Most notably, in *Regina v. Immigration Officer at Prague Airport and another (Respondents) ex parte European Roma Rights Centre and others (Appellants)*, a case involving Roma from the Czech Republic stopped from travelling to the United Kingdom by UK border officials stationed at Prague Airport. The House of Lords, the highest appeals court in the United Kingdom, ruled that UK Immigration Officers operating under the authority of the Home Secretary at Prague Airport discriminated against Roma who were seeking to travel from that airport to the United Kingdom by treating them less favourably on racial grounds than they treated others who were seeking to travel from that airport to the United Kingdom, in contravention of the law.[50] The ban on racial discrimination in border matters has also been affirmed by the ECtHR.[51] The UN Committee on the Elimination of Racial Discrimination has recently—for the second time—attempted to elaborate where the ban on racial discrimination intersects with the rights of non-citizens.[52] As noted above, Article 6 of the Schengen Borders Code explicitly bans discrimination at the border based on, among other grounds, racial or ethnic origin.

OSCE

There is a strong political commitment to the principle of non-discrimination among the OSCE participating States. The 1990 Copenhagen Conference document states that "[t]he participating States clearly and unequivocally condemn totalitarianism, racial and ethnic hatred, anti-semitism, xenophobia and discrimination against anyone as well as persecution on religious and ideological grounds. In this context, they also recognize the particular problems of Roma (gypsies)" (para 40). This commitment was renewed in 1991 in the Geneva Report on National Minorities and again at the Moscow Conference the same year, and "[r]eaffirmed, in this context, the need to develop appropriate programmes addressing problems of their respective nationals belonging to Roma and other groups traditionally identified as Gypsies and to create conditions for them to have equal opportunities to participate fully in the life of society, and will consider how to co- operate to this end." The 1999 Istanbul Summit document states "[w]e will reinforce our efforts to ensure that Roma and Sinti are able to play a full and equal part in our societies and to eradicate discrimination against them." The Berlin Declaration of the OSCE Parliamentary Assembly refers to the Istanbul Summit's commitment to adopt anti-discrimination legislation and urges Member States to promote anti-discrimination. The political will as expressed by the OSCE is unequivocal. The problem is delivery on these commitments.

Council of Europe

The Council of Europe instruments, as well as regular political pronouncements, make clear that combating discrimination is among the most central commitments of the Council of Europe. A general prohibition on discrimination on prohibited grounds is contained in Article 14 of the ECHR. Protocol No 12 to the European Convention, adopted in 2000, provides that "[t]he enjoyment of any right set forth by law shall be secured without discrimination on any ground such as sex, race, colour, language, religion, political or other opinion, national or social origin, association with a national minority, property, birth or other status". For the moment 17 states have ratified Protocol No 12.[53]

The ECtHR has applied Article 14 in numerous cases concerning migrants. For Article 14 to apply, there must be another ECHR right at stake—for migrants this is often Article 8, the right to respect for private and family life. As discussed above, the ECtHR has found that prohibition on discrimination can also apply to the ground of nationality. On this basis, it has held that discrimination against migrants in the provision of social benefits breaches Article 14.[54]

The Court has also repeatedly called racial discrimination a "particularly invidious" form of discrimination.[55] In a series of decisions since 2004, the Court has applied the Article 14 ban on discrimination in a number of findings against Council of Europe Member States in cases concerning Roma in the following areas: inadequate investigation of possible racial motivation in police killings;[56] inadequate investigation of racial motive in other police abuse cases;[57] inadequate investigation of racial motive in cases of vigilante "skinhead" violence against Roma;[58] and racial segregation or other racial discrimination in education.[59] The Court has also held that degrading living conditions, combined with evident racism on the part of the public authority, can amount to degrading treatment in the sense of Article 3 ECHR, in cases concerning the failure to remedy extreme community violence against Roma.[60] In addition, the European Committee of Social Rights, the arbiter of Council of Europe law under the European Social Charter and Revised Social Charter, has on a number of occasions found systemic discrimination and related violations in cases against Charter parties in the field of housing of Roma.[61] This jurisprudence includes the finding that, "for the integration of an ethnic minority as Roma into main-stream society measures of positive action are needed".[62]

The European Union

The EU has prohibited discrimination on the basis of nationality since its inception. Currently, Article 12 TEC contains this general provision which has been upheld by the EU court as directly effective. The prohibition of discrimination on the basis of nationality has been included in most secondary legislation and applies to all citizens of the Union. The comparator is the treatment that a national of the state enjoys. Thus, for instance, if under national law citizens are entitled to benefits, in principle these must be extended also to nationals of the other Member States. The most sensitive area of application of the non-discrimination principle vis-à-vis citizens of the Union has been in respect of social benefits. Here, EU secondary legislation limits equal treatment to workers and the self-employed. Students, pensioners and the economically inactive must reside for five years in the state before they acquire a right to equal access to social benefits (Article 24, Directive 2004/38). So far there has been no answer to the question whether Article 12 TEC restricts or limits in any way discrimination on the basis of nationality among those who are not EU nationals. However, the EU has proceeded on the basis that discrimination among foreigners on the basis of nationality is permitted (for instance the establishment of the visa black list).

The EU Charter of Fundamental Rights adopted in 2000 prohibits discrimination. Article 21 provides that "[a]ny discrimination based on any ground such as sex, race, colour, ethnic or social origin, genetic features, language, religion or belief, political or any other opinion, membership of a national minority, property, birth, disability, age or sexual orientation shall be prohibited."

In 1999 the EU introduced a new non-discrimination provision into the EC Treaty—TEC Article 13, which states that "the Council may establish the measures needed to combat discrimination based on sex, racial or ethnic origin, religion or belief, disability, age or sexual orientation". Under this new power, the EU adopted two directives in 2000. The first, Directive 2000/43, provides for equal treatment on grounds of racial and ethnic origin. There is a common definition of unlawful discrimination, which includes less favourable treatment of a person on the basis of race or ethnic origin or a provision, criterion or practice which appears neutral but is likely to have an unfavourable outcome for a person or a specific group of persons on a prohibited ground. Directive 2000/43 applies to employment, training, working conditions, professional organizations, social protection and social security, as well as social advantages and access to supply of goods and services, including housing. This Directive had to be implemented in all the Member States by 19 July 2003.

The second Directive adopted under the new EC Treaty Article 13, Directive 2000/78, had to be transposed into national law by 2 December 2003. This directive prohibits discrimination on the basis of religion or belief, disability, age or sexual orientation, as regards employment or occupation and membership of organizations. It applies to the field of economic activities, whether employed or self-employed, including promotion, vocational training, working conditions, membership of organizations and applies both to the public and private sectors.

The two Directives ban the following forms of discrimination:
• Direct discrimination, or treating similarly situated persons differently in similar situations, for arbitrary reasons including perceived race or ethnicity;[63]
• Indirect discrimination, meaning where persons are placed at a particular disadvantage as a result of an apparently neutral rule, criterion or practice, provided there is no objective justification for the disadvantage;
• "Harassment", meaning "unwanted conduct related to racial or ethnic origin takes place with the purpose or effect of violating the dignity of a person and of creating an intimidating, hostile, degrading, humiliating or offensive environment";
• An instruction to discriminate against persons on grounds of racial or ethnic origin;
• Adverse treatment or adverse consequences as a reaction to a complaint or to proceedings aimed at enforcing compliance with the principle of equal treatment.

In July 2008, the European Commission proposed a new Directive to implement the principle of equal treatment irrespective of religion or belief, disability, age or sexual orientation outside the labour market. This is currently under consideration in the EU institutions. So far the EU institutions have been monitoring the Member States' transposition of the new Directives and taking action in cases of non-transposition or wrongful transposition into domestic law. There has only been one decision by the European Court of Justice—the final arbiter of EU law—on matters concerning one of the anti-discrimination Directives of the new Article 13 TEC. This decision is related to disability. Throughout 2008, the European Commission has been extensively examining how the Member States are handling the transposition into domestic law related to EU gender discrimination bans.

Further discussion of the European law ban on discrimination in the particular sectoral fields of education, employment, health care and housing is provided in the relevant sections of Part II of this study.

[...]

VIII. Conclusion

The intensification of EU integration from the mid-1980s onward has brought about unprecedented changes to the real and potential mobility of Europeans. Europe's most powerful regional entity—the European Union—as a matter of original purpose acts to facilitate the movement of Europeans within the greater EU space. The end of Communism and the changes following 1989, combined with the rapid pace of technological change globally, has further fundamentally altered the demography of European societies. Today, with some exceptions, most European societies are more multicultural than they ever have been. Migration has never been a more significant fact for the public and policymaker alike in Europe.

At the same time, the three European regional organizations—the Organization for Security and Co-operation in Europe, the Council of Europe and the European Union—have acted as leaders for the development of new laws and policies banning discrimination based on perceived race or ethnicity. This undertaking is not yet even partially complete, and is in a current state of dynamic growth. All three organizations have separate roles in securing peace, respect for and protection of human rights and economic prosperity in Europe. However, they are all committed to combating racial, religious and ethnic origin discrimination and ensuring that everyone in Europe has an equal chance of personal fulfilment within their community and the wider society. As outlined in this study, there are numerous sources for this commitment and the obligations undertaken by all the states in the region towards this goal.

Nevertheless, it is apparent that a massive gap exists between European efforts to challenge racial discrimination, on the one hand, and policies concerning Romani migration, on the other. Within Europe, major efforts have been made to force Roma to go to or to stay in the East, away from the economically dynamic parts of Europe. Where this has not proven possible, certain public authorities' action or inaction has led to a worsening of the situation of Romani migrants or to a neglect of their plight, even when living conditions may be degrading.

There is a need to reinvigorate the European project, to ensure that the benefits of European integration are enjoyed at all levels, and without regard to ethnic origin. In particular, there is an urgent need to ensure that all Europeans moving from one part of Europe to another have their human dignity respected and protected and are able to access in practice all fundamental human rights, as well as those rights accruing as a result of the relevant European treaties. As this study has also endeavoured to show, there is an urgent need to extend an effective ban on all forms of discrimination based on perceived race or ethnicity, including matters involving border administration, immigration control and related decisions pertaining to the treatment of non-citizens. Specific recommendations for action follow below.

IX. Recommendations

On the basis of the findings of the research, the authors of this study have made the following recommendations for action:

To OSCE participating States:

Without delay, ratify the International Convention on the Protection of the Rights of All Migrant Workers and Members of their Families.

Ensure that a comprehensive and effective ban on racial discrimination extends to all areas secured by law. Ensure that the ban on the particularly serious harm of racial discrimination extends, inter alia, to decisions concerning access to and expulsion from the territory, including decisions on such key matters as visa allocation, where such are required.

Ensure that all decisions concerning personal status—including immigration status—are based on the personal circumstances of the person concerned; ensure that decisions at all levels on matters concerning status, as well as decisions concerning related integration measures, are individual and not collective.

Ensure that international law requirements on the treatment of non-citizens, particularly those set out under General Recommendation 30 of the United Nations Committee on the Elimination of Racial Discrimination concerning discrimination against non-citizens[193] are adequately and effectively secured under domestic law.

Take proactive measures to resolve the immigration status of persons who would otherwise benefit from measures of inclusion, were it not for their belonging or perceived belonging to excluded Romani or related groups. Persons factually on the territory for periods of five years should enjoy a residence status leading progressively and without undue delay to permanent residence and/or citizenship, where the latter status is sought.

Take proactive measures to ensure that the physical integrity and security of migrants is ensured; in those states where attacks on migrants have occurred, ensure that all perpetrators are brought swiftly to justice; undertake public campaigns to ensure understanding of the value of multicultural societies.

Ensure equal and effective access to all persons, regardless of ethnicity or perceived race, to key services required for the realization of fundamental rights, including but not limited to education, employment, health care and housing. Where necessary, undertake proactive, positive measures to assist persons from marginalized groups in exercising fundamental rights.

Take steps, without delay, to extend social assistance and welfare measures to groups currently falling outside these protections, including excluded migrants. Ensure that Roma suffer no direct or indirect discrimination in access to social assistance and/or welfare benefits.

End practices of racial profiling of migrants and related groups.

Ensure that, where expulsion from the territory is absolutely unavoidable, expulsion measures do not result in human rights violations for any person affected by the expulsion, including family members of the person expelled. Ensure that, in all cases where minors in particular are expelled from the territory, complete education and health records travel with the person concerned.

To Council of Europe Member States:

Ratify, without delay, the First, Fourth, Seventh and Twelfth Protocols to the ECHR, where this has not yet been done.

Ratify, without delay, all elements of the Revised European Social Charter, including the mechanism providing for a system of collective complaints.

Ratify, without delay, the FCNM and the European Charter for Regional or Minority Languages, and provide explicit recognition of Roma and, depending on the facts of demography in the state at issue, other relevant groups regarded as "Gypsies".

Ratify and integrate into domestic law all aspects of the European Convention on Nationality, the Council of Europe Convention on the Avoidance of Statelessness in Relation to State Succession, the Council of Europe Convention on Action against Trafficking in Human Beings and the Council of Europe Convention for the Protection of Individuals with regard to Automatic Processing of Personal Data.

Ratify the European Convention on the Legal Status of Migrant Workers as well as the International Convention on the Protection of the Rights of All Migrant Workers and Members of their Families and provide training to officials at all levels, as well as other relevant parties, on the requirements of Council of Europe law as it relates to migrants, migrant workers and other non-citizens on the territory.

Disseminate at national, regional and local level and ensure effective implementation notably of the Council of Europe Committee of Ministers' Recommendation CM/Rec(2008)5 *on policies for Roma and/or Travellers in Europe* and of the FCNM Advisory Committee guidelines contained in its 2008 Commentary on the Effective Participation of Persons Belong to National Minorities in Cultural, Social and Economic Life and in Public Affairs.

To Member States of the European Union:

Cease immediately—and at the same time adopt effective measures to prevent—all efforts to expel EU citizens in contravention of EU law, as well as other measures aimed at hindering access to the territory for certain groups, where these are undertaken.

Provide training to officials at all levels on the requirements of EU law as concerns the rights of entry to the territory and establishment of citizens of other EU Member States.

Prioritize effective implementation of the EU anti-discrimination legislation and contribute to the efforts under way aimed at its further strengthening.

To the OSCE Institutions:

Develop inter-State mechanisms to ensure that no person legally expelled from the territory lacks any relevant documents—including relevant education, employment, health and other records—to ensure speedy establishment and reintegration.

Establish regular and systematic monitoring, jointly or together with the Council of Europe and/or relevant EU institutions, of expulsions carried out to Serbia, Montenegro and Kosovo, with a view to ending race-based expulsions of Roma and other persons regarded as "Gypsies".

To the Council of Europe:

With a mind, inter alia, to strengthening the legal protection of migrants in the Council of Europe Member States, reinvigorate efforts to promote ratification of the First, Fourth, Seventh and Twelfth Protocols to the European Convention, as well as ratification of the Revised European Social Charter, including the mechanism establishing a system for collective complaints, as well as of the European Convention on the Legal Status of Migrant Workers.

To the European Union:

Establish a Roma Unit in the European Commission to provide particular policy focus to matters concerning the inclusion of Roma and others regarded as "Gypsies", and ensure this unit's continued function until such time as systemic, racially discriminatory exclusion of Roma is overcome in Europe.

With a view to ensuring the implementation of best practice in all relevant areas, continue effective collaboration with the OSCE and the Council of Europe and prioritize monitoring of the situation of Roma and others regarded as "Gypsies" in (i) the work of the Fundamental Rights Agency; (ii) the reports toward accession of candidate countries to the EU; (iii) other relevant mechanisms.

Review current EU policies and rules with a view to strengthening policies at Union level to assist EU citizens without health insurance to get access to health insurance, with a particular focus on those EU citizens factually resident in an EU Member State other than their own.

NOTES

[...]

4. For a general history of Roma, see Fraser, Sir Angus, *The Gypsies*, Oxford: Blackwell, 1992. See also Council of Europe, *Factsheets on Roma History*, www.coe.int/education/roma and http://romafacts.uni-graz.at/.

5. On the Romani language, see especially Matras, Yaron, *Romani: A Linguistic Introduction*, Cambridge: Cambridge University Press, 2002.

6. Ibid.

7. The Council of Europe provides an "average estimate" of Roma in Europe of 11,166,500, with upper estimates of over 16,000,000 (see Council of European Roma and Travellers Division, "Number of Roma and Travellers in Europe, July 2008 Update", included here as Appendix 1).

8. A discussion of this issue is found in Margalit, Gilad and Matras, Yaron, "Gypsies in Germany—German Gypsies? Identity and Politics of Sinti and Roma in Germany", in Stauber, Roni and Vago, Raphael (eds.) *The Roma: A Minority in Europe: Historical, Political and Social*

Perspectives, Budapest: Central European University Press, 2007, pp. 103–116. Margalit and Matras refer to "Gypsy I" as "a common term associated with a lifestyle or socio-economic organisational form, irrespective of origin, language or traditions" and "Gypsy II" "for a population which shares a language (albeit split into several dialect groups), traditions and beliefs, and ultimately originating in India" (pp. 102–103). The borders between "Gypsy I" and "Gypsy II" may not in all cases be as fixed as the authors contend, and in any case are not noticed in cases in which persons regarded as "Gypsies" are singled out for negative treatment.

9. At least one series of government policies—those of Italy—are based on the idea that all Roma are "nomads" and any claim otherwise—for example including requests for mainstream housing, is invalid and to be resisted (see European Roma Rights Centre, *Campland: Racial Segregation of Roma in Italy*, Budapest, 2000).

10. A useful account of stereotypes about Roma is provided in Hancock, Ian, *The Pariah Syndrome: An Account of Gypsy Slavery and Persecution*, Ann Arbor: Karoma Publishers, 1987.

11. On the enslavement of Roma in Romania, see Viorel, Achim, *The Roma in Romanian History*, Budapest: Central European University Press, 2004, pp. 27–132.

12. European Commission, DG Employment and Social Affairs, *The Situation of Roma in an Enlarged European Union*, European Commission, 2004, pp. 9–10.

13. See *inter alia* Council of Europe Committee of Ministers, *Recommendation* CM/Rec(2008)5 *on policies for Roma and/or Travellers in Europe*, 20/02/2008, www.coe.int/t/cm.

14. See European Commission, DG Employment and Social Affairs, *The Situation of Roma in an Enlarged European Union*, 2004; European Commission, "Commission Staff Working Document accompanying the Communication from the Commission to the European Parliament, the Council the European Economic and Social Committee of the Regions; Non-discrimination and equal opportunities: A renewed commitment; Community Instruments and Policies for Roma Inclusion", {COM(2008) 420}.

15. See *inter alia* Parliamentary Assembly of the Council of Europe, Committee on Legal Affairs and Human Rights, "The situation of Roma in Europe and relevant activities of the Council of Europe, Introductory memorandum", Rapporteur: Mr József Berényi, Slovak Republic, EPP/CD, AS/Jur (2008) 29 rev 3 September 2008).

16. See *inter alia* declarations by OSCE participating States, as well as Ministerial Council Decision No. 3/03, "Action Plan on Improving the Situation of Roma and Sinti within the OSCE Area", 2 December 2003.

17. The situation of Roma has been addressed by Charter-based bodies such as the Special Rapporteur on the Right to Adequate Housing, the Special Rapporteur on Racism, the Independent Expert on Minority issues, as well as in the context of the Universal Periodic Review mechanism. The Treaty Bodies have extensively addressed human rights issues facing Roma in the national context. The Committee on the Elimination of Racial Discrimination (CERD) has issued a General Comment on discrimination against Roma, (General Recommendation No. 27: Discrimination against Roma: 16/08/2000. Gen. Rec. No. 27.). An extensive review of approaches by intergovernmental agencies to Roma issues is the subject of Rooker, Marcia, *The International Supervision of Protection of Romani People in Europe*, Nijmegen: Nijmegen University Press, 2002.

18. A useful summary of the "Zamoly" episode is provided in Desi, Janos, "In League with the Romas against the Hungarians", in Gero, Andras, Laszlo Varga and Vince Matyas (eds.) *Anti-Semitic Discourse in Hungary in 2001*, B'nai B'rith Budapest Lodge, Budapest, 2002, pp. 209–216.

19. The United Kingdom introduced a visa regime on Slovak citizens in October 1998; Finland followed suit in June 1999, after the arrival of a group of Roma from Slovakia, who were subsequently summarily expelled. During 2001 and 2002, a number of countries, particularly in northern Europe, introduced a visa regime for Slovak citizens as a result of purported "ethno-tourism" by Roma from Slovakia (see Vasecka, Imrich and Michal Vasecka, "Recent Romani Migration from Slovakia to EU Member States: Romani Reaction to Discrimination or Romani Ethno-tourism?", *Nationalities Papers*, Vol. 31, No. 1, 2003).

20. A report commissioned by the Union institutions to assess the efficacy of measures in the period 2001–2003 was less than praiseworthy in its conclusions (see EMS Consortium, "Review of the European Union Phare Assistance to Roma Minorities, Countries: Bulgaria, Czech Republic, Hungary, Romania, Slovakia", 1 April 2004).

21. Previously the Commission for Security and Co-operation in Europe (CSCE).

22. See European Commission, Special Eurobarometer 296, *Discrimination in the EU: Perceptions, Experiences and Attitudes*, July 2008, http://ec.europa.eu/public_opinion/archives/ebs/ebs_296_en.pdf.

23. All reference to Kosovo, whether to the territory, institutions or population, in this study shall be understood in full compliance with United Nations Security Council Resolution 1244 and without prejudice to the status of Kosovo.

24. Article 12(4) International Covenant on Civil and Political Rights; also found in Protocol 4 European Convention on Human Rights and elsewhere.

25. UN Convention relating to the status of refugees 1951; UN convention against Torture 1984; Article 3 ECHR.

26. In respect of persons fearing persecution, there is an exception on national security grounds. However, for those fearing torture there is no exception (see ECtHR, judgment, *Saadi v Italy*, 28 February 2008).

27. Article 27 International Covenant on Civil and Political Rights; Framework Convention for the Protection of National Minorities.

28. Helsinki Final Act 1975 (CSCE).

29. Report by the Chairman of the Committee of Ministers in view of the Informal Meeting of Ministers for Foreign Affairs of the Council of Europe, New York, 24 September 2008.

30. Article 16: The Parties shall refrain from measures which alter the proportions of the population in areas inhabited by persons belonging to national minorities and are aimed at restricting the rights and freedoms flowing from the principles enshrined in the present framework Convention; Article 17: The Parties undertake not to interfere with the right of persons belonging to national minorities to establish and maintain free and peaceful contacts across frontiers with persons lawfully staying in other States, in particular those with whom they share an ethnic, cultural, linguistic or religious identity, or a common cultural heritage, See text at http://conventions.coe.int.

31. *Boultif v Switzerland*, 2 August 2001.

32. *Sen v Netherlands*, 21 December 2001; *Tuquabo-Tekle v Netherlands*, 1 December 2005; *Rodrigues da Silva and Hoogkamer v Netherlands*, 31 January 2006.

33. C-413/99 *Baumbast*, 17 September 2002; C-291/05 *Eind*, 11 December 2007.

34. C-213/05 *Geven*, 18 July 2008.

35. C-268/99 *Jany*, 20 November 2001.

36. C-55/94 *Gebhard*, 30 November 1995.

37. 186/87 *Cowan* 1991.

38. C-127/08 *Metock*, 25 July 2008.

39. C-1/05 *Jia*, 9 January 2007.

40. "Intra-EU borders" are borders between the EU Member States, not including Ireland and the United Kingdom.

41. Denmark, Ireland and the United Kingdom are not party to this Directive.

42. Note this is a different test than applies to EU citizens who are economically inactive where the test is whether their resources are sufficient so that they will not become a burden on the social assistance or security system of the host state. The test for EU nationals can onl y be applied to the economically inactive and only after three months residence.

43. Ireland and the United Kingdom do not participate in the system. Denmark participates by way of a separate agreement.

44. The "visa black list" is officially Regulation 539/2001 of 15 March 2001 "listing the third countries whose nationals must be in possession of visas when crossing the external borders and those whose nationals are exempt from that requirement" as subsequently amended. The black list in the regulation itself is described as: ANNEX II Common List referred to in Article 1(2).

45. Beaudu, G., "L'externalisation dans le domaine des visas Schengen", Cultures et Conflits, Hivers 2007, pp. 85–109; Boratynski, J. and A. Szymborska, *Neighbours and Visas: Recommendations for a Friendly European Union Visa Policy*, Warsaw: Stefan Batory Foundation, September 2006.

46. Denmark participates by way of a separate treaty, Ireland and the United Kingdom do not participate by choice. Bulgaria and Romania have not yet been admitted.

47. Article 2 International Covenant on Civil and Political Rights 1966.

48. *Gaygusuz v Austria*, 16 September 1996.

49. *Stec and Others v United Kingdom*, 12 April 2006.

50. House of Lords, Judgments— *Regina v. Immigration Officer at Prague Airport and another (Respondents) ex parte European Roma Rights Centre and others (Appellants)*, SESSION 2004–05, [2004] UKHL 55, on appeal from: [2003]EWCA Civ 666.

51. See former European Commission of Human Rights, *East African Asians v the UK*, Report of the Commission, 14 December 1973, esp. paras 207–208.

52. United Nations Committee on the Elimination of Racial Discrimination, General Comment 30, "Discrimination and Non-Citizens", CERD/ C/64/Misc.11/rev.3.

53. Albania, Andorra, Armenia, Bosnia, Croatia, Cyprus, Finland, Georgia, Luxembourg, Montenegro, the Netherlands, Romania, San Marino, Serbia, Spain, the former Yugoslav Republic of Macedonia and Ukraine.

54. See *Gaygusuz v Austria*, 16 September 1996 and *Okpisz v Germany*, 25 October 2005.

55. See for example *Timishev v. Russia*, 13 December 2005, para. 56.

56. *Nachova v Bulgaria*, 26 February 2004.

57. *Bekos and Koutropoulos v Greece*, 13 December 2005; *Cobzaru v Romania*, 26 July 2007.

58. *Secic v Croatia*, 31 May 2007.

59. *D.H. and others v Czech Republic*, 13 November 2007; *Sampanis and others v Greece*, 5 June 2008.

60. *Moldovan and others v Romania*, 12 July 2005; see also collection of Roma-related case law of the ECtHR at: http://www.coe.int/t/dg3/romatravellers/jurisprudence/echr_en.asp.

61. See European Committee of Social Rights, decisions on the merits in Collective Complaints 15, 27, 31 and 39 against Greece, Italy, Bulgaria and France respectively.

62. See European Committee of Social Rights, *European Roma Rights Centre v. Bulgaria*, Complaint No. 31/2005, Report to the Committee of Ministers, Strasbourg, 30 November 2006, http://www.coe.int/t/e/human_rights/esc/4_collective_complaints/list_of_collective_complaints/default.asp#P121_10046.

63. The ECtHR, in *Thlimmenos v Greece*, judgment of 6 April 2000, has established the complementary principle that, "[t]he right not to be discriminated against . . . is also violated when States without an objective and reasonable justification fail to treat differently persons whose situations are significantly different."

[...]

193. http://www.unhchr.ch/tbs/doc.nsf/(Symbol)/e3980a673769e229c1256f8d0057cd3d?Opendocument.

SELECTED BIBLIOGRAPHY

Atkinson, A.B., Cantillon, B., Marlier, E., and Nolan, B., "Taking Forward the EU Social Inclusion Process: An Independent Report Commissioned by the Luxembourg Presidency of the Council of the European Union", 31 July 2005

Brouwer, Evelien, *Digital Borders and Real Rights: Effective Remedies for Third-Country Nationals in the Schengen Information System*, Nijmegen: Willem-Jan en Rene van der Wolf Publishers, 2006

Cahn, Claude and Skenderovska, Sebihana, "Roma, Citizenship, Statelessness and Related Status Issues in Europe", paper presented at meeting on citizenship and minorities convened by the UN Independent Expert on Minority Issues Gay McDougall, December 2007

Commissaire aux droits de l'homme du Conseil de l'Europe, "Memorandum faisant suite à sa visite en France du 21 au 23 mai 2008", CommDH(2008)34 Strasbourg, 20 novembre 2008

Council of Europe Commissioner for Human Rights, *Memorandum following his visit to Italy on 19-20 June 2008*, CommDH(2008)18, Strasbourg, 28 July 2008

Ecumenical Humanitarian Organization (EHO), "Violations of the Rights of Roma Returned to Serbia under Readmission Agreements", Novi Sad, April 2007

European Citizen Action Service, *Who's Afraid of the EU's Latest Enlargement?: The Impact of Bulgaria and Romania Joining the Union on Free Movement of Persons*, ECAS 2008

European Commission, DG Employment and Social Affairs, *The Situation of Roma in an Enlarged European Union*, 2004

European Commission, DG Employment and Social Affairs, *The Situation of Roma in an Enlarged European Union*, 2004; European Commission, "Commission Staff Working Document accompanying the Communication from the Commission to the European Parliament, the Council the European Economic and Social Committee of the Regions; Non-discrimination and equal opportunities: A renewed commitment; Community Instruments and Policies for Roma Inclusion", {COM(2008) 420}

European Roma Rights Centre, "Written Comments of the European Roma Rights Centre Concerning Germany for Consideration by the United Nations Human Rights Committee at its 80th Session, March 16, 2003–April 3, 2004", Budapest, March 8, 2004

European Union Agency for Fundamental Rights, "Incident Report: Violent attacks against Roma in the Ponticelli district of Naples, Italy", FRA 2008, 5 August 2008

Herm, Anna, "Recent Migration Trends: Citizens of EU-27 Member States Become Ever More Mobile While EU Remains Attractive to Non-EU Citizens", Luxembourg: Eurostat, Population and Social Conditions, Statistics in Focus 98/2008

Matras, Yaron, "Romani Migrations in the Post-Communist Era: Their Historical and Political Significance", *Cambridge Review of International Affairs*, Vol.XIII, No.2, pp. 32–50

Open Society Institute, "Security a la Italiana: Fingerprinting, Extreme Violence and Harassment of Roma in Italy", Budapest, July 2008

Organization for Security and Co-operation in Europe, Ministerial Council Decision No. 3/03, "Action Plan on Improving the Situation of Roma and Sinti within the OSCE Area", 2 December 2003

Organization for Security and Co-operation in Europe, Office for Democratic Institutions and Human Rights "Implementation of the Action Plan on Improving the Situation of Roma and Sinti within the OSCE Area", Status Report 2008, OSCE/ODIHR 2008

Parliamentary Assembly of the Council of Europe, Committee on Legal Affairs and Human Rights, "The situation of Roma in Europe and relevant activities of the Council of Europe, Introductory memorandum", Rapporteur: Mr. József Berényi, Slovak Republic, EPP/CD, AS/Jur (2008) 29 rev 3 September 2008

Richard, Jérôme, "Situation and problems of Roma immigrants in the Nantes Metropolitan Area". Document prepared by Mr. Richard following on from the request of the Committee of Experts on Roma and Travellers (MG-S-ROM) at its 25th meeting (Strasbourg, 3–4 April 2008), 30 June 2008

United Nations Committee on the Elimination of Racial Discrimination (CERD), "General Recommendation No. 27: Discrimination against Roma": 16/08/2000. Gen. Rec. No. 27. (General Comments)

United Nations Committee on the Elimination of Racial Discrimination (CERD), "General Recommendation No. 30: Discrimination against non-citizens", CERD/C/64/Misc.11/rev.3, 23 February–12 March 2004

United Nations Development Programme, *The Roma in Central and Eastern Europe. Avoiding the Dependency Trap*, Bratislava, 2003, UNDP

United Nations Development Programme and the Agency for Human and Minority Rights Government of the Republic of Serbia, "Reintegration of Returnees in Serbia: An Overview of Awareness Raising Activities of the Agency for Human and Minority Rights", Belgrade, March 2008

*Claude Cahn and Elspeth Guild, "Recent Migration of Roma in Europe Report for the Commissioner for Human Rights, Organization for Security and Co-operation in Europe," 2nd ed. (October 2010): 13–33, 80–88. Available at: http://www.osce.org/hcnm/78034.

Used by Permission.